UNCONDITIONAL SURRENDER

The Impact of the Casablanca Policy upon World War II

ANNE ARMSTRONG

RUTGERS UNIVERSITY PRESS
New Brunswick New Jersey

Library of Congress Catalogue Card Number: 61-10253

Manufactured in the United States of America
by Quinn & Boden Company, Inc., Rahway, N. J.

To the Memory of
C. C. H.

George had heard it said that good books could no longer be published and read in Germany. This, he found, was not true, as some of the other things he had heard about Germany were not true. And about Hitler's Germany he felt that one must be very true. And the reason one needed to be very true was that the thing in it which every decent person must be against was false. You could not turn the other cheek to wrong, but also, it seemed to him, you could not be wrong about wrong. You had to be right about it. You could not meet lies and trickery with lies and trickery, although there were some people who argued that you should.—Thomas Wolfe, *You Can't Go Home Again*

Preface

At about noon on January 24, 1943, at the conclusion of the Casablanca Conference President Franklin Roosevelt spoke for about fifteen minutes before a press conference attended by correspondents and photographers. After summarizing the decisions of the conference he added that he and Prime Minister Churchill "were determined to accept nothing less than the unconditional surrender of Germany, Japan, and Italy." [1]

The announcement was casual and informal, but the formula of Unconditional Surrender was the reflection of considered policy. It represented not only the American war aim in the Second World War but also a basic American attitude toward the enemy, toward international politics, and toward war. The policy of Unconditional Surrender, casually announced at Casablanca, was to dominate Anglo-American relations with Germany, Italy, and Japan throughout the war and was destined to have a profound, if not precisely measurable, effect on the postwar world.

Critics of the Casablanca Formula have contended that the unrelenting Allied demand for Unconditional Surrender prolonged the war, undermined the efficacy of the anti-Nazi forces within Germany, and perhaps led to the failure of the tragic July 20, 1944, attempt against the life of Hitler. The critics say that the total destruction of German military power created a

[1] Robert E. Sherwood, *Roosevelt and Hopkins* (New York: Harper & Brothers, rev. ed., 1950), pp. 693-94.

vacuum in Central Europe into which the Red Army could and did sweep unopposed and has thus been a basic cause of the present bipolarity in world politics and of the Cold War.

Defenders of Unconditional Surrender maintain that the Second World War was a moral crusade of the forces of democracy and of international justice against National Socialism and aggression, that the very nature of the Hitler regime and the Nazi party made any compromise or negotiation unthinkable. Further, they hold that a major cause of the Second World War had been the German insistence that in the First World War their army had never been defeated by carrying the war to German soil, by the literal destruction of the German capacity to resist, and that therefore there was no practicable alternative to the demand for Unconditional Surrender.

Political leaders and scholars have debated this question since 1943. By now perhaps a sufficient number of years has elapsed to allow a degree of historical perspective and detachment from the emotions of war and from commitments of loyalty to the partisan politics of the time. In the years since the Second World War many of the pertinent facts concerning the military and diplomatic conduct of the war have gradually come to light. Many of the surviving military and political leaders, both Allied and Axis, have published papers, commentaries, and memoirs and many official documents have been released by the governments concerned. Perhaps it is only now, eighteen years after the Casablanca announcement, that a factual and dispassionate examination of the possible historical consequences of the policy of Unconditional Surrender can be attempted. Even now many documents are still unavailable, many witnesses are silent. An exhaustive study of even the available documents and interviews with all the still living men who participated in the formulation of wartime policy for all belligerents would require the facilities of a research foundation. A single writer can hope to investigate only selected and representative material and to discuss limited aspects of the question of the consequences of the policy of Unconditional Surrender. This study, then, will be not a detailed history of the policy but rather an examination and an analysis.

The purpose of this inquiry will be to look into the methods by which the United States adopted the policy of Unconditional

Surrender in the Second World War, to try to discover the aims and motives of the policy, the nature of the American policy makers' thinking about European history, and about war and wartime policy which this demand reveals, and to explore the question of the validity of that thinking in terms of the results which the policy seems to have produced. Was the Casablanca formula historically necessary and politically sound or was it the product of wartime emotion and of propaganda-inspired misconceptions? Did it reflect a realistic appraisal of the causes of the Second World War and further the legitimate war aims of the Anglo-American alliance or was it symptomatic of a genus of thinking which can hold dangerous portent for the Western world?

What, specifically, were the effects of the policy on Germany? Did the demand lengthen and intensify the war? Did it destroy the possibility that an anti-Nazi resistance movement within Germany might overthrow the Hitler government and bring about a solution to the problem of Central Europe which would have suited Allied interests? These are some of the questions which will be posed and examined in the following chapters.

There are no absolute answers to these questions. There is no way in which the historian or political scientist can conduct laboratory experiments to determine the precise results of policy. It is difficult to isolate the effects of one phase of war and of policy from the total effects of the war itself and of the time and atmosphere of the war period. It is impossible to measure with historic accuracy the precise effect of any specific policy. At best the investigator can accumulate and evaluate available data, analyze the commentaries of those experts on war and diplomacy who have contributed to the discussion of Unconditional Surrender, and offer conclusions which point to probable effects. On a question as vital as this, a question which reflects a basic American attitude toward war and diplomacy and which illuminates the method by which American policy was formulated during the Second World War, perhaps even this modest service is worthwhile.

This, then, is the question posed by this inquiry: What were the probable effects on Germany of the Casablanca demand for unconditional surrender?

Acknowledgments

So many people have been helpful to me in the preparation of this study that it would be difficult for me and tedious to the reader if I were to attempt to list and thank them all publicly. My present adviser, Professor Dankwart Rustow, merits special gratitude for having taken on the dissertation in its final stage. My previous advisers, Professors Nathaniel Peffer and Lindsay Rogers, were always unfailing in offering sound counsel and courteous encouragement. My original adviser, Professor Franz Neumann, I can thank only in memory and I do so in full recognition of his example of meticulous scholarship. I should like to thank all four and also add a very personal thank you to Edith Black for her many kindnesses.

Following is a partial list of the people who have contributed data for my research, who have submitted to interview, or who have read and criticized parts of the manuscript: Professor Friedrich Berber of the University of Munich, General (ret.) Guenther Blumentritt, Axel Freiherr von dem Bussche-Streithorst, Senator Clifford P. Case, Eugene Davidson, Senator James O. Eastland, George Fielding Eliot, the late General (ret.) Heinz Guderian, General (ret.) Franz Halder, Luise Jodl, Albrecht von Kessel, the late Field Marshal (ret.) Albert Kesselring, Basil Liddell Hart, Louis P. Lochner, Field Marshal (ret.) Erich von Manstein, Professor Hans Rothfels, George Eric Rosden, Henning von Royk-Lewinski, Fabian Freiherr von Schlabrendorff, General Hans Speidel, John R. Steelman, Ralph de Toledano, General (ret.) Walter Warlimont, and General (ret.) Hermann von Witzleben. My sincere thanks to them all.

The library staffs at Columbia, at the Wiener Library in London, at the Institut für Völkerrecht and the Institut für Zeitgeschichte in Munich, at the Council on Foreign Relations and the Goethe House in New York, and at Fairleigh Dickinson in Rutherford, New Jersey, have all been exceptionally courteous and helpful. My typing aides, Carlene Lowry, Claire Mitchell, and Hazel Sheridan, all deserve my warmest appreciation and thanks.

The man who first suggested the theme *Unconditional Surrender* to me was the late and most loved Charles Cheney Hyde. It was he who first posed the question to me: What were the effects of the demand for Unconditional Surrender? It was he who encouraged a frank examination of the subject at a time when frankness still required courage. For this, and for his friendship and example, I dedicate my thanks and my work.

To my friends, my colleagues, and my mother, whose encouragement and criticism, patience and impatience have helped me to complete this work, my thanks.

A. A.

Rutherford, New Jersey
Spring, 1961

Contents

Unconditional Surrender

CHRONOLOGY
of
Major Political Events of the Second World War

1 September 1939	German troops cross the Polish border
3 September 1939	Great Britain and France declare war on Germany
10 May 1940	Churchill becomes British Prime Minister
3 September 1940	United States and Great Britain arrange Destroyer-Bases Agreement
16 September 1940	United States Selective Service Bill
11 March 1941	United States Lend-Lease Bill
22 June 1941	German invasion of U.S.S.R.: Operation Barbarossa
14 August 1941	United States and Great Britain sign Atlantic Charter
7 December 1941	Japanese attack on Pearl Harbor
1 January 1942	United Nations Declaration
14-28 January 1943	Casablanca Conference: Unconditional Surrender
17-24 August 1943	First Quebec Conference

19 October-1 November 1943	Moscow Conference
23-26 November 1943	Cairo Conference
28 November-1 December 1943	Teheran Conference
20 July 1944	Attempted assassination of Hitler
11-16 September 1944	Second Quebec Conference: Morgenthau Plan
4-12 February 1945	Yalta Conference
7/8 May 1945	Colonel General Jodl signs Unconditional Surrender document at Reims; surrender in Berlin
6 July-7 August 1945	Potsdam Conference

CHAPTER 1

The Background of Unconditional Surrender

THE CASABLANCA ANNOUNCEMENT

War, wrote Clausewitz, is nothing more than the continuation of policy with a mixture of other means. In other words, war is the implementation of policy by force, it is the violence to which a state resorts when diplomatic means have failed to achieve a political objective. If this is true, the aim of the war will be to compel the enemy to accede to the original political demand, the aim of strategy will be to reduce his strength to the point at which he is forced to accede. A successful war will be one in which the original political objective is achieved at a military cost which is roughly proportionate to the value of the objective. From this point of view let us inquire how successfully the military victory of the Allies in the Second World War served the ends of Allied diplomacy and how efficiently the policy of Unconditional Surrender contributed to the victory of both strategy and diplomacy.

According to Clausewitz, policy is "woven into the very fabric of war," and strategy, if it is sound, is the handmaiden of diplomacy.[1] The accounts of the major Allied conferences of the Sec-

[1] Karl von Clausewitz, *On War*, tran. by Colonel J. J. Graham (London: Kegan, Trench, Trubner, 1911), Vol. III, p. 121; see also pp. 79, 87, 123 ff.

ond World War seem to indicate that President Roosevelt and many of his advisers thought otherwise. The major decisions, at least during the first years of the war, were military. The major conferences were devoted to strategic planning and were often attended by the Commanders in Chief and their military staffs to the exclusion of ranking diplomatic advisers. Policy trailed in the wake of strategy, and strategy seemed to be aimed solely at the destruction of the enemy. The policy of Unconditional Surrender is both a reflection and a symptom of the nature of the thinking of the Anglo-American policy makers on the conduct of war and the role of policy in wartime. The Casablanca Conference in January, 1943, was a case in point, illustrative of the priority given to military planning. Policy, to the extent that it figured at all in the meetings of the conference, was a by-product and an afterthought. The decision to call for nothing less than the unconditional surrender of Germany, Japan, and Italy—a decision which was basically in the realm of policy and was to have far-reaching political implications—was made by the President and the Prime Minister after consultation with their military chiefs and advisers as an appendage to military discussions. Neither the American Secretary of State, Cordell Hull, nor the British Foreign Secretary, Anthony Eden, had attended the Casablanca Conference and neither was consulted in the decision of Unconditional Surrender. This was not an accident. It reflected a basic attitude, and perhaps a basic situation in the relations among the Allies. Let us first examine the Casablanca decision and then probe into its background and implications.

Although at the President's suggestion the Casablanca Conference has won the title of "the Unconditional Surrender meeting," [2] the decision to make this historic demand was incidental to the initial aims of the conference. Basically the Casablanca Conference was a military meeting. The decision to demand Unconditional Surrender was discussed by the chiefs briefly between urgent discussions of the planned Second Front, the all-out air offensive against the German homeland, and the status of the sea war. The atmosphere at the conference was one of urgency and

[2] Reported by Lord Hankey, *Politics: Trials and Errors* (Chicago: Henry Regnery, 1950), p. 29.

gravity, and perhaps to a large extent the Unconditional Surrender demand reflects this mood of urgency and gravity. Perhaps, as Churchill later explained, this was a gesture of defiance evoked by a grim situation in which victory seemed distant.[3]

The Casablanca Conference convened on January 14, 1943. From the Allied viewpoint, the military situation at the opening of 1943 was promising, but still uncertain. Hopes for eventual victory were stronger, but Germany, Japan, and even Italy were still formidable opponents and the price of victory would be high. The Allied planners still operated in the mood of the early months of the war, which had witnessed an unbroken series of Axis triumphs.

By January, 1943, the German advance in North Africa had been halted. At the beginning of November, 1942, the English counterattack in Tunisia had broken through the German defenses at El Alamein. A few days later the Allied amphibious landing in North Africa had further endangered the German Afrika Korps. On November 13 Tobruk had fallen to the British Eighth Army. On the Eastern Front the German advance had been stopped at Stalingrad. By November 22 the entire German Sixth Army had been encircled and cut off. By January the fate of 250,000 Germans had been sealed. The tide of the war had begun to turn.

However, many grave threats still haunted the Allied chiefs, many serious obstacles still stood between them and eventual victory. The German Wehrmacht remained a formidable weapon and it still straddled a vast space in Western Russia stretching from Leningrad in the north to Stalingrad in the south. It held Poland, the Baltic States, the Ukraine, and the Crimea and occupied Europe from the Atlantic through the Balkans, from Norway to the Mediterranean. Rommel's Afrika Korps, although badly injured by the English breakthrough and suffering from severe shortage of supply, was still a dangerous opponent. Throughout 1942 German submarines had taken a heavy toll of Allied shipping in the North Atlantic; sinkings had outstripped replacements by a million tons.[4] The German homeland was intact and German

[3] Robert E. Sherwood, *Roosevelt and Hopkins,* p. 696.
[4] Arthur Bryant, *The Turn of the Tide,* based on the diaries of Field

production, although hampered by inherent limitations of raw materials, was reaching new levels of expansion. All in all, although the tide had perceptibly turned, the end of the war was certainly not in sight. The questions of how victory could be achieved and what its cost would be were still unanswered. It was in this context that the English and American military leaders met at Casablanca. Perhaps in this context it is easy to understand that they were preoccupied with the immediate problem of military victory, that they were urgently concerned with strategic means, not with political ends.

The Allied political situation in January, 1943, was far from clear. The weaknesses of coalition warfare were already apparent and the basic suspicions lurking between the Eastern and Western Allies contributed to the uneasiness of the atmosphere at Casablanca. Stalin had criticized his allies openly and severely for their delays in opening a second front to relieve pressure on the Red Army; the Anglo-Americans were haunted by the fear that the Soviet Union would desert the alliance and make peace with Hitler. Even the English and the Americans, although firmly determined to fight to ultimate victory, were by no means clearly in agreement on the methods of achieving that victory or on the terms of the peace that would follow. Not only was there a natural rivalry for leadership in the coalition between the British and the American chiefs, but also there was a genuine divergence of viewpoint on basic strategy which strained the temper of the planners if not the alliance itself.[5] These political factors also had their influence at Casablanca and probably played a role in the call for Unconditional Surrender.

Let us examine briefly the milieu that produced the Casablanca Formula. The major problems which faced the British and Americans at Casablanca were as follows: the relative importance of the war in the Pacific as opposed to the war in Europe; the control and ending of the U-boat menace; the dispute between the rival Free French generals, de Gaulle and Giraud; the question

Marshal Lord Alanbrooke, Chief of the Imperial General Staff (New York: Doubleday, 1957), p. 440.

[5] See especially Bryant, *op. cit.*, pp. 434-93, 507-9, 554-75. See also Albert C. Wedemeyer, *Wedemeyer Reports!* (New York: Henry Holt, 1958), pp. 77-96, 163-80, 187-89.

of future operations in the Mediterranean; the method and scope of the proposed bombing offensive against Germany; and perhaps most decisive and most controversial, the decision of where and when to launch a second front invasion.[6] The British and American chiefs were divided on their answers to almost all of these questions. The major work of the meetings at Casablanca involved ironing out disagreements. The atmosphere often became strained, the rift in viewpoint seemed basic. On one point, however, the Anglo-Americans clearly agreed: that the war must be pursued to the point of final victory. Perhaps in an atmosphere of division the one point of total accord needed to be stated unequivocally. Perhaps to some extent this explains "Unconditional Surrender."

Underlying many of the differences in approach to strategic plans was a basic American mistrust of British diplomacy and especially of imperialism. For example, the American military men seemed to fear that, since the major British interests lay in the Middle East and in Europe, the English would exploit American strength for the defeat of Germany and would then leave the work of defeating Japan largely to the United States, and, further, that British interest in continuing military operations in the Mediterranean resulted more from concern for the lifeline of the Empire and for postwar political advantage than from a desire to relieve pressure on the Red Army and to defeat the German Wehrmacht as quickly and economically as possible.[7] The British, on the other hand, seemed suspicious of American enthusiasm and lack of experience. RAF Marshal Sir John Slessor put it succinctly: he said that the American attitude was simple, "in fact rather too much so." He felt that the American chiefs wanted action in Europe even though in the British view their troops were not yet battleworthy. The Americans criticized the British for their caution in wishing to postpone the projected invasion of the European Continent until the battle for shipping had been won, until a sufficient buildup of men and matériel in the British Isles had been accomplished, and until German resistance had

[6] See, for example, Wedemeyer, *op. cit.*, pp. 169 ff., and Sherwood, *op. cit.*, pp. 667-97.

[7] Wedemeyer, *op. cit.*, pp. 174-75, 187-88.

been softened by strategic bombing of industrial centers. Slessor explained that the English had been "once bitten (or rather twice, having had nearly a million men killed last time) and were twice shy about that particular dog." [8] The Americans, relatively new to land warfare on the European Continent, seemed fresh, eager and naïve to the more skeptical and seasoned British.

The discussions on all phases of the disagreement were sometimes heated and acrimonious. The British Chief of the Imperial General Staff, Lord Alanbrooke, recorded the Casablanca wrangling in his diary and noted: "There is no doubt that we are too closely related to the Americans to make co-operation easy." In a later entry he wrote of the Americans that they "are difficult, though charming people to work with." [9] Agreement could be obtained only by concessions and compromise. For example, the British agreed formally to the target date of fall, 1943, or spring, 1944, for the cross-channel invasion even though they doubted the feasibility of the earlier date. In return the Americans accepted the British plan for the invasion of Sicily as a means of clearing the Mediterranean for Allied shipping and perhaps of forcing Italy out of the war.[10] There was a long controversy over the nature and scale of the bombing offensive to be launched against German war production centers, but there too a compromise was effected.

In the perspective of these bitter debates, the question of whether or not to demand the Unconditional Surrender of the enemy seemed a minor issue. Neither Alanbrooke nor Slessor mentions any discussion of the issue in his book. General Wedemeyer states that the American Joint Chiefs took up the proposal at a morning meeting at Casablanca and notes that both he and General Deane opposed the plan, but the chiefs took no official stand on the matter.[11] Apparently the final decision to issue the demand was made unofficially by the President and the Prime Minister.

[8] Sir John Slessor, *The Central Blue,* Autobiography of Sir John Slessor, Marshal of the RAF (New York: Praeger, 1957), p. 434; see also pp. 408, 433 ff.

[9] Bryant, *op. cit.,* pp. 447, 454.

[10] *Ibid.,* pp. 440, 456-58.

[11] Wedemeyer, *op. cit.,* pp. 186-87.

Elliott Roosevelt, who had accompanied his father to the conference, reports that the President suggested the phrase informally at lunch on the next to last day of the conference. Although this account is not confirmed in other sources, he writes that both Harry Hopkins and the Prime Minister reacted favorably to the phrase, that Churchill looked thoughtful, grinned, and then said "Perfect! And I can just see how Goebbels and the rest of 'em'll squeal!" The President thought that the formula would be "just the thing for the Russians . . . Uncle Joe might have made it up himself." Later that day when cocktails were passed around Elliott Roosevelt says that Churchill proposed a toast: "Unconditional Surrender." [12]

On the following day, January 24, at the press conference which marked the conclusion of the official meetings President Roosevelt read the communiqué which announced the Anglo-American decisions. The phrase "Unconditional Surrender" was not included. The President then went on to explain that there was a matter which had long been in the hearts and minds of people but had never before been expressed explicitly, and this was that peace could come only by the elimination of German and Japanese war potential. He said that the unconditional surrender of Germany, Italy, and Japan would mean a reasonable assurance of world peace. This, he explained, did not imply the destruction of the population of these countries, but rather the destruction of their philosophies of fear and hate and the subjection of other peoples. He suggested that the Casablanca Conference be named "the Unconditional Surrender meeting" and reportedly Prime Minister Churchill cheered "Hear! Hear!" [13] In this informal way the policy of Unconditional Surrender was announced and endorsed.

For some reason both Churchill and Roosevelt later maintained that the press conference announcement of the demand for Unconditional Surrender had been a spontaneous remark of the President's. Roosevelt later explained that during the course of

[12] Elliott Roosevelt, *As He Saw It* (New York: Duell, Sloan, Pearce, 1946), pp. 117-19.

[13] Lord Hankey, *op. cit.*, pp. 29-30, quoted from the (London) *Times*, Jan. 27, 1943.

reading the communiqué, General Grant's phrase "unconditional surrender" had suddenly flashed through his mind and he had said it without reflection.[14] Actually the phrase seems to have been discussed at a meeting of the American Joint Chiefs of Staff in Washington as early as January 7,[15] and Robert Sherwood writes that the notes which President Roosevelt had carried to the press conference had contained the following paragraph:

> The President and the Prime Minister, after a complete survey of the world situation, are more than ever determined that peace can come to the world only by a total elimination of German and Japanese war power. This involves the simple formula of placing the objective of this war in terms of an unconditional surrender by Germany, Italy and Japan. Unconditional surrender means not the destruction of the German populace, nor of the Italian or Japanese populace, but does mean the destruction of a philosophy in Germany, Italy and Japan which is based on the conquest and subjugation of other peoples.[16]

Sherwood concludes that, far from being a chance phrase, the formula Unconditional Surrender was "very deeply deliberated . . . a true statement of Roosevelt's considered policy."[17] This seems to be so. Despite severe criticism of the policy by political opponents and even by members of his own Cabinet and by his military advisers, the President consistently refused all demands or suggestions to retract or modify the demand. Again and again in speeches and communiqués throughout the war he repeated the phrase. He refused all suggestions of compromise, and until his death his war aim remained the Unconditional Surrender of Germany and Japan.

THE ORIGINS OF THE POLICY OF UNCONDITIONAL SURRENDER

Historical Background

The doctrine of Unconditional Surrender propounded at Casablanca seems to have originated with President Roosevelt or in

[14] Sherwood, *op. cit.*, p. 693.
[15] Wedemeyer, *op. cit.*, p. 186.
[16] Sherwood, *op. cit.*, pp. 696-97.
[17] *Ibid.*

his immediate circle. It was Roosevelt who proposed the idea to the American Joint Chiefs of Staff and later to Prime Minister Churchill, and since Secretary of State Hull writes that he and his colleagues at the Department of State had been greatly surprised by the Casablanca announcement,[18] it seems clear that the policy had not originated there. Very possibly it was the President's own phrase.

Roosevelt's account of the origin of the phrase is given by Robert Sherwood. Roosevelt explained that during difficult negotiations between the two Free French generals, Giraud and de Gaulle, he had been reminded of the negotiations between Generals Lee and Grant and he remembered that Grant had been called "old Unconditional Surrender." The phrase had pleased Roosevelt. At the press conference he explained to the correspondents that his meaning of Unconditional Surrender was the same as Grant's at Appomattox.[19]

Psychologically the account may be correct. Roosevelt may have been reminded of Grant and Lee at Appomattox and of the phrase "Unconditional Surrender." If so, he did not check into the accuracy of his memory. It is true that General Grant was called "Unconditional Surrender," but the phrase comes not from Appomattox but rather dates back to 1862. In that year Grant had launched a surprise attack against Fort Donelson in Tennessee, a key Confederate garrison in the crucial border states. When the fort's commander requested terms, Grant brusquely demanded and won unconditional surrender. This victory, the first after an unbroken series of defeats, was received with wild enthusiasm by the press and public in the North. Grant became a popular hero. Journalists made much of the coincidence that Grant's initials were the same as those of his demand: Unconditional Surrender. The term became a northern byword.[20]

Grant's demand at Fort Donelson provided the precedent for the use of the phrase, but it does not constitute a historic prece-

[18] Cordell Hull, *Memoirs* (New York: Macmillan, 1948), Vol. II, p. 1367.
[19] Sherwood, *op. cit.*, p. 696.
[20] B. H. Liddell Hart, unpublished memorandum, "The Background of 'Unconditional Surrender,'" July 31, 1943; see also his *The Defence of the West* (New York: Morrow, 1950), pp. 52-61.

dent for the demand of the unconditional surrender of an enemy state. In the history of warfare the demand for the unconditional surrender of a single garrison is not infrequent. This means that the military personnel of the captured fort will be taken prisoner and confined under the rules of war until the end of hostilities. The method by which this procedure could be extended to the surrender of an entire state is not clear; the precise legal meaning of Unconditional Surrender when applied to a state is still not clear. There were few precedents for such a demand in 1943.

In ancient history perhaps the most famous example of a demand for unconditional surrender occurred in the Third Punic War when Rome ordered Carthage to surrender unconditionally in order to prevent the destruction of the city. The Romans defined "unconditional surrender" as the surrender of all territory, cities, and citizens. The Carthaginians refused the demand and a costly and bitter war ensued. It ended with the storming, sacking, and obliteration of Carthage in 146 B.C.

Lord Hankey, who has investigated the historical background of Unconditional Surrender, contends that not one of the fifteen wars in which Great Britain participated between the end of the sixteenth century and 1943 ended in unconditional surrender. During the Boer War in South Africa Lord Milner reportedly suggested that the Boers be compelled to surrender unconditionally, but Joseph Chamberlain objected, writing that "there seems to be a flavour of medieval cruelty about unconditional surrender from which we shrink." However, even the rumor that unconditional surrender was to have been demanded seems to have aroused great bitterness among the Boers. Later at the Paris Peace Conference Boer General Botha was unable to mention the words "unconditional surrender" without exasperation.[21]

The phrase "unconditional surrender" arose again during the negotiations that preceded the armistice which ended the First World War. In the fall of 1918 in answer to an inquiry of the German High Command regarding the possibility of negotiating peace on the basis of the Fourteen Points, President Wilson had stated that if the United States was required to deal with the

[21] Hankey, *op. cit.*, pp. 35 f.

German imperial government it would have to demand "not peace negotiations but surrender." The reaction of the German Generals Hindenburg and Ludendorff was violent. They regarded the Wilson Note as a demand for unconditional surrender, a demand unacceptable to honorable soldiers. They insisted that their government reject the proposal, but the civilian arm of government was already committed to peace.[22] Although the Paris Conference, which followed the Armistice, did not allow for negotiations in the traditional manner of past European peace conferences, the words "unconditional surrender" were not employed.

Traditionally the European wars of modern times had ended in negotiation between victor and vanquished. The announcement at Casablanca that the United States and Great Britain would accept nothing less than the unconditional surrender of their enemies established a precedent. Established international law governing armistices and occupation rights had grown up around the concept of negotiated peace. The legal implications, in fact the precise legal meaning of Unconditional Surrender, were not clear in 1943. There is still no general agreement on these questions. These are only a few of the repercussions of the Casablanca pronouncement. However, before discussing the results of the policy, let us look more closely into its origins.

Psychological Roots of the Policy

It is probable that the decision to demand unconditional surrender was President Roosevelt's own and very probable that, as he said, he borrowed the phrase from General Grant. However, whatever its origin the philosophy of war and of policy in wartime which the phrase reflects did not originate at Casablanca and did not belong exclusively to Roosevelt. Unconditional Surrender seems to stem from a basic American attitude toward war and from a view of German history which apparently was widespread in both American and British official circles during the Second World War. Let us examine briefly some of the bases for the policy.

[22] *Ibid.*, p. 37.

The Doctrine of Moral War and Total Victory

Even before the Japanese attack on Pearl Harbor had brought the United States into the Second World War as a full belligerent, President Roosevelt had committed himself and his nation to a policy which rejected the very thought of compromise as a basis for peace. In November, 1941, Admiral Leahy, then American ambassador to the Vichy French government, reported that he had been approached in Vichy by both public officials and private citizens who had urged him to request President Roosevelt to use his good offices as a neutral or to encourage the intervention of the Vatican to bring about a negotiated peace between Great Britain and the Axis powers. The President categorically rejected this suggestion.[23]

Two days after Pearl Harbor Roosevelt stated his position openly in a radio address:

> Powerful and resourceful gangsters have banded together to make war upon the whole human race. . . .
>
> . . . I repeat that the United States can accept no result save victory, final and complete. Not only must the shame of Japanese treachery be wiped out, but the sources of international brutality, wherever they exist, must be absolutely and finally broken. . . . We are now in the midst of war, not for conquest, not for vengeance, but for a world in which this nation, and all this nation represents, will be safe for our children.[24]

In his annual Message to Congress on January 6, 1942, the President repeated these objectives:

> The militarists in Berlin and Tokyo started this war. But the massed, angered forces of common humanity will finish it.
>
> Our own objectives are clear: the objectives of smashing the militarism imposed by war lords upon their enslaved peoples—the objective of liberating the subjugated nations—the objective of establishing and securing freedom of speech, freedom of religion, freedom from want and freedom from fear everywhere in the world.

[23] Admiral William Leahy, *I Was There* (New York: McGraw-Hill, 1950), pp. 40, 52. See also pp. 127 ff. and 206 ff.

[24] *War Messages of Franklin D. Roosevelt: December 8, 1941 to April 13, 1945* (Washington: U.S. Government Printing Office); Address of Dec. 9, 1941, pp. 14 ff.

We shall not stop short of these objectives—nor shall we be satisfied merely to gain them and then call it a day. I know that I speak for the American people—and I have good reason to believe I speak also for all the other peoples who fight with us—when I say that this time we are determined not only to win the war, but also to maintain the security of the peace which will follow. . . .

. . . Many people ask, "When will this war end?" There is only one answer to that. It will end just as soon as we make it end, by our combined efforts, our combined strength, our combined determination to fight through and work through until the end—the end of militarism in Germany and Italy and Japan. Most certainly, we shall not settle for less. . . .

. . . We are fighting today for security, for progress and for peace, not only for ourselves but for all men, not only for one generation, but for all generations. We are fighting to cleanse the world of ancient evils, ancient ills.

. . . Our enemies are guided by brutal cynicism, by unholy contempt for the human race. We are inspired by a faith which goes back through all the years to the first chapter of the Book of Genesis: God created man in His own image. . . .

. . . This is the conflict that day and night now pervades our lives. No compromise can end that conflict. There never has been—there never can be—successful compromise between good and evil. Only total victory can reward the champions of tolerance, and decency, and faith.[25]

This message, a year before the Casablanca Conference, heralded the policy of Unconditional Surrender: it rejected any thought of compromise and called for total victory. From this time on the theme of total victory recurred in the President's statements. He repeatedly pointed out that the objective of the war was the total destruction of the military power of the enemy states so that they might not again rise to menace the United States and her allies "a generation hence."

The emphasis on the postwar punishment of war criminals in the Axis states is another evidence of the doctrine of moral war. In October, 1942, the President connected the concept of war crimes trials with his goal of victory:

The United Nations have decided to establish the identity of those Nazi leaders who are responsible for the innumerable acts of savagery.

[25] *Ibid.*, pp. 27-30.

As each of these criminal deeds is committed, it is being carefully investigated: and the evidence is being relentlessly piled up for the future purposes of justice.

We have made it entirely clear that the United Nations seek no mass reprisals against the populations of Germany or Italy or Japan. But the ringleaders and their brutal henchmen must be named, and apprehended, and tried in accordance with the judicial processes of criminal law. . . .

We are united in seeking the kind of victory that will guarantee that our grandchildren can grow and, under God, may live their lives, free from the constant threat of invasion, destruction, slavery, and violent death.[26]

One of the elements of total victory was the ability to disarm and demilitarize the defeated powers. The President stated:

We have learned that if we do not pull the fangs of the predatory animals of the world, they will multiply and grow in strength—and they will be at our throats once more in a short generation. . . . It is clear to us that if Germany and Italy and Japan—or any one of them—remain armed at the end of this war, or are permitted to rearm, they will again, and inevitably, embark upon an ambitious career of world conquest. They must be disarmed and kept disarmed, and they must abandon the philosophy which has brought so much suffering to the world.[27]

He went on to remind the citizens of the United States that after the First World War American policy had been dedicated to building a permanent peace on the basis of idealism, but this had failed.[28] He warned that after the Second World War the United Nations must remain vigilant to prevent rearmament in Germany, Japan, or Italy, "or in any other nation which seeks to violate the Tenth Commandment, 'Thou shalt not covet.'" He summarized as the nation's war aim "to fight this war through to the finish—to the day when United Nations forces march in triumph through the streets of Berlin, Rome, and Tokyo." [29]

[26] *War Messages,* pp. 48-51, from radio address of Oct. 12, 1942.

[27] *Ibid.,* p. 66.

[28] The accuracy of the President's statements is not discussed or implied; the statements are presented as a reflection of the climate of wartime thinking.

[29] *War Messages,* pp. 66 and 68.

To Roosevelt, moral war implied not only total victory followed by total disarmament of the enemy and the punishment of war criminals, but it also involved the re-education of the enemy population. In his words, the people of Germany, Italy, and Japan must be "taught a lesson":

Now we are going to teach Japan a lesson. We have the will and the power to teach her the cost of treachery and deceit, and the cost of stealing from her neighbors. With our steadfast Allies, we shall teach this lesson so that Japan will never forget it. We shall free the enslaved peoples. We shall restore stolen lands and looted wealth to their rightful owners. We shall strangle the black Dragon of Japanese militarism forever.

Regarding Germany, he said:

Obviously we could have come to terms with Hitler, and accepted a minor role in his totalitarian world. We rejected that! . . . The decision not to bargain with the tyrants rose from the hearts and souls and sinews of the American people. They faced reality; they appraised reality; and they knew what freedom meant. . . .

. . . As for Germany, that tragic nation which has sown the wind is now reaping the whirlwind—we and our Allies are entirely agreed that we shall not bargain with the Nazi conspirators, or leave them a shred of control—open or secret—of the instruments of government. We shall not leave them a single element of military power—or of potential military power. . . .

The German people are not going to be enslaved—because the United Nations do not traffic in human slavery. But it will be necessary for them to earn their way back into the fellowship of peace-loving and law-abiding nations. And, in their climb up that steep road, we shall certainly see to it that they are not encumbered by having to carry guns. They will be relieved of that burden, we hope, forever.[30]

Although to a certain extent both the style and the content of the President's speeches can probably be attributed to his desire to stir public enthusiasm for the war and so must be considered simply propaganda, certain basic themes which recur throughout the speeches also appear in official communiqués and policy state-

[30] *Ibid.*, p. 145.

ments. Thus, although they may have begun as propaganda slogans, they ended as aims of policy, and they contributed to the President's insistence throughout the war on the aim of Unconditional Surrender, that is, on achieving nothing less than total victory through the total destruction of enemy power.

There were many of these themes. In a paper dedicated to exploring the background and causes of the demand for Germany's Unconditional Surrender we cannot examine the content of more than the major theme, the Leitmotif, and even in this case we can make only a cursory study of the charge and the facts.

Throughout the President's statements there is one underlying concept regarding the war with Germany: the war must be fought to its final conclusion, until Allied troops march triumphantly through Berlin, because the war is dedicated to a moral purpose and its results must teach a moral lesson. Not only must the Nazi regime be defeated and removed from power and those charged with war crimes tried and punished, but also the people of Germany must be taught the cost of waging aggressive warfare, Germany must be disarmed and demilitarized and forcibly prevented from rearming in the future. In the President's view, the Second World War was dedicated to the aim of preventing future wars by destroying "the sources of international brutality" and by "smashing militarism." Behind these objectives lay certain assumptions which must be examined briefly:

1. the assumption that a major cause of the Second World War was militarism in Japan and Germany;
2. the assumption that Germany was traditionally an aggressor nation;
3. the assumption that the core of German militarism and aggression was Prussia.

The investigation of these assumptions in detail would form a separate study, but let us look into them briefly.

German Militarism

In his message to Congress on September 17, 1943, Roosevelt said:

This is one thing that I want to make perfectly clear: when Hitler and the Nazis go out, the Prussian military clique must go with them. The war-breeding gangs of militarists must be rooted out of Germany . . . if we are to have any real assurance of future peace.[31]

This attitude is reflected in the official Yalta communiqué of February, 1945:

It is our inflexible purpose to destroy German militarism and Nazism and so insure that Germany will never again be able to disturb the peace of the world. We are determined to disarm all German armed forces: break up for all time the German General Staff that has repeatedly contrived the resurgence of militarism . . . remove all Nazi and militarist influences from public office and from the cultural and economic life of the German people . . . only when Nazism and militarism have been extirpated will there be hope for a decent life for Germans, and a place for them in the comity of nations.[32]

The President seems to have singled out the German General Staff as the pivotal point of German militarism. In his report to Congress on the Yalta Conference he demanded the destruction of militarism and the "permanent dismemberment of the German General Staff which has so often shattered the peace of the world." He concluded: "there is not enough room on earth for both the German militarism and Christian decency." [33]

Dwight Eisenhower at the time that he was Allied Supreme Commander European Theater apparently shared the President's view of the German General Staff. On July 10, 1944, he stated his view that the German General Staff regarded "this war and the preceding one as military campaigns in their dogged determination, first to dominate Europe and eventually the world." [34] His aide, Captain Butcher, reports a conversation between Eisenhower and his chief of staff, General Walter Bedell Smith, in which the two generals discussed the postwar disposition of the 3,500 officers which, they estimated, were members of the German General Staff. He writes that Eisenhower advocated extermi-

[31] *Ibid.*, p. 85.
[32] *Ibid.*, p. 183.
[33] *Ibid.*, p. 190.
[34] Captain Harry C. Butcher, *My Three Years with Eisenhower* (New York: Simon and Schuster, 1946), p. 609.

nation or exile and that Bedell Smith warned that imprisonment would be useless because within six or eight years the Anglo-American public would grow "soft-hearted and conciliatory"; however, both generals apparently agreed that punishment of the Staff could be "left to nature if the Russians had a free hand."[35]

Plans for the destruction of the institution of the German General Staff and perhaps also for the extermination of its members played a significant role in the American view of the peace settlement. The view of the German General Staff as a criminal organization and of the German, and specifically the Prussian, professional officers as militarists and warmongers and enemies of democracy played a crucial role in the policy of Unconditional Surrender. Not only did such a view imply that the American war aims must embrace far-reaching changes in German society, but also, more immediately, it precluded an alternative to Unconditional Surrender. A negotiated armistice with an enemy ruled by a dictatorship was probable only by an arrangement made with the military command. If the military commanders were as bad as or worse than the Nazis, then obviously no compromise was feasible. The validity of the policy of Unconditional Surrender to a large extent rests on the assumption that there was no reasonable alternative. One possible alternative was the encouragement of the overthrow of the Hitler government by the German military. For this reason one must inquire whether the evaluation of the General Staff as warmongers and aggressors was historically sound, whether the prevalent attitude toward militarism and Prussianism was grounded in fact or in propaganda.

Let us begin by asking, What is militarism? Webster gives two definitions for militarism: the predominance of the military class or of their ideals; second, the subordination of civilian ideals or of the policies of the government to the military.[36] In other words, the term "militarism" may be used in two very different senses: (a) a militaristic society may be one in which the soldier is

[35] *Ibid.*, pp. 609-10.

[36] Unabridged Dictionary. See also Alfred Vagts, "Bedingungslose Kapitulation als geschichtliches Phänomen," *Vierteljahrshefte für Zeitgeschichte* (7 Jahrgang, 1959, 3 Heft, July), pp. 280-309.

accorded great social esteem and in which military virtues such as courage and loyalty and discipline are highly valued; (b) militarism may signify that the policies of the state are directed or strongly influenced by the military.

Prussian society from the time of the Great Elector has been traditionally militaristic in the former sense: respect for the uniform, for military achievement, for courage and discipline permeated all levels of Prussian life, and professional military families ranked high in the Prussian social elite. Much of this tradition passed into the social life of unified Germany after 1871 and some of these values survived after the revolution of 1918. This form of militarism may contribute to the morale and discipline of a fighting force once war has begun and it may lead to a mood of popular romanticism about war but this quality in itself, although it may contribute to the spiritual toughness of a people and thus render it a more dangerous enemy, does not in itself cause wars. Respect for soldierly virtues does not necessarily imply eagerness for war, certainly not if the professional soldiers as a class oppose the war. Social militarism may be a factor in creating a climate of popular acceptance of war but this is effective only if the policies of the state are directed toward war. The "militarists," that is, the professional soldiers, are responsible for the outbreak of war not simply by virtue of their profession, or because their profession is popularly admired, but only if they are instrumental in influencing policy, and if their influence is used in the direction of war.[37]

Did militarism in the second and more significant sense exist in Germany? Did the professional soldiers traditionally influence or direct German policy and did they guide it in the direction of war, as President Roosevelt's charges seem to indicate? During the Bismarck era of the German Empire, decisions of policy were held firmly in the hands of the Iron Chancellor and of his civilian government. Bismarck had many disagreements and wrangles with his generals, and occasionally he deferred to their judgment in matters of a primarily military nature, but by and large he vigilantly prevented military interference in political matters.

[37] See, for example, Gordon A. Craig, *The Politics of the Prussian Army: 1640-1945* (New York: Oxford Univ. Press, 1956).

Final policy decisions were solely in civilian hands, usually in Bismarck's.[38]

During the reign of William II, German military preparedness assumed greater importance and the armed forces received increased appropriations, but policy making remained in civilian hands. In the pre-World War I period of crisis the German generals advocated a strong national defense, but the 1914 German Foreign Minister, Gottlieb Günther von Jagow, denied that the military leaders had advocated war. In a 1929 interview with the British historian G. P. Gooch, Jagow stated: "Tirpitz was on holiday and was not consulted. Nor was Moltke consulted till the end. The control of our policy was entirely in civilian hands." [39]

During the crisis which preceded the actual declarations of war in 1914 the German General Staff prepared a memorandum for its government warning that events had been set in motion as a result of Russia's announcement of her intent to mobilize, which would precipitate "the mutual butchery of the civilized nations of Europe" and could "annihilate for decades the civilization of almost all Europe." [40] It does not appear, then, that the German General Staff welcomed the outbreak of war with any fervor of enthusiasm, certainly not that they urged it.

In the days of the Weimar Republic even the social militarism of the imperial period declined. The military defeat of the First World War and the period of economic unrest and moral dislocation of the postwar period undermined the position of the former social elite, including that of the aristocratic military families. The mood of democratic socialist and pacifist feeling diminished the popular admiration for military ideals and for the military profession. Immediately following 1919 citizens paraded through the streets of many German towns under banners which proclaimed "Nie Wieder Krieg!"—"Never Again War." Both the arms restrictions of the Versailles Treaty and the scanty Weimar budg-

[38] See, for example, Bismarck's *Briefe an Seine Gattin aus dem Kriege: 1870-71* (Stuttgart and Berlin: Cotta'sche Buchhandlung Nachfolger, 1903), pp. 63-74.

[39] G. P. Gooch, *Studies in Diplomacy and Statecraft* (London: Longmans, Green, 1942), p. 85.

[40] Captain Russell Grenfell, R.N., *Unconditional Hatred* (New York: Devin-Adair, 1953), pp. 76-77.

ets limited the size and power of the Republic's army and of its General Staff. During these years the Chief of the General Staff, General Hans von Seeckt, dedicated himself to two goals: (a) to rehabilitate the professional status of his 100,000-man army and (b) to keep his officers scrupulously out of political affairs. In matters of military appropriations the army was dependent on the Reichstag in which a powerful voting bloc of Socialists and Pacifists kept vigilant watch over expenditures which might lead to rearmament. The principle of civilian control of the War Ministry and of foreign policy was scrupulously maintained. Not only did the professional soldier disdain party politics but he also viewed policy formation, that is, the formulation of Grand Strategy, as the realm of the civilian.[41]

During the Nazi regime the role of the General Staff and of the regular army was very different from the image conveyed by the American President's speeches. We have the testimony of an expert, if not otherwise reliable, witness. During a visit to the Eastern Front early in the campaign against Russia, Adolf Hitler made the following statement:

> Before I was head of the German Government I thought the German General Staff was like a butcher's dog—something to be held tight by the collar because it threatened to attack all and sundry. Since then I have had to recognize that the General Staff is anything but that. It has consistently tried to impede every action that I have thought necessary. It objected to the military occupation of the Rhineland, to the march into Austria, to the occupation of Czechoslovakia, and finally even to the war against Poland. The General Staff

[41] During the long history of the Prussian, later German, General Staff there were, of course, exceptions to the Schlieffen-Seeckt principle of military abstention from politics. Notably Generals von Waldersee and Schleicher demonstrated interest and ambition in political as well as in purely military matters, but the overwhelming tendency of the Prussian-German professional officer corps was against such activity. For details see, for example: Samuel P. Huntington, *The Soldier and the State: the Theory and Politics of Civil-Military Relations* (Cambridge, Mass.: Belknap Press of Harvard Univ. Press, 1958); Liddell Hart, *The Other Side of the Hill* (London: Cassell), Chap. II, "The Mould of Seeckt," pp. 17-26; Hans Rothfels, *The German Opposition to Hitler* (Chicago: Henry Regnery, 1948), pp. 64 ff; and Gustav Stolper, *German Realities* (New York: Reynal and Hitchcock, 1948), pp. 154 ff.

warned me against offensive action in France, and against the war with Russia. It is I who have always had to goad on this "butcher's dog." [42]

Hitler put it succinctly. The Austrian who had served as a noncommissioned officer in the First World War always resented the aloofness and implied sense of superiority of his professional generals. He consistently rejected their advice and their warnings and reversed their decisions. He resented the resistance of the army to Nazi ideological influence and to penetration of its officer corps by party members; he resented the moral disdain of Prussian officers reared in the Schlieffen tradition for Nazi posturing and flamboyance, he resented the conservatism and legalism and what he considered pessimism and defeatism which impelled the generals to disagree with all his plans for expansion.[43]

There is no question that the soldiers welcomed the larger military budgets which Hitler's program of rearming in repudiation of the Versailles system meant. There is also little question that some of the soldiers were delighted with the increased prestige abroad and morale at home that rearmament brought to Germany, that some of them regarded Hitler as something better than a lesser evil. By and large, however, the army as a whole remained nonpolitical regarding domestic issues and used its influence to oppose rather than to encourage the steps which led Hitler to war in 1939. The Chief of the General Staff, General Ludwig Beck, was adamant in opposing the drift to war, and he resigned in indignant protest when Hitler violated the Munich Pact by marching into Prague in the spring of 1939.[44] From this point of view the Germany of Hitler was less "militaristic" than Imperial Germany had been: the military had still less effective influence on the policies of government. Even before the war

[42] Fabian von Schlabrendorff, *They Almost Killed Hitler* (New York: Macmillan, 1947), pp. 34-35.

[43] The Schlieffen idea of the Prussian officer is described in Friedrich von Boetticher, *Schlieffen* (Göttingen: Musterschmidt Verlag, 1957); see also, Wolfgang Foerster, *Ein General Kämpft gegen den Krieg* (Munich: Münchener Dom Verlag, *c.* 1949), pp. 24 ff.

[44] Foerster, *op. cit.*, pp. 90 ff.

broke out the anti-Nazi resistance forces had begun to crystallize, and the center of this resistance was in the German Wehrmacht, in the General Staff in particular. The opposition culminated in the July 20 attempt which pivoted around the General Staff officer who would carry a bomb into a staff meeting with the hope of blowing up the Führer and around the officers who planned to assume control of the government until peace could be made and a new government elected. The activities of the German generals in opposing war and in opposing Hitler and his party were well known in London and Washington, and yet both Churchill and Roosevelt regularly referred to the militarists as a war-breeding gang, as bad or worse than the Nazis.

There is not much doubt that Nazi Germany was a society which aimed at military power, nor is there doubt that uniforms, parades, and military demonstrations were an important adjunct to propaganda, a vital aspect of the Nazi apparatus. The Nazi party created its own military force in the Hitler Youth, the SA and the SS, and there is no question that these party military forces exerted a formidable influence over the government. Himmler, commander of the SS and the Gestapo, ranked second only to Hitler in power by the end of the war. If there was a form of militarism to be rooted out of Germany it was the militarism of the party forces, but the wartime speeches of Roosevelt and Churchill do not distinguish between the Wehrmacht and the SS, and they distinctly aim their attack at the General Staff of the regular army. Militarism existed, but it was not the conservative offspring of orthodox military organizations. The target at which Anglo-American policy was aimed did not, in fact, exist. There is reason to believe that the makers of policy knew that it did not exist.[45]

Prussian-German War Guilt

Anglo-American policy toward Prussia is reflected in a statement by Prime Minister Churchill:

[45] It is one of the puzzles of the Second World War that President Roosevelt steadfastly refused to recognize the existence and importance of the anti-Nazi movement in Germany and particularly within the German Wehrmacht. See Chapter 4.

> The core of Germany is Prussia. There is the source of the pestilence. . . . Nazi tyranny and Prussian militarism are the two main elements in German life which must be absolutely destroyed. They must be rooted out if Europe and the world are to be spared a third and still more frightful conflict.

In the same speech Churchill charged that "twice within our lifetime, and three times counting that of our fathers" the German people "have plunged the world into their wars of expansion and aggression." [46]

The implication is that German and especially Prussian society is warlike and aggressive by nature, that Prussia-Germany had been morally responsible for the three preceding wars, and that therefore the aim of the Second World War was to destroy this aggressive Prusso-German spirit. This made the war a moral crusade, and it made only one war aim possible—the total defeat of the enemy. The truth or falsehood of the charge against Prussia and Germany cannot be determined without exhaustive examination of the diplomatic events which led up to the three most recent European wars, but let us examine the most obvious facts of the case.

The Franco-Prussian War: 1870-1871. The view of the English and American governments on war guilt in 1870 was somewhat different at the time of the outbreak of the war between France and Prussia than it appears to have been in 1943. For example, on October 12, 1870, the American Minister to Berlin, Bancroft, informed the German Foreign Secretary that both official and public opinion in the United States regarded the war as an act of self-defense on the part of Prussia. He said that his countrymen remembered past wars of aggression against the German states by their western neighbors, "of which the past three centuries have brought so large a number." [47] There is little question that the declaration of war was issued by France, and that the powers in 1870-1871 viewed the cause of German national unification with sympathy. Bismarck, who fought to further the principle of nationality, was not criticized by contemporary journal-

[46] From a speech of Sept. 21, 1943, Winston Churchill, *Closing the Ring* (Boston: Houghton Mifflin, 1951), p. 159.

[47] Stolper, *op. cit.*, p. 218.

ists and diplomats for having resorted to war to unite his nation any more than Abraham Lincoln had been criticized for waging a war of national unity a decade earlier. In the nineteenth century national unity was conceived of as a moral goal of policy, and war, if necessary, counted as a legitimate means of achieving that goal, especially if the war was declared by the enemy. There is little question that Bismarck welcomed the French declaration of war: he called the war a "national necessity,"[48] but there is also little question that his attitude was not regarded as unjustified or aggressive in his own time.

Unified Germany under Bismarck's guidance was a singularly peaceful state. Under the Bismarck policy of limited liability Germany was the only great power of the period between 1871 and 1914 to avoid war: the United States fought Mexico and Spain; Russia was at war with Turkey and Japan; England fought the Boer War; France was engaged in warfare in her colonies. Although Germany, too, acquired colonies during these years, German policy avoided war.

World War I. The Versailles Treaty attributes the sole guilt in inciting and provoking the First World War to Germany. The Churchill speech and similar speeches by Roosevelt imply that the charge is fully true. The views of diplomatic historians are by no means unanimous, and the welter of facts concerning the actual outbreak of war in 1914 indicates a multiplicity of causes. Although the analysts disagree in apportioning guilt for the war, the literal facts of the case are that the assassination of the Austrian Archduke by a Serbian national provoked a sharp ultimatum by Austria-Hungary to Serbia, which was declined by Serbia, and, therefore, Austria-Hungary declared war on Serbia. The German entry into the war came only after the declaration of intent to mobilize by Russia, and it came despite the German General Staff's warning that war would mean the devastation of European culture.

The purpose of this discussion is not to assert that Germany had no part in the responsibility for the outbreak of war in 1914, or even to allocate to her a lesser burden of guilt, but merely to cast some doubt on the easy assumption of sole German guilt.

[48] Fürst Otto von Bismarck, *Gedanken und Erinnerungen* (Stuttgart: Verlag der J. G. Cotta'schen Buchhandlung, 1898), Vol. II, pp. 85 ff.

Subsequent to the war the Allied governments admitted that many of the atrocity charges against the enemy had been false. The charge "twice within our lifetime, and three times counting that of our fathers" is by no means above question. It carries the earmarks of wartime propaganda rather than of scholarly historical analysis, a fact which is understandable in that it derives from a public speech of a wartime political leader. It is natural that the British Prime Minister and the American President should have used moral charges against the German enemy to fire the Allied public with war zeal. Propaganda had become an accepted weapon of warfare, and the accepted ammunition of that weapon is the distortion and oversimplification of truth. Perhaps in modern war, which depends for its success on the enthusiastic support of broad segments of the public, such distortions are justified, but however reasonable it may have been to lay the accusation of perpetual aggression against Prussia and Germany in propaganda attacks, it seems not only unreasonable but dangerous to national interest to have allowed policy to be directed by a propaganda slogan. The Anglo-American propaganda offensive proclaimed Prussia-Germany, not just Nazi Germany, a warmongering, outlaw society; therefore, Allied policy had to be directed toward the total defeat, punishment, and reconstruction of German society rather than toward the simple goal of the overthrow of the Nazi government. Such far-reaching war aims seem to have been a basic factor underlying the doctrine of total victory and of Unconditional Surrender.

The Concept of Prussia

The core of Germany is Prussia. This was Churchill's view not merely in his public proclamations but also at the conference table. Throughout the war both Churchill and Eden proposed peace terms which would reduce the size of Prussia or abolish it altogether and isolate the smaller German states from Prussian influence. They seem to have found sympathy for these suggestions in Roosevelt and Hull. The concept of the Prussian menace seems to have been another vital factor in the policy of total victory. Once more, not merely the Nazi regime must be overthrown but Germany must be totally defeated so that territorial and constitutional changes could be effected with the aim of weakening or destroying the Prussian spirit.

The exact nature of the Anglo-American image of Prussia and of Prussianism is not revealed in detail by the speeches and statements of Churchill and Roosevelt, but it seems to include two elements: that Prussia is basically militaristic and, therefore, aggressive and warlike and that Prussian society is antidemocratic. It further includes a belief that the Prussian core of Germany propelled the more passive, peace-loving, and democratic areas of Germany into rearming and into war and implies Prussian moral and political responsibility for Hitlerism.

Few writers, especially not the most stanchly Prussian, will deny that there is a Prussian spirit, nor that, by and large, the characteristics of this spirit are orderliness and respect for law and for established authority, nor, indeed, that soldierly virtues and respect for the military profession have always played a significant role in the Prussian tradition. However, the conclusions that respect for order leads automatically to a negation of democracy and that military virtues automatically militate toward war and especially aggressive war would be further examples of a form of logic more appropriate to propaganda than to historical analysis or to policy formation. We have already discussed briefly the role of Prussian militarism in the task of policy formation and in relation to aggressive warfare. Let us look briefly at the charge that Prussia has been traditionally antidemocratic and that Prussianism contributed to the growth and success of the National Socialist movement.

While it certainly seems true that Prussia was the home of a particularly stern form of conservatism, it was also a stronghold of Socialism and of democratic forces. Under the monarchy the power of the German Social Democratic party grew gradually, and during the Weimar Republic, at least until 1930, the SPD was the most powerful single party in Germany on the basis of election returns. The center of SPD strength was Prussia, especially Berlin. When the Weimar Constitution had been drafted, the state of Prussia had been preserved not at the insistence of

German nationalists but on pleas of the Socialists because the source of their power was Prussia.[49]

It is interesting to look at the election figures for Berlin during the years 1920 to 1931. In all but one election, the SPD polled more votes than any other single party. Throughout the first seven years of the period, the German National party, the conservative monarchist group, was generally the second party, polling fewer votes than the SPD but more than the Communists, the Democrats, or the Catholic (Centrist) party. The German National party, however, consistently polled only a small minority of the total vote cast and usually substantially less than half the total of the Weimar Coalition, that is, of the SPD, Centrists, Democrats, and German People's party together. After 1928 the German Nationals dropped to third place in Berlin elections, giving way to the Communists.[50] Thus, although the Conservatives formed a politically significant segment of Prussian life and perhaps exercised more social influence than the statistics indicate, the Prussian electorate was firmly and consistently and overwhelmingly democratic. In Berlin the NSDAP remained in seventh place until 1929, and even at its height in 1932 it polled fewer votes than the Communists or than the democratic coalition.[51] Prussia was never a Nazi bastion. In August, 1931, the

[49] Prince Hubertus zu Loewenstein, *The Germans in History* (New York: Columbia Univ. Press, 1945), p. 467.

[50] Statistical Office of Berlin, *Berlin in Zahlen: Taschenbuch* (Berlin: Das Neue Berlin Verlagsgesellschaft m.b.H., 1947), p. 372, table of election results by party, 1921-1932.

[51] Loewenstein, *op. cit.*, pp. 467, 477. For example, the Reichstag election statistics indicate that the NSDAP polled substantially more votes in Upper Bavaria than in the Prussian election districts in the elections of 1924 and 1928: 2.83 per cent and 1.3 per cent on the average in the ten Prussian districts as compared to 4.8 per cent and 6.2 per cent in Upper Bavaria. In Prussia, as elsewhere in Germany, National Socialist strength increased sharply in the wake of the 1929 crash. In the elections of 1930 and 1932, the Nazis polled a higher percentage of votes in Prussia than in Bavaria, possibly because the basically agrarian economy of Bavaria suffered less severely from the depression, or because Communist strength, greater in Prussia and concentrated in Berlin, seemed the greater and more apparent evil to many Prussian voters. See Wilhelm Dittmann, *Das Politische Deutschland vor Hitler* (Zurich and New York: Europa Verlag, 1945; pages unnumbered). See also G. Franz, "Munich, Birthplace and Center of the NSDAP," *Journal of Modern History*, December, 1957.

NSDAP joined forces with the Communists to try to overthrow the democratic coalition in Prussia by plebiscite, but the attempt failed.

On July 20, 1932, Chancellor Franz von Papen dismissed the legitimate Prussian state government by decree and had the German President appoint him commissar for Prussia. The Prussian government appealed its case to the German Supreme Court, which ruled in October, 1932, that the Chancellor's act had been unconstitutional. Papen was forced to withdraw as commissar and to permit the re-establishment of the coalition government.

When Hitler became chancellor in January, 1933, he forcibly expelled the Prussian government and appointed Hermann Goering as Prussian prime minister and so achieved by force what could not be accomplished in free elections or by constitutional means.[52] The stronghold of National Socialism was Bavaria, not Prussia. It was in Munich and not in Berlin that Hitler first organized the NSDAP and attempted his first Putsch. The leaders of this movement were predominantly non-Prussian: Hitler himself was Austrian, Ribbentrop and Goebbels were from the Rhineland, an overwhelming number of the Nazi hierarchy were South Germans, although of course there were some Prussians among them. The general atmosphere of the Nazi party and of the Nazi era in German public life, the ostentation and display, the rule by the party as distinguished from rule by the law, the cynical contempt of the party leaders for the constitution, the vulgarity and excess revealed in the public behavior and private lives of many of the Nazi chiefs, were in direct opposition to the Prussian spirit of simplicity and restraint, of self-discipline, and of respect for the law and for tradition. To a great extent it was this basic dichotomy between the spirit of Prussia and the atmosphere and ideology of the Nazi regime which gave impetus to the rise of an anti-Nazi movement within Germany. To a great extent, it seems to have been the failure to perceive this dichotomy between Prussianism and National Socialism which prevented the Anglo-American leadership from exploiting the rift in German society by giving support to the anti-Nazi Germans.

[52] Loewenstein, *op. cit.*, pp. 467, 477.

Instead, the English and the Americans equated Prussianism with aggression, militarism, and totalitarianism and demanded the destruction of Prussia along with the destruction of National Socialism; instead, they continued to demand Unconditional Surrender.

The Necessities of Alliance

The concept of Total Victory may have sprung from many sources. To judge from presidential statements and from speeches by Churchill, the will to punish aggressive nations, to eradicate militarism, and to abolish Prussia and Prussianism certainly contributed to the Anglo-American view that the Second World War must be pursued to the point of absolute victory, until the victorious Allied armies marched through the streets of Tokyo and Berlin. Total victory was a necessary prerequisite to carrying out the sweeping changes in the enemy societies which their policy envisioned. Other factors, however, also seem to have contributed to the policy. One of these was difficulty of arriving at any concrete peace plans to which the three major Allies, Great Britain, the U.S.S.R., and the United States, could agree in advance. Since specific agreements could not be made, the general commitment to fight on until total victory had been achieved, to fight for Unconditional Surrender, served as a substitute for war aims.

The fear that the Soviet Union would withdraw from the war and arrange a separate peace with Germany haunted the British and American governments during the early years of the alliance. This fear was especially acute just prior to the Casablanca Conference before the Red Army's victory at Stalingrad. During the weeks before Casablanca the British Ambassador in Moscow, Clark Kerr, warned his government that the Soviets were threatening to withdraw from the war unless the Anglo-Americans committed themselves to a speedy opening of a second front in France. Although the British chiefs apparently took this threat with some skepticism, the Prime Minister and the American President regarded the danger as a matter of serious concern.[53]

[53] Bryant, *op. cit.*, pp. 436 f.

From the viewpoint of the Allied planners, the strategic picture had begun to brighten, and there was little question at Casablanca that the long-range prognosis was good. The combined potential of manpower, resources, and production of the Anglo-Americans alone probably could have ensured eventual victory over Germany, but the memory of the unbroken succession of German victories of the early war years clouded the optimism of the combined chiefs. In January, 1943, the U-boat war was at its height and the German Wehrmacht still dominated the entire European Continent. Soviet defection would have released a substantial proportion of the German forces in Russia to fight on the Western Fronts and would have left the Germans in control of the land and resources of a large part of European U.S.S.R. At the beginning of 1943 this prospect constituted a genuine threat and apparently the Soviet leaders understood how to exploit this threat.

The decision that the three-power coalition must be preserved, that the war must be fought in a close alliance with Great Britain and the Soviet Union formed the basic policy of the war as far as the United States government was concerned. Secretary of War Stimson has written that neither he nor any administration leader with whose views he was familiar had ever questioned that decision. His view was that the three Allies together "formed the indispensable team for victory over Germany. Together . . . they could not lose. Apart or at cross purposes . . . they could hardly win." [54]

Republican Senator Vandenberg, on the Senate Foreign Relations Committee, not always a firm supporter of presidential foreign policy, also endorsed this view. Although he was wary of the Soviet Union's long-range peace aims, especially of Soviet ambitions in Eastern Europe, he warned against entering into arguments which might undermine the unity of the military alliance. He wrote:

> . . . now that we are in the war up to our eyes, I think the first job is to *win the war*. . . . I am unwilling to do *anything* which might

[54] Henry L. Stimson, *On Active Service in Peace and War* (New York: Harper, 1948), p. 525.

disunite the war effort by premature peace efforts. . . . I do not want to end up fighting this war all alone. If we must quarrel with our Allies, I'd rather do it *after victory.*[55]

Vandenberg opposed any open debate on the Senate floor on the details of postwar planning which might emphasize the opposition of the senators to Soviet war aims and he warned that such discussion "could re-divide Americans at home. It could easily divide our Allies abroad . . . it could jeopardize victory itself." [56] In March, 1943, Secretary of State Hull also expressed fear of any American statement or action which might endanger the alliance. He felt that relations with the U.S.S.R. were extremely delicate.[57]

At least one high-ranking official in Washington opposed this trend. Undersecretary of State Sumner Welles writes that he favored a policy of winning concessions regarding postwar commitments from the U.S.S.R. precisely at a time when the Red Army was critically dependent on American Lend-Lease aid and while American moral authority was at its highest. He pointed to Wilson's failure to achieve binding commitments from the Allies prior to the Armistice in 1918 and warned that delays in securing inter-Allied agreement might lead to a result similar to that of the Paris Peace Conference: once the Allies no longer required American production to aid in the defeat of the enemy they would be in a position to reject American political demands.[58]

General John R. Deane, chief of the United States Military Mission in Moscow, attempted to warn the American government that many of the Soviet threats to withdraw from the war were simply tactical maneuvers designed to win concessions from the Western Allies. Deane learned the secret of Soviet bargaining techniques through day-to-day experience in Moscow. He describes Russian negotiating tactics in his book, *The Strange Alli-*

[55] *The Private Papers of Senator Vandenberg,* ed. Arthur H. Vandenberg, Jr. (Boston: Houghton Mifflin, 1952), pp. 45-46, entry of April 15, 1943.

[56] *Ibid.,* p. 40.

[57] *Ibid.,* p. 41.

[58] Sumner Welles, *Seven Decisions That Shaped History* (New York: Harper, 1951), pp. 123-26.

ance: the Soviet representative would usually begin discussions by launching a long and outspoken criticism of Western policy and strategy, questioning both methods and intentions, then he would issue a blunt demand for increased military aid. At the next official Moscow dinner Soviet and Western officers would drink a hearty toast to Allied unity, and the following morning the United States would dispatch a thousand planes for the Soviet Air Force; the U.S.S.R. would reciprocate by granting a visa which had been promised and pending for months. Deane warned that the Russians admired hard bargaining and despised gullibility. He advised his superiors that one-sided concessions to Soviet demands would arouse more suspicion than gratitude. Unquestioning generosity might have been understandable during the early days of the alliance when the Red Army was in danger of imminent collapse, but with the victory at Stalingrad both the military and the psychological situation in the U.S.S.R. had changed. Deane advocated a firm policy of demanding political concessions in return for our aid, but other counsels prevailed.[59]

President Roosevelt rejected proposals that United States relations with the Soviet Union be conducted on the basis of hard bargaining. He seemed confident of his ability to deal with Stalin. Although he assumed that Soviet influence would be greater in postwar Europe and even that the Soviet Union would be likely to dominate the European Continent, he confided to William C. Bullitt:

> I have a hunch that Stalin . . . doesn't want anything but security for his country, and I think that if I give him everything I possibly can and ask for nothing in return, noblesse oblige.[60]

Roosevelt's policy toward the Soviet Union was based on the attempt to win Soviet gratitude and friendship and he opposed any public statement of war aims which might arouse Soviet suspicion or destroy the working alliance. He considered any overt criticism of the Soviet ally a threat to the unity he felt

[59] General John R. Deane, *The Strange Alliance* (New York: Viking, 1947), p. 84.

[60] William C. Bullitt, "How We Won the War and Lost the Peace," *Life,* Aug. 30, 1948, p. 94. See also Hull, *op. cit.,* p. 1452.

was essential to the war effort. He tended to regard suspicion of Soviet war aims as Nazi propaganda. For example, in February, 1942, he warned in a radio address that

> . . . the object of the Nazis and Japanese is to separate the United States, Britain, China, and Russia and to isolate them one from another so that each will be surrounded and cut off from sources of supply and reinforcements. It is the old familiar Axis policy of "divide and conquer." [61]

In February, 1943, he repeated the warning. He said that the Axis propagandists were "trying all of their old tricks" to divide the Allies by intimating that after the war Russia, England, China, and the United States would turn on each other. He said that none of the Allies would be so gullible as to be duped into making deals at the expense of all the others:

> The Nazis must be frantic indeed if they believe they can devise any propaganda which would turn the British and American and Chinese governments and people against Russia—or Russia against the rest of us.[62]

Even as late as January, 1945, he told the American Congress not to give credit to "evil and baseless rumors against the Russians." He said that examination of such rumors will show "that every one of them bears the same trademark—'made in Germany.'" Certainly Roosevelt was aware that differences in ideology and interest separated the goals of the Eastern and the Western Allies but he warned the Congress that "we must not let those differences divide us and blind us to our more important common and continuing interest in winning the war and building the peace." [63] Throughout the war Roosevelt continued to appeal for a policy of solidarity with all the Allies. During the early years of the war he favored postponing controversial questions which might tend to disrupt the alliance.[64]

In this context the policy of Unconditional Surrender may be viewed as a war aim which committed the two Western Allies

[61] *War Messages,* p. 31.
[62] *Ibid.,* p. 71.
[63] *Ibid.,* pp. 158-64.
[64] See, for example, the Yalta communiqué Feb. 11, 1945.

to fight on until total victory was achieved and thus offered moral support to the U.S.S.R. at a time when Stalin had been complaining of the delays in opening a second front. It further offered a simple slogan on which all three major Allies could agree even though their political aims in Europe differed sharply. Unconditional Surrender was diplomatically ambiguous; it avoided precipitating open disagreements among the Allies. It represented a policy of lowest common denominator.

Conclusions

The policy of Unconditional Surrender was essentially a policy of total victory. Such a war aim is a logical outgrowth of the concept of war as a moral struggle to punish aggressive nations and is inevitable if the war aims include reconstruction of enemy society in order to destroy such elements as militarism and the Prussian spirit. It was also a policy of the lowest common denominator, which aimed at uniting disunited Allies at least upon the goal of common victory. Perhaps, too, other factors lay behind the demand.

There is no indication in either Roosevelt's statements or in the diaries of participants at the Casablanca Conference that the matter of domestic American politics had been a consideration in the President's announcement of the policy, but the desire to represent American war aims in a simple formula on which all facets of American political thought could unite may have contributed to his continued endorsement of the Casablanca Formula. There is no question that isolationism was still a factor in internal American politics. There is also no question that the United States Senate was by no means agreed on the exact nature of the peace which ought to have constituted American war aims. The debates of the Foreign Relations Committee reveal a wide divergence of views. Here again Unconditional Surrender was the lowest common denominator; all factions could agree upon winning the war, of pursuing it to total victory.[65]

Robert Sherwood, who has investigated the question of Unconditional Surrender in his book *Roosevelt and Hopkins,* states

[65] See, for example, Vandenberg, *op. cit.,* pp. 38 ff.

that the ghost of Woodrow Wilson had been at Roosevelt's shoulder at Casablanca. Roosevelt wanted to avoid the errors of Wilson.[66] By allowing the Axis enemy no "escape clauses" he hoped to prevent a repetition of the tragedy of the Fourteen Points: if no terms were offered or accepted, there could be no charge later that the eventual peace treaty had failed to fulfill the promised terms. Apparently Roosevelt attributed the rise of Hitler to a great extent at least to German public bitterness over the discrepancies between the promise of the Fourteen Points and the actuality of the Versailles Treaty and to the slogan exploited by the Nazis that in the First World War the German Army had not been defeated in the field but rather had been stabbed in the back by the revolt on the home front in 1918. He was determined that in the Second World War there would be no promises to be broken and no occasion for a new "stab in the back" legend. Unconditional Surrender would mean that the German Army would be totally defeated in the field, that Allied troops would penetrate German territory and march through the streets of Berlin.

Winston Churchill added another explanation for the announcement. The mood of depression which had surrounded the Allied governments had begun to lift after the British victory at El Alamein, but at the time of the Casablanca Conference the military situation was still grave. Although the tide of the war had turned, Allied victory was by no means yet in sight. Allied morale was still shaken. Therefore Churchill said defiance was the note. This, in part, may explain the resounding demand: Unconditional Surrender.

THE REACTION OF CHURCHILL AND STALIN TO UNCONDITIONAL SURRENDER

The decision at Casablanca to call for the unconditional surrender of the Axis enemy, although endorsed and accepted by Churchill, was clearly an American responsibility. It was Franklin Roosevelt's phrase and policy and seems to have grown naturally, perhaps inevitably, out of the American experience and the American tradition of warfare. It reflected the basic American

[66] *Op. cit.*, p. 697.

war aim of total victory. It will be interesting to examine the question as to what extent the phrase and policy reflected the war aims of the two other major Allies of the wartime coalition. How enthusiastic was Churchill's acceptance of the formula? How correct was Roosevelt's surmise that the phrase would be just the thing for the Soviets, that Stalin himself might have originated it?

An examination of Churchill's subsequent speeches and writings does not reveal any forceful opposition to the Casablanca phrase, in fact, Churchill defends it, but it is clear that the Churchillian view of the aims of the war differed from Roosevelt's, that the simple aim of total victory never adequately represented the British goal of warfare.

Churchill's View of Unconditional Surrender

Churchill attributed the phrase "Unconditional Surrender" unequivocally to the American President. In a House of Commons debate subsequent to the Casablanca Conference the Prime Minister referred to the Casablanca Formula as "a statement which the President wished to make." Later, in a 1949 House of Commons debate, Churchill offered an explanation of the Casablanca decision which he later found to be in error. He said:

> The statement was made by President Roosevelt without consultation with me. I was there on the spot, and I had very rapidly to consider whether the state of our position in the world was such as would justify me in not giving support to it. I did give support to it, but it was not the idea which I had formed in my own mind. In the same way, when it came to the Cabinet at home, I have not the slightest doubt that if the British Cabinet had considered the phrase, it is likely that they would have advised against it, but working with great, loyal, and powerful friends from across the ocean, we had to accommodate ourselves.[67]

In *Roosevelt and Hopkins* Robert Sherwood reported that he received a letter from Prime Minister Churchill in which he stated:

> I heard the words "Unconditional Surrender" for the first time from the President's lips at the Conference. It must be remembered that

[67] Hankey, *op. cit.*, pp. 30, 31.

at that moment no one had a right to proclaim that Victory was assured. Therefore Defiance was the note. I would not myself have used these words, but I immediately stood by the President and have frequently defended the decision. It is false to suggest that it prolonged the war. Negotiation with Hitler was impossible. He was a maniac with supreme power to play his hand to the end, which he did; and so did we.[68]

Although he later admitted that his memory had been in error, that indeed he had discussed the phrase with the President prior to the announcement, the letter may indicate Churchill's basic attitude toward Unconditional Surrender. Although he defended the demand against the charge that it may have lengthened the war, he endorsed the policy with only faint praise. The words "Unconditional Surrender" were not those he would have used.

Robert Sherwood writes that cables on file at the British Foreign Office show that the British Cabinet had been consulted about the decision to demand unconditional surrender. The cable file contains a message from Churchill at Casablanca dated January 19, 1943, to Clement Attlee requesting the War Cabinet's views on the inclusion of a demand for the unconditional surrender of Germany and Japan in the Casablanca press release and stating, "the President liked this idea and it would stimulate our friends in every country." Attlee's reply cable of January 21 gave the War Cabinet's endorsement of the plan but suggested that the demand be extended to Italy as well as to Germany and Japan.[69]

In his *Memoirs* Churchill admits that his first recollection that he had never heard the phrase "Unconditional Surrender" until the President announced it at the press conference had been incorrect, that the cables indicate that the matter must have been discussed. He explains that the omission of the phrase from the official communiqué had convinced him that the President had abandoned the plan, and so he was surprised at the press conference announcement.[70] The Prime Minister's forgetfulness may

[68] Sherwood, *op. cit.*, p. 696.
[69] *Ibid.*, p. 973.
[70] Winston Churchill, *The Hinge of Fate* (Boston: Houghton Mifflin, 1950), pp. 685-87.

indicate that the discussion of the phrase had not impressed him as of major importance at Casablanca.

Although Churchill was not the author of Unconditional Surrender and had not endorsed the policy with any degree of enthusiasm, his wartime speeches made it clear that he supported the underlying policy of the total defeat of Germany and Japan. Throughout the war he insisted that

> . . . justice must be done upon the wicked and the guilty, and within her proper bounds justice must be stern and implacable. No vestige of Nazi . . . power . . . will be left to us when the work is done, and done it certainly will be.[71]

On June 30, 1943, Churchill made an address at the Guild Hall. He stated that the will of the enemy powers to resist must be completely broken, that "they must yield themselves absolutely to our justice and mercy." He warned that the Allies intended to take all steps necessary to prevent

> . . . the world from being again convulsed, wrecked and blackened by their calculated plots and ferocious aggressions. It does not mean . . . that we are to stain our victorious arms by inhumanity or by mere lust of vengeance.[72]

In an address before the House of Commons on September 21, 1943, Churchill further explained his view of the policy. He welcomed the recent overthrow of the Mussolini government by the Italians and he expressed the hope that the Italian people would be permitted "in due course to regain their rightful place among the free democracies of the modern world." Regarding the German people Churchill entertained no such charitable hopes. "The case is different," he asserted:

> Twice within our lifetime, and three times counting that of our fathers, they have plunged the world into their wars of expansion and aggression. They combine in the most deadly manner the qualities of the warrior and the slave. They do not value freedom themselves, and the spectacle of it in others is hateful to them. Whenever they become strong, they seek their prey, and will follow with an iron discipline anyone who will lead them to it. The core of Germany

[71] Hankey, *op. cit.*, pp. 32 f.
[72] *Hinge of Fate*, p. 688.

is Prussia. There is the source of the pestilence. But we do not war with races as such. We war against tyranny, and we seek to preserve ourselves from destruction. I am convinced that the British, American and Russian peoples, who have suffered measureless waste, peril and bloodshed twice in the quarter of a century through the Teutonic urge for domination, will this time take steps to put it beyond the power of Prussia or of all Germany to come at them again with pent-up vengeance and long-nurtured plans. Nazi tyranny and Prussian militarism are the two main elements in German life which must be absolutely destroyed. They must be rooted out if Europe and the world are to be spared a third and still more frightful conflict.[73]

Although he believed that compromise with Axis satellite states might be possible, he insisted that "the twin root of all our evils, Nazi tyranny and Prussian militarism, must be extirpated." [74]

In February, 1944, the Prime Minister explained his interpretation of the policy of Unconditional Surrender. He said that it did not mean that the German people would be enslaved or destroyed, but rather it meant simply that the Allies would not be bound by any specific prior commitment. For example, there would be no question of the Atlantic Charter's applying to Germany as a matter of right and no chance for misunderstanding or recrimination arising from pre-Armistice agreements such as the Fourteen Points. He said that Unconditional Surrender meant simply that

the victors have a free hand. It doesn't mean that they are entitled to behave in a barbarous manner, nor that they wish to blot out Germany from among the nations of Europe. If we are bound, we are bound by our own consciences to civilization, we are not bound as a result of a bargain struck, that is the meaning of "Unconditional Surrender." [75]

In May, 1944, he repeated his defense of the Unconditional Surrender formula on grounds that it eliminated the danger "of anything like Mr. Wilson's Fourteen Points being brought up by the Germans after their defeat, claiming that they surrendered in

[73] *Closing the Ring,* p. 159. See also Hankey, *op. cit.,* p. 34.
[74] *Closing the Ring,* p. 142.
[75] *Ibid.* See also Hankey, *op. cit.,* p. 34.

consideration of them." [76] These statements reveal a somewhat stronger tendency on the part of the Prime Minister than of President Roosevelt to assure the German people and world public opinion that Unconditional Surrender did not mean a barbarous and vindictive peace, but they also indicate that Churchill too advocated the doctrine of a moral war fought to an uncompromising conclusion.

Churchill's Strategy Reservation

If Winston Churchill was as sensitive as Franklin Roosevelt to the threat of Prussian militarism and of German aggression and if he too seems to have believed that the objective of the Second World War was to punish aggression and extirpate militarism, he did not share the American President's confidence that these were the only likely menaces to future world peace. His preoccupation with a plan to invade Southeastern Europe and so prevent the Balkans and the Danube Valley from falling under Soviet occupation indicates not only a view of postwar diplomacy which differed from that entertained by Roosevelt, but also a basically different view of war. Apparently he believed with Clausewitz that strategy should serve the ends of policy. Apparently Churchill had no desire to see German hegemony in Europe supplanted by Soviet domination of the Continent.

This basic divergence of views between the American President and the British Prime Minister was reflected in divergent strategy proposals by the American and British military chiefs. The battle continued through most of the war. The American attitude can be summed up in General George Marshall's argument that the Anglo-Americans should plan an invasion of the European mainland by the shortest possible route at the earliest possible date to end the war quickly. The English attitude is reflected in Chief of Staff Alanbrooke's reply that this would end the war quickly "but not the way we hope to finish it." [77] The American goal was to defeat the German Army in the field; the British goal was to achieve political objectives.

[76] William Henry Chamberlin, *America's Second Crusade* (Chicago: Henry Regnery, 1950), p. 290.

[77] Bryant, *op. cit.*, p. 508.

The conflict of views became apparent as early as 1942 when the American Joint Chiefs of Staff proposed *Operation Sledgehammer,* a small-scale Anglo-American invasion of France in order to divert sufficient German troops from the Eastern Front to prevent the collapse of the Red Army. Churchill and the British chiefs rejected the proposal as rash and premature, and suggested instead a plan to invade North Africa.[78] The Americans acceded to the British proposal. The conflict bobbed to the surface again at Casablanca when once again the British opposed American plans for an early invasion of the French coast as premature, and instead urged the invasion of Sicily. It became clear to the American chiefs that their British colleagues favored operations in the Mediterranean as a preliminary to an eventual invasion of the Balkans. At Casablanca the Americans agreed to the plan to invade Sicily, but reserved decision on a Balkan invasion.

In May, 1943, the Prime Minister and his aides arrived in Washington for the *Trident* conference and again the British propounded the view that the Mediterranean offered more favorable opportunities for Allied operations than the French coast. They advocated a campaign against Italy to knock the Italians out of the war with a view to an eventual trans-Adriatic invasion of Yugoslavia, penetrating north up the Danube to Prague and Vienna and into the southeastern door of the German homeland. The Americans, led by Marshall, championed the plan of immediate concentration on the proposed cross-channel invasion of France. *Trident* accepted a compromise three-pronged solution:

1. A cross-channel invasion of France with a target date of May, 1944, to be launched with an initial force of twenty-nine divisions.

2. Intensified Anglo-American bombing attacks against both Italy and Germany.

3. The invasion of Sicily and later of Italy from North African bases with a view to eliminating Italy from the war.

[78] For further details of the Anglo-American conflict on this subject see, for example, Dwight D. Eisenhower, *Crusade in Europe* (New York: Doubleday, 1948), pp. 138, 225-28; William L. Neumann, *Making the Peace* (Washington, D. C.: Foundation for Foreign Affairs, 1950), p. 42; Wedemeyer, *op. cit.*, pp. 185, 211, 218, 230-36.

Thus, although the American plan carried the day, the way was left open for a later Balkan invasion from Italian soil. At subsequent conferences the British continued to press for further Mediterranean operations and the Americans, generally, continued to demur.

At Teheran in November, 1943, Churchill once more urged the plan of an Anglo-American invasion of the Balkans. He argued that the twenty Allied divisions in the Mediterranean which could not be deployed to the Atlantic because of lack of shipping could be exploited in an invasion of Yugoslavia where the aid of Marshal Tito and his partisan forces would greatly increase the efficiency of the Allied force and so relieve pressure on the Red Army immediately. Stalin, however, strongly opposed any plan of this sort on the grounds that it would delay *Operation Overlord,* the cross-channel invasion of France. Churchill replied that a trans-Adriatic invasion need not preclude the cross-channel project, that at worst it would delay it a few weeks. Stalin objected strenuously to even a day's delay and impugned the seriousness of the Anglo-American intentions to launch a second front.[79]

Roosevelt added his support to Stalin's position. The American chiefs advised the President that the quickest way to defeat the Wehrmacht with the smallest loss of Allied life would be to mount a major invasion, concentrate the full mass of Allied strength at that point, and penetrate from the coast of France straight into the heartland of Germany. This, the President explained at the conference, was the way "to kill the most Germans with the least loss of American soldiers . . . it makes sense to Uncle Joe. It makes sense to all our generals. . . . It makes sense to the Red Army people. That's that." [80]

Privately Roosevelt confided to his son Elliott and to Harry Hopkins that he attributed Churchill's enthusiasm for a Balkan operation to British imperialistic ambitions. He said that he feared Churchill was more interested in preserving the British lifeline of empire in the Eastern Mediterranean and in carving out a British sphere of influence in postwar Southeast Europe than in

[79] Deane, *op. cit.,* pp. 41-44. See also Sherwood, *op. cit.,* p. 185.
[80] Elliott Roosevelt, *op. cit.,* p. 185.

defeating the Germans. He also feared that the Churchill policy would destroy Soviet confidence in the good faith of the Anglo-Americans and would thus weaken Big Three unity and perhaps discourage the U.S.S.R. from entering the war against Japan.[81]

Most of the President's military advisers, including Secretary of War Stimson, General Marshall, and his personal Chief of Staff, Admiral Leahy, supported the direct cross-channel assault as the simplest, least costly means of achieving military victory. Leahy wrote that only by engaging the German Army in defense of its own homeland could German strength be broken and only then would "the road to Berlin and victory in Europe" be in sight. Leahy shared Roosevelt's belief that Churchill was motivated by desire to preserve the power of the British Empire in the Eastern Mediterranean.[82] Even Generals Deane and Wedemeyer, who were less confident than the President of the friendly intentions of the Soviet ally, advocated the cross-channel invasion instead of the Balkan project on grounds of military advantage: shorter supply lines, better protection of lines of communication, and the most direct route to the heart of industrial Germany.[83]

Churchill was forced to accede to the demands of his allies. The Teheran Conference accepted the plan for a cross-channel invasion of France, *Operation Overlord,* to be followed by a secondary invasion of Southern France, *Operation Anvil.* Unofficially the British Prime Minister continued to press for his own plan. It was Churchill and the British chiefs who persuaded their American allies to invade the Italian peninsula after the attack on Sicily, and until July, 1944, they kept urging the abandonment of the secondary invasion of France from the south, *Anvil,* in favor of a trans-Adriatic attack from Italy into Yugoslavia.

The American general immediately concerned in the implementation of *Operation Anvil* was General Mark Clark, commander of the Fifth Army in Italy. It would be elements of his forces which would have to be diverted to Southern France. He

[81] *Ibid.,* pp. 109, 156, 163-65, 176, 185-86; see also Chester Wilmot, *The Struggle for Europe* (New York: Harper, 1952), p. 447.

[82] Leahy, *op. cit.,* p. 209.

[83] Deane, *op. cit.,* p. 44. See also Wedemeyer, *op. cit.,* pp. 231-36, 240-46.

complained that the diversion left such gaps in his front in Italy that the German commander, Field Marshal Kesselring, had become confused and had sent out scouts to find out "where the hell the Fifth Army was."[84] Clark criticized the implementation of *Anvil* not only because it slowed down the Allied advance in Italy and was costly and inefficient but also because it defeated the political aim of securing Western influence in the Balkans. Clark favored a plan for a trans-Adriatic invasion from Italy which would enter Yugoslavia and press on toward Vienna, Budapest, and Prague. He writes that Roosevelt had initially expressed interest in the idea but had been dissuaded by Harry Hopkins.[85] When General Ira Eaker, Allied air commander in the Mediterranean, also advocated the trans-Adriatic invasion he was rebuffed by General Marshall with the comment, "You've been too damned long with the British."[86]

The Intelligence Division of the United States War Department prepared a memorandum warning of the dangers of Soviet predominance in the Balkans. The authors of the memorandum were told by their superiors that they were in error, that "the Russians have no political objectives in the Balkans; they are there for military reasons only."[87]

In general the attitude of the American military planners seems to have been that strategy is designed to achieve one purpose, the destruction of the armed power of the enemy, that strategy has no connection with political ends. That this viewpoint was dominant is reflected in the fact that Secretary of State Cordell Hull, who had been included in the President's War Council before the attack on Pearl Harbor, was never invited to attend any of the wartime Allied meetings or conferences when the primary purpose of the meeting was military. In his *Memoirs* Hull writes:

> The question of where the armies would land and what routes they would take across the continent in the grand military movement to

[84] Mark Clark, *Calculated Risk* (New York: Harper, 1950), pp. 367-69.
[85] *Ibid.*, p. 371.
[86] Hanson W. Baldwin, *Great Mistakes of the War* (New York: Harper, 1950), p. 39; see also pp. 34-44.
[87] *Ibid.*, p. 45.

conquer Hitler was a subject never discussed with me by the President or any of his top military advisors.[88]

President Roosevelt, who obviously thought with his military men that the primary task was to defeat the German Wehrmacht in order to accomplish political ends in Germany, also thought beyond Germany and beyond the war. His long-range goal seems to have been the establishment of peace on the basis of trust and friendship among the wartime Big Three—Great Britain, the Soviet Union, and the United States—and to this end he sought to avoid any moves which would engender suspicion. "Win the war first" was also his attitude, but he emphasized the need to win it in a spirit of co-operation and confidence.

British Policy in the Second World War

The Americans who negotiated with the British chiefs during the Second World War often disagreed with their colleagues' views of strategy and with their proposals, but they write with admiration of the British skill in negotiation, of the unity of the British team, of the superior co-ordination between the civilian and military spheres. General Wedemeyer points out that the British chiefs had frequent, almost daily, access to Churchill as well as to officials in all branches of government. Churchill was always well-informed of military intelligence reports and kept in close personal as well as intellectual touch with military affairs.[89] Thus in Great Britain strategy was a joint product of the civilian and military arms. The military chiefs were in constant touch with political leaders and were informed of British political aims and requirements and the civilian leaders were in constant touch with military developments, with the strength at their disposal. This produced not only unity at planning conferences but strategy dedicated to political ends.

For centuries the British had maintained an extensive empire, had preserved a world-wide network of trade and communication, had ranked among the world's great powers, and had often been dominant in world affairs without ever having maintained large concentrations of land power. The manpower and resources

[88] Hull, *op. cit.*, Vol. II, p. 1110. See also Wilmot, *op. cit.*, p. 131.
[89] Wedemeyer, *op. cit.*, p. 179.

of the British Isles are comparatively small. Great Britain had maintained her position of pre-eminence through the use of sea-power and diplomacy. During the decades of responsibility, often of danger, Britain had developed a tradition and a skill in diplomacy which often stood in the stead of physical force.

The fact of Britain's relatively small land mass and population led to the traditional balance of power concept, a policy of preventing any single power from achieving hegemony on the Continent. For centuries the power which threatened to do this was France, and so for centuries the enemy of England was France. After 1871 it was Germany who emerged as the chief land power, and so it was German hegemony which was to be prevented by British policy. It was to this end that the pre-World War I entente with France and later with Imperial Russia had been dedicated, this was the aim of British policy in the First World War.

In 1939 Great Britain declared war on Nazi Germany immediately after German tanks crossed the border to invade Poland. Under the Ribbentrop-Molotov Agreement, the Soviet Union co-operated with Germany in the invasion of Poland. The Red Army marched into Eastern Poland and the Baltic States, and so the U.S.S.R. was equally responsible with Germany for the resort to force and the violation of small states, but Great Britain did not declare war on the Soviet Union, only on Germany. This indicates that the British aim in entering the war was not legalistic, not merely the punishment of aggression, but rather that it was the restoration of the power equilibrium on the Continent, the prevention of German hegemony. Realistic British policy had to take into account in 1939 that the U.S.S.R. posed a long-range threat to European equilibrium but the German threat was immediate and imminent. Britain could not fight a united German-Soviet enemy; therefore, her policy had to be to divide the U.S.S.R. from Germany, reduce German power first, and then work to prevent the excessive increase of Soviet power. Churchill had no desire to help release the European Continent from German domination only to have it fall under the domination of the Soviet Union. It was for this reason that the British Prime Minister urged Anglo-American operations in Eastern Europe. To Churchill and to his government and chiefs, war was a continuation of policy, an implementation of the policy of equilibrium.

An example of English thinking on the aims of war can be found in a study prepared by Percy Corbett for the Royal Institute of International Affairs titled *War Aims and Postwar Plans.*[90] Let us examine the method of reasoning of this study to see whether it sheds light on the divergence of plans of the English and American allies.

The analysis of the question of what British war aims regarding Germany ought to be begins with an examination of the relative power of the world's great powers. Corbett maintains that the basic requirements of a first-class military power at the time of the Second World War were a large and adaptable engineering industry and the capacity to produce the highest quality industrial goods in mass quantity. By these standards only the United States, Great Britain, and Germany ranked as first-class military powers in the years before the ending of the Second World War. The U.S.S.R. and Japan had the capacity to produce industrial goods in large quantities, but their goods were of inferior quality; Sweden, Switzerland, and Czechoslovakia produced goods of excellent quality but in insufficient quantity and diversity to rank as first-class powers; France had never fully industrialized and so had never evolved into a modern first-rate power. Therefore, a realistic policy vis-à-vis Germany must be based on a factual understanding of her source of status as a military power.

The real source of German military strength lay in her pool of highly skilled workers and in her highly developed technology especially in the fields of toolmaking, drafting, designing, and construction engineering. One example of this source of strength can be seen in the relative numbers of skilled metalworkers among European nations in 1941:

Germany	4.1 million skilled metalworkers
France	1.6 million skilled metalworkers
Belgium	.3 million skilled metalworkers
Holland	.3 million skilled metalworkers
Poland	.3 million skilled metalworkers

[90] London: Chatham House, 1941.

In other still more highly skilled trades the German advantage was greater. Germany also possessed a pool of highly trained civil servants, industrial administrators and engineers, as well as facilities for training technical workers and for educating scientific and engineering personnel. Although the German economy suffered basic disadvantages, such as the shortage of vital raw materials including oil, metals, fat, rubber, and textile goods, Germany had nevertheless been Europe's chief source of capital goods. Corbett concluded that, despite the destruction that war would bring, Germany would inevitably play a major role in postwar European economic recovery and that the maintenance of German productive capacity was an essential element of European economic well-being. He further concluded that a reasonable degree of prosperity in Germany was essential to European political stability since large-scale unemployment resulting from depression could lead to political crisis and might compel the postwar German government to resort to the Hitler policy of drafting the unemployed and of stimulating economic recovery by arms contracts.

In consideration of these basic factors the paper outlines three policies which Great Britain might pursue as war aims:

1. *A policy of complete repression.* This, the paper concludes, would be extremely dangerous unless the repression were truly complete. Such a policy would necessitate the total destruction of German war potential; otherwise it would breed desire for revenge and leave Germany the power to wreak that vengeance. However, destruction of German war potential would also destroy Germany's capacity to contribute to postwar economic reconstruction in Europe and would weaken European economic prosperity. Conclusion: a policy of total repression would be both dangerous and wasteful.

2. *A policy of political repression without the destruction of economic power.* The disadvantages of such an alternative would lie in the shortage of trained personnel to administer a long-range occupation of Germany by a military government and in the tendency of public opinion in both Great Britain and the United States to weary of the duties and expense of maintaining such political supervision. Vigilance might ultimately lag, with disastrous results.

3. *A policy of reconciliation.* This alternative would call for the preservation of both the German economy and the German state with the possible exception of territorial losses, such as the detachment of the Sudetenland and/or East Prussia. After an initial postwar period the Germans would co-operate in economic and political reconstruction on an equal footing with the victors. A final peace treaty would not be signed until after the completion of the initial period.

There are two dangers inherent in this policy: the possibility that Germany will achieve ultimate hegemony in Europe and the danger that Germany might use her economic power to weaken the economies of other states, for example those of Southeastern Europe.[91]

On the basis of the facts and arguments presented, the paper concludes with a five-point recommendation:

British war policy vis-à-vis Germany should include:

1. The punishment of war criminals, dissolution of the Wehrmacht, expulsion of the Nazi government; Allied inspection to prevent rearmament.

2. Maintenance of the German economy at a healthy level. A degree of prosperity and a rising standard of living in Germany will help prevent demands for political expansion.

3. The Allies should encourage German participation in international associations, especially in those which deal with economic questions.

4. German arms factories should be closed or, preferably, converted to the production of consumers' goods; monopolies and cartels should be regulated.

5. Close economic co-operation between Great Britain and the United States should be fostered in the postwar period; both powers should co-operate closely with other European states in economic affairs.[92]

Again it must be emphasized that this study of war aims does not represent official British government policy, nor is its analysis presented as an ideal solution to the problem of what Allied policy

[91] Paraphrased from Percy Corbett, *War Aims and Postwar Plans.*
[92] *Ibid.*

vis-à-vis Germany in the Second World War ought to have been, but rather an example of English thought on the relationship between war and policy. The Corbett paper indicates that any war policy must take into account long-range economic, psychological, and political factors and must be designed to achieve a practical, realizable, and ultimately desirable goal. The strategy pursued in the war must serve the ends of that goal. Although there were certainly individual Americans, including government officials and military men, who shared this British view, the men who made American policy in the Second World War did not. Perhaps it was this fundamental difference in the philosophy of war which led to the division between Roosevelt and Churchill. Churchill accepted with reservations the slogan of Unconditional Surrender and, indeed, part of the policy which that slogan represented, the doctrine of moral war fought to total victory, but he never accepted the American view that the goal of strategy was simply to destroy German power totally nor the view of the American President that world peace could rest eventually on good will alone. Churchill conceived of war as a means to a political end.

Stalin's Attitude toward Unconditional Surrender

Roosevelt had predicted that Unconditional Surrender would be "just the thing for the Russians" and that "Uncle Joe might have made it up himself." [93] However, Stalin's reaction to the Casablanca announcement was less than enthusiastic. The Soviet Marshal, who had very clear war aims in the Second World War, refused to adhere to the Unconditional Surrender doctrine until the final months of the war when he allowed the phrase to be included in the Yalta Declaration, which he joined in signing.

Stalin, the apt pupil of Lenin, was also a student of Clausewitz. He considered the Red Army an instrument of Soviet policy and, conversely, he also considered wartime policy a weapon of the Red Army. He had no desire to increase the military burden of the war by sharpening enemy resistance. On the contrary, instead of calling uncompromisingly for Unconditional Surrender,

[93] Elliott Roosevelt, *op. cit.*, p. 117.

Stalin repeatedly issued assurances to the German people that the victory of the Red Army would not mean their destruction. His statements and proclamations were intended to divide the German people from the Nazi leadership, not to weld all Germans together into a unity born of desperation.

For example, in his Order of the Day of November 6, 1942, Stalin announced:

> It is not our aim to destroy all military force in Germany, for every literate person will understand that this is not only impossible in regard to Germany . . . but it is also inadvisable from the point of view of the future.[94]

Following the Russian victory at Stalingrad, just one month after the Anglo-American pronouncement at Casablanca, Stalin declared:

> Occasionally the foreign press engages in prattle to the effect that the Red Army's aim is to exterminate the German people and destroy the German state. This is, of course, a stupid lie and a senseless slander against the Red Army. . . . It would be ridiculous to identify Hitler's clique with the German people and the German state. History shows that Hitlers come and go, but the German people and the German state remain.[95]

At Stalingrad Field Marshal Paulus had surrendered together with the remnants of his Sixth Army, including more than twenty generals. Stalin sought to convert his high-ranking prisoners of war to a policy of co-operation with the U.S.S.R. In July, 1943, the National Committee of Free Germans was organized in Moscow, and subsequently high-ranking German prisoners of war addressed radio appeals to their former comrades to end the senseless slaughter. These Germans emphasized not the ideological goals of Communism but simply the survival of the German state and of the German people.[96]

On November 6, 1943, when the German forces were in full retreat beyond the Dnieper line, Stalin again appealed to ele-

[94] Quoted in Felix Wittmer, *The Yalta Betrayal* (Caldwell, Idaho: Caxton Press, 1954), p. 32.

[95] Chamberlin, *op. cit.*, p. 289; Wittmer, *op. cit.*, p. 32; Veit Valentin, *The German People* (New York: Knopf, 1946), p. 674.

[96] *Ibid.*

ments of the Wehrmacht to end the war and rebel against the Nazi government:

> It is not our aim to destroy Germany, for it is impossible to destroy Germany, just as it is impossible to destroy Russia. But the Hitler state can and should be destroyed. It is not our aim to destroy all organized military force in Germany, for every literate person will understand that this is not only impossible in regard to Germany, as it is in regard to Russia, but it is also inadmissible from the viewpoint of the victor.[97]

Thus, while Franklin Roosevelt insisted that "the United Nations would never negotiate an armistice with the Nazi Government, the German High Command, or any other group or individual in Germany" and wished to make a public pronouncement to that effect, Stalin pursued a very different policy of trying to divide the people from the Nazis and especially of trying to divide the German soldiers from the government. In May, 1943, Churchill dissuaded Roosevelt from proclaiming his uncompromising stand on the grounds that Stalin would not have agreed, and when subsequent appeals were made by the Allies to the Axis satellite states of Hungary, Rumania, Bulgaria, and Finland, it has been reported that the words "unconditional surrender" were omitted under the influence of Stalin.[98]

Stalin's opposition to the proclamation of the intention to call for the unconditional surrender of Germany by no means indicates that he envisioned eventual peace terms for Germany less severe than those planned by the English and the Americans. The demands of Soviet ambassadors in London and Washington and those presented by Stalin and Molotov at Big Three Conferences indicate that Stalin sought to secure as much from the peace settlement as the traffic would bear in the realm of reparations, territory, and political concessions. His views regarding the punishment of war criminals were at least as stringent as those of Roosevelt and his desire to revamp German society was at least as strong as the American's, but the Soviet Marshal was cautious enough not to proclaim his drastic war aims until the

[97] *Ibid.*

[98] Reported by the diplomatic correspondent of the *Daily Telegraph,* issue of May 9 and 13, 1944. See also Hankey, *op. cit.,* p. 32.

power to resist of the German Wehrmacht had clearly begun to crumble, until will to resist alone could no longer defend the German frontier against the onslaught of the Red Army. Stalin sought total victory, if possible, but he sought it at the lowest possible price.

In evaluating Roosevelt's prediction that Unconditional Surrender was just the thing for the Russians one is tempted to compare the Casablanca Formula to the wine of Burgundy, which the French say is good for women when men drink it, and conclude that perhaps the phrase was just the thing for the Russians as long as it was American policy. In subsequent chapters we shall examine the effect on both American and Soviet policy.

CHAPTER 2

The Implementation of the Policy of Unconditional Surrender in the Second World War

THE MEANING OF UNCONDITIONAL SURRENDER

At Casablanca on January 24, 1943, President Roosevelt announced that the Anglo-American alliance would accept nothing less than the unconditional surrender of the Axis enemy, and so was born the formula and the policy of Unconditional Surrender. It arose from a complex background, grew from complex causes, evoked complex reactions. It implied that the Allies would bind themselves to no prior commitments to the enemy regarding the peace settlement. It implied that the Allies intended to keep a free hand to shape the peace terms, that they wanted to preserve unlimited scope in remaking the postwar world in closer accord with their ideals. Beyond this, the exact meaning and implications of Unconditional Surrender were not clear. What precisely did the phrase portend for the future of Germany? For what sort of peace terms was the free hand reserved? An evaluation of the effect of the Casablanca Formula on Germany and the Germans must take into account the implication given the phrase by the Allied plans for postwar Europe. These plans became manifest in the decisions and communiqués of the series of conferences which took place between January, 1943, and May, 1945. Let us examine the Allied postwar design for Germany as it took shape and revealed itself between the time of the Casablanca announcement and the final unconditional surrender of Germany, for in this design is woven the meaning imparted to Unconditional Surrender in the Second World War.

THE DEVELOPMENT OF AMERICAN AIMS FOR GERMANY

Before Casablanca the United States and Great Britain had participated in two major policy announcements regarding their peace aims, the Atlantic Charter and the United Nations Declaration. Since both statements refer to the enemy, we should examine their content. The Atlantic Charter, a joint declaration by the American President and the British Prime Minister, issued in August, 1941, before Pearl Harbor, proclaimed several postwar intentions which impinge on Germany:

1. The United States and the United Kingdom seek no aggrandizement, territorial or otherwise.
2. They desire no territorial changes not in accord with the freely expressed wishes of the people concerned.
3. They will respect the right of all people to choose their own form of government.
4. They will endeavor to afford to all states, "great or small, victor or vanquished," access on equal terms to the world's trade and raw materials as required for their economic prosperity.
5. After the destruction of Nazi tyranny, they desire the establishment of a peaceful world which will guarantee freedom from fear and freedom from want.[1]

In brief, the Atlantic Charter indicated that the Anglo-American policy aim in Germany was the overthrow of the National Socialist government, but it extended the promise that ultimate

[1] Paraphrased from *The Atlantic Charter*, "Toward the Peace," Department of State (Washington, D. C.: U.S. Government Printing Office, 1945), p. 1.

peace terms would ensure economic prosperity to the vanquished enemy.

These principles were reaffirmed in the United Nations Declaration, signed on January 1, 1942, by the United Kingdom, the United States, the U.S.S.R., China, and twenty-two Allied states. The declaration endorses the ideals of the Atlantic Charter and asserts that the signatory powers agree that "complete victory over their enemies is essential to defend life, liberty, independence and religious freedom, and to preserve human rights and justice in their own lands as well as in other lands" and that they pledge themselves to commit their full resources to the war effort. Each adherent agreed not to make an armistice or a separate peace with the enemy.[2] The words "complete victory" and the rejection of separate peace negotiations foreshadowed Unconditional Surrender.

By the time of the Casablanca Conference the United States had committed itself to an all-out war effort aimed at the complete defeat of the enemy and the overthrow of the Nazi government. Beyond that, the war aims of the United States and its allies were not clear.

The vagueness of the goal of American policy led to a demand in the Senate and House of Representatives for clarification. Throughout the year which had begun with the Casablanca Conference the American Congress, and in particular the Senate Foreign Relations Committee, studied proposals designed to commit the United States and its allies, especially the Soviet Union, to peace conditions which would embody the ideals of the Atlantic Charter. The series of draft resolutions discussed during these months reveal an emphasis on "no territorial aggrandizement," on postwar economic reconstruction in both Allied and Axis states, and on the establishment of international machinery for the preservation of future peace. It is interesting to note that during the long months of discussion none of the proposed resolutions included any reference to a possible compromise settlement with the enemy. The Ball-Burton-Hatch-Hill Draft Resolution, for example, called for temporary Allied mili-

[2] *Ibid.*, p. 2.

tary occupation of the defeated Axis states but promised eventual local self-government.[3]

Apparently the chief concerns of the Senate were the fear that isolationism would be resurgent after the war and would prevent the United States from assuming its place with the United Kingdom and the Soviet Union as one of the guardians of the new international community and the fear that Soviet ambitions in Eastern Europe, specifically in the Baltic States, Poland, and the Balkans, would undermine the idealism envisioned in the Atlantic Charter. The Congressional discussions of this period reveal very little concern with the question of the details of the peace to be concluded with Germany.

Both American Secretary of State Hull and British Foreign Secretary Eden, who visited Washington in March, 1943, and met with the Senate Foreign Relations Committee, warned the senators not to precipitate a discussion of issues which might tend to divide the Big Three Alliance. Hull used his influence to prevent a debate on the Senate floor which might jeopardize the extremely delicate relations with both England and the U.S.S.R. at a time when he regarded the final outcome of the war as still uncertain. Within the Senate the moderates of both parties sought to prevent debate on issues which might provoke an open split between the isolationists and the internationalists, and so for these two reasons public Senate discussion of postwar conditions was restricted to the most general terms on which all the Allies and both major elements of the Senate could agree. It amounted to a policy of "win the war first," in other words, to a restatement of the Casablanca Formula.[4]

The result of the almost yearlong discussions was the Connally Resolution, adopted by the Senate in November, 1943.

Resolved, That the war against all our enemies be waged until complete victory is achieved.

That the United States co-operate with its comrades-in-arms in securing a just and honorable peace.

That the United States, acting through its constitutional processes, join with free and sovereign nations in the establishment and main-

[3] Vandenberg, *Private Papers,* pp. 38 f.

[4] *Ibid.,* pp. 37-65.

tenance of international authority with power to prevent aggression and to preserve the peace of the world.[5]

The Connally Resolution committed the United States Senate to the policy of total victory and to co-operation in plans to establish some form of international machinery to preserve peace, but it did not recommend any specific proposals for a settlement with Germany. In the Senate as at the international conferences fear of splitting the precarious wartime alliance led to the policy of the lowest common denominator, the policy of defining the war aim as that on which all Allies and almost all factions could agree—the defeat of the enemy.

Gradually, however, an Allied plan to implement the demand for unconditional surrender with specific terms to be imposed upon the vanquished enemy emerged. Since we are concerned with the effect within Germany of the Allied plans, we need not discuss in detail unpublished draft peace proposals, such as the series evolved by the United States Department of State's Advisory Committee on postwar foreign policy. Of immediate concern are the decisions of the major inter-Allied conferences which first gave world public opinion and German public opinion in particular an indication of the meaning of Unconditional Surrender.

There was some discussion of postwar plans for Germany between British Foreign Secretary Eden and American Secretary of State Hull at *Quadrant,* the first Quebec Conference in August, 1943. No decision was arrived at and no announcement of policy was made, but the two men discussed the possibility of weakening German political and military power by some form of decentralization. Eden advocated a plan of dividing Germany into several small independent states. Hull seems to have agreed to a form of decentralization but he opposed forced separation, arguing that compulsory dismemberment would create nationalism and foster a spirit of vengeance. He suggested, instead, an encouragement of voluntary federalism.[6] No specific plans for administering enemy territory were drafted at Quebec, but it

[5] "Toward the Peace," *op. cit.,* p. 8.
[6] Hull, *Memoirs,* p. 1233.

is clear that the Anglo-Americans clearly envisioned a period of military occupation of the defeated enemy.[7]

Before the *Quadrant* conference closed a wire arrived from Stalin inviting the British and American Foreign Ministers to a tripartite conference at Moscow. This meeting convened on October 18, 1943, with Soviet Foreign Minister Molotov presiding. The agenda contained items the scope of which spanned the globe. It included the question of the division of the Italian Navy, the plan to induce Turkey to enter the war, the future status of Poland, the possibility of a Soviet declaration of war against Japan, and plans for a subsequent meeting of Churchill, Stalin, and Roosevelt. There was also a detailed discussion of the German question.

Regarding the immediate problem of the war, the Soviet delegate demanded the opening of a second front by the Anglo-Americans in the near future. The Soviets had long been contending that the Red Army alone was bearing the full military burden of the war and Molotov indicated his suspicion of the seriousness of the Western Allies' intentions. The British and American military delegates, Lieutenant General Ismay and Major General Deane, assured the Soviets of Western plans to launch an invasion against the French coast in the spring of 1944. They explained that planning had been under way since the Casablanca Conference and that the plans would surely be implemented provided that the necessary preconditions could be achieved: air superiority, no major increase of German ground forces in the West, and continued pressure from the Red Army in the East.[8]

Regarding the postwar treatment of Germany, Hull presented a State Department statement proposing the following points:

1. Unconditional Surrender. The war would be pursued until the total defeat of Germany, following which the United Nations would be empowered to exercise all power in Germany and would assume all the rights of occupying powers. The German government would deliver all prisoners of war and all United Nations nationals, turn over all war criminals, disband its armed

[7] William L. Neumann, *Making the Peace*, p. 55.
[8] Deane, *The Strange Alliance*, pp. 16-19.

forces, permit the United Nations to supervise all German economic activities.

2. During an interim period the terms of surrender would be carried out by an Inter-Allied Control Council. The Nazi party would be disbanded and all Nazi officials would be dismissed; otherwise there would be minimum United Nations interference with local government.

3. Germany would pay reparations for war damages in an amount to be determined by a Reparations Commission.

4. Germany would be totally disarmed.

5. Future military controls would permit no German standing army, would eliminate the military caste, dismantle arms manufacturing plants, prohibit the production or importation of war material, prohibit the production of aircraft even for civilian purposes. These controls would be supervised by the United Nations.

6. The United States suggested a decentralized German state in which the influence of Prussia would be minimized. The new Germany would be governed on a broad democratic base allowing for individual liberties and a tolerable standard of living. Controls should be limited to those essential for Allied future security. Freedom of speech and press should be restored as quickly as feasible to all but Nazi party members.[9]

Hull records that the Allied delegates endorsed the general tenor of the memorandum and that Molotov reported Stalin's enthusiastic approval and his agreement to accept the proposals as Soviet policy.[10] To implement the general agreement the Foreign Ministers decided to establish the European Advisory Commission, which would meet in London to draft specific details of the German settlement.

At Moscow the Allied Foreign Ministers further determined that Nazi officers and government officials accused of war crimes would be apprehended and tried. The Declaration on German Atrocities issued at the close of the conference on November 1, 1943, warned that all Germans, military or civilian, who committed acts of atrocity in any Allied state would be returned

[9] Paraphrased from text in Hull, *op. cit.*, pp. 1285-86.
[10] *Ibid.*

following the war to the state in which the atrocity had been committed for trial under the laws of that state.[11]

The conference concluded with the issuance of the Moscow Declaration on General Security signed by the representatives of Great Britain, the United States, the U.S.S.R., and China, which pledged the four powers to pursue the war until the unconditional surrender of their enemies was achieved.[12]

At the end of November, 1943, Roosevelt met with Churchill and Chiang Kai-shek at Cairo in a meeting preliminary to a conference with Stalin at Teheran. Discussions at Cairo concerned the war in Asia only. Once again the Allies pledged themselves to continue the war against Japan until her unconditional surrender was achieved.

The Teheran meeting of the Big Three opened on November 28, 1943. At this meeting decisions portentous for Germany were arrived at. Roosevelt, accompanied by a party of about seventy aides including Harry Hopkins, Admiral Leahy, the Joint Chiefs of Staff, and military and civilian experts, had intended to reside at the American Legation, but on the invitation of Stalin, who assured them that their security would be more adequately safeguarded by the NKVD, the entire party transferred their headquarters to the compound of the Soviet Embassy. The relations between the American President and his party and the Soviet hosts seem to have been cordial on this occasion.[13]

Stalin took the occasion of the friendly atmosphere to insist once more that the Western Allies open their second front in France in the immediate future. At his first private welcoming meeting with Roosevelt and at later plenary meetings he opposed any deviation from the plan of an Anglo-American invasion of France and contended against any scheme which would delay that invasion for as much as a single day.[14] These debates on strategy, chiefly against Churchill, may have lent acrimony to the later discussions concerning the disposition of Germany.

Once again in the meetings devoted to drafting plans for the

[11] "Toward the Peace," *op. cit.*, p. 7.
[12] *Ibid.*, p. 6.
[13] Sherwood, *Roosevelt and Hopkins*, pp. 776-77.
[14] Deane, *op. cit.*, p. 43.

postwar treatment of Germany the lines were drawn between Churchill and Stalin. Stalin confided privately to Roosevelt that he feared the British Prime Minister took too optimistic a view of Germany. He said he had little faith in the probability of the reform of the German people, that even the German workers were too docile, too well disciplined, too obedient as tools of their government. He warned the American President that German power would be resurgent within fifteen or twenty years unless the Allies imposed severe postwar economic controls. He further warned that such controls would have to be carefully enforced because of the German skill at deception and their ability to convert peaceful industries almost overnight to war production. Therefore, he suggested that the three Allies obtain and maintain military bases within Germany, along the German borders, and at key points throughout the world in order to safeguard their future security. Roosevelt apparently expressed enthusiastic agreement with these suggestions.[15]

Churchill agreed that the peace settlement should provide for the elimination of German war production, but he warned that a punitive peace which proved economically unviable would be self-defeating in that it would arouse desire for revenge. He pointed to Prussia as the crux of the German problem and suggested that perhaps Prussia could be separated from the rest of Germany and isolated and controlled but that the South German states could be encouraged to federate, perhaps form a Danubian Confederation with Austria and Hungary. Stalin opposed this on the ground that the Germans would soon dominate any Danubian Confederation and maintained that all Germans, not merely Prussians, were dangerous and that, although the Prussian officers provided the cement, "all Germans fought like fierce beasts."[16]

At the final Teheran meeting Roosevelt formally introduced an American plan under which Germany would be divided into five autonomous states, one of which would be Prussia, reduced in size. Churchill did not agree to this plan and even Stalin was

[15] Sherwood, *op. cit.*, pp. 782, 786-87.
[16] Churchill, *Closing the Ring*, pp. 401 f.

not in full accord, and so the question was tabled and referred for final solution to the European Advisory Commission.[17]

The American plans, which seem drastic in retrospect, were mild compared to those proposed by the Soviet Union. For example, at one of the official dinners at Teheran, Stalin raised his glass in a toast to swift justice for all German war criminals, proposing that at least 50,000 of them be dispatched by firing squads as quickly as they could be captured. Churchill, who writes in his *Memoirs* that he was not sure at the time whether Stalin was serious—"the atmosphere was jovial but he was grim"—was incensed by the suggestion. He branded it mass murder, contrary to Anglo-Saxon standards of justice. Roosevelt tried to breach the gap between the Prime Minister and Stalin by suggesting humorously that only 49,500 instead of 50,000 Germans should be shot, but apparently the President's levity made Churchill still angrier.[18]

Stalin was not speaking humorously when he demanded that four million German men be assigned to forced labor in the Soviet Union after the war to aid in rebuilding devastated areas nor when he suggested that Germany be stripped of East Prussia and of territory as far west as the Oder River. These were the serious aims of Soviet policy. No agreement was arrived at at Teheran and so these questions, too, were referred to the European Advisory Commission.[19] It was clear after Teheran that the Stalin definition of Unconditional Surrender had a Carthaginian flavor.

When the conference closed on December 1, 1943, the three powers issued a declaration restating their common determination to co-operate both during the war and in the peace to follow. They expressed confidence in ultimate victory and in their ability to "banish the scourge and terror of war for many generations" and to eliminate "tyranny and slavery, oppression and intolerance." [20]

The Second Quebec Conference, which occurred approximately

[17] Sherwood, *op. cit.*, p. 797.

[18] Leahy, *op. cit.*, pp. 189-206; E. Roosevelt, *As He Saw It*, p. 189.

[19] Churchill, *op. cit.*, p. 706. See also Herbert Feis, *Churchill, Roosevelt, Stalin: the War They Waged and the Peace They Sought* (Princeton, N. J.: Princeton Univ. Press, 1957), pp. 269 ff.

[20] "Toward the Peace," *op. cit.*, p. 15.

nine months after Teheran, was probably the most significant of all the wartime conferences from the point of view of effect on Germany. It was at Quebec in September, 1944, that the Morgenthau Plan was accepted.

Like the First Quebec Conference, the Second was a two-power meeting between Roosevelt and Churchill. The meeting had been intended as a purely military conference and so for this reason and also because of poor health Secretary of State Hull did not attend. Secretary of War Stimson and Harry Hopkins also were absent from the Second Quebec Conference, but Secretary of the Treasury Henry Morgenthau, Jr., was in attendance. Churchill was accompanied by Foreign Secretary Anthony Eden.

The conference convened on September 11, 1944. By then the issue of the war was no longer in doubt. The Anglo-American invasion in Normandy, *Operation Overlord,* had been successfully launched in June, and in July General Patton's forces had broken out of the bridgehead onto the plain leading to Paris. By September the Allies were driving forward toward the German border. The Red Army had penetrated the Balkans in the south and was threatening East Prussia in the north. Italy had capitulated early in September. The Allies found themselves confronted with the urgent necessity to prepare for peace.

The European Advisory Commission, which had been in session since the Moscow Conference, had drafted and discussed many possible plans for dealing with Germany but it had not arrived at any final agreement. The United States Department of State had prepared a series of draft plans and representatives of the State Department had met frequently with War Department planners to discuss the issue, but no over-all American policy had been adopted. Into this vacuum of indecision the American Secretary of the Treasury injected his plan for the deindustrialization of Germany which has become known as the Morgenthau Plan.

The Origin of the Morgenthau Plan

In August, 1944, shortly before Morgenthau was to fly on an official visit to England a former Treasury attorney, Colonel Bernard Bernstein, who was then on military leave serving at SHAEF headquarters, procured a draft of the War Department's proposed plan for administering postwar Germany. Morgenthau read the plan during his flight and was shocked by the mildness of the proposals. The plan apparently envisioned a relatively high standard of living for the German people once Nazi control had been destroyed and war criminals had been punished; it promised free, democratic institutions, the encouragement of a free trade-union movement and it provided for limited controls of the German economy designed only to prevent war production.

When he arrived in London Secretary Morgenthau, together with his assistant, Harry Dexter White, had lunch with General Eisenhower to sound out his views on the German question. Morgenthau reports that he found Eisenhower sympathetic to his own views, that the General described the German nation as "a synthetic paranoid" and saw no reason for treating a paranoid gently, that he did not advocate restoring the German economy simply to improve the standard of living of the German people. Regarding the Soviet Union, Eisenhower reportedly said that, since Russia would have acquired as much new territory as she could digest for some time, she would not be a menace in the immediate postwar period.[21]

Following this lunch, Morgenthau met with American Ambassador Winant and others to discuss official British views on the German question. The Secretary reports that Winant described the opinions of three groups in England: (1) Eden's group, which favored close co-operation with the U.S.S.R. and sponsored severe terms for Germany; (2) an opposition group, which feared the postwar power of the Soviet Union and so wished to preserve some element of German power as a potential counterweight; and (3) a middle group, which seemed to center around Churchill.[22]

Morgenthau sought out Eden and, as Winant had predicted, found him basically sympathetic to his own severe views. Eden reportedly feared that should the United Kingdom and the United States pursue a soft policy in regard to Germany this would arouse the suspicion of the Soviet Union.[23]

[21] Henry Morgenthau, Jr., "Our Policy toward Germany," New York *Post*, Nov. 24, 1947.

[22] *Ibid.*

[23] *Ibid.* See also W. H. Chamberlin, *America's Second Crusade*, p. 303.

On August 17 Morgenthau returned to Washington and immediately took up the question of the German peace settlement with President Roosevelt. Roosevelt, too, objected to the mildness of the War Department plan. He sent a memorandum to the Secretary of War in which he stated that the German people must be taught a lesson; he complained that many Americans held the view that the German people as a whole were not responsible for the war, that only a few Nazi leaders were responsible, but he did not agree. He insisted that the German people must "have it driven home to them that the whole nation has been engaged in a lawless conspiracy against the decencies of modern civilization." He did not propose to let the German people starve, but if the Germans would require more food than could be supplied by their own economy they should be fed three times a day with soup from army soup kitchens. That, he asserted, "will keep them perfectly healthy, and they will remember that experience all their lives. The fact that they are a defeated nation, collectively and individually, will be so impressed upon them that they will hesitate to start any new war." [24] Roosevelt said that the German people should live at a level of subsistence not above that of the poorest of the people they had conquered.

The President appointed a Cabinet Committee composed of the Secretaries of War, State, Treasury, and Navy to be coordinated by Harry Hopkins to undertake a study of the German problem in the light of these views. It was at the first meeting of this committee on September 2, 1944, that Harry Dexter White presented the Treasury Department's proposal for the postwar treatment of Germany—the Morgenthau Plan.

The plan contained the following major proposals:

1. Reduction of the size of Germany by cession of border lands to her neighbors.

2. Division of the remaining area into three parts, one of which, comprising the Ruhr, the Saar and Kiel, would be placed

[24] Memorandum of Aug. 26, 1944, *Interlocking Subversion in Government Departments: The Harry Dexter White Papers,* Committee on the Judiciary, U.S. Senate (Washington, D. C.: U.S. Government Printing Office, 1956), pp. 2580-82. See also Hull, *op. cit.,* pp. 1602 f.

under international control. The internationalized area would not be permitted to trade with the rest of Germany.

3. The two remaining areas would comprise two states, a southern state, which might be permitted to join a customs union with Austria, and a northern state, centered around Prussia.

4. Industrial plants in all three German areas would be destroyed or dismantled and delivered to the victors.

5. The Ruhr would "not only be stripped of all presently existing industries but so weakened and controlled that it cannot in the foreseeable future become an industrial area . . . all industrial plants and equipment not destroyed by military action shall either be completely dismantled or removed from the area or completely destroyed, all equipment should be removed from the mines and the mines shall be thoroughly wrecked." [25]

Dr. White further proposed that this program be supervised by an international commission in which primary responsibility would rest with Germany's immediate neighbors: France, the Soviet Union, Poland, Czechoslovakia, Greece, Yugoslavia, Norway, the Netherlands, and Belgium. The United States would be a member of the commission but American troops would be withdrawn from the area in "a relatively short time." White went on to interpret the Treasury Plan, explaining that the resources of the Ruhr ought not be allowed to add to the living standard of the rest of Germany.[26]

James W. Riddleberger, representing the State Department, opposed any drastic program of dismantling which would undermine the European economy. He pointed out that the German population could not be fed solely on food grown in Germany even with the old boundaries, and that such punitive terms would breed such deep resentment that its enforcement would require burdensome and never-ending supervision. The State Department felt that adequate protection could be achieved by federalization, that is, by decentralization.

Secretary Hull rejected the Morgenthau proposals: "Essentially,

[25] Paraphrased from Hull, *op. cit.*, pp. 1605 ff. See also *Interlocking Subversion in Government Departments: The Harry Dexter White Papers*, pp. 2693-2730.

[26] *Ibid.*, pp. 1605-6.

this was a plan of blind vengeance . . . it failed to see that in striking at Germany, it was striking at all of Europe." He called the plan to destroy the Ruhr mines "breath-taking in its implications for all Europe." [27] The War Department representatives, John J. McCloy and General Hilldring, joined in opposing the Treasury Plan, contending that the enforcement of such proposals would place a tremendous burden on the Army of Occupation.

Secretary of War Stimson vigorously condemned the Morgenthau Plan. Stimson tended to agree with the viewpoint of Keynes that the Versailles peace settlement had foundered because it had been economically unsound. He, therefore, strongly opposed the creation of a Central Europe which would be economically bankrupt and he tended to regard Morgenthau's view as emotional, rising from a bitterness he described as not unnatural. When the Cabinet Committee reconvened on September 5, Stimson sided with Hull in opposing a plan he regarded as "frankly Carthaginian." [28]

On behalf of the Department of State Hull suggested that an American High Commissioner for Germany be appointed as soon as possible in order to be able to confer with appropriate Allied representatives regarding German policy. He proposed the following program for dealing with Germany:

1. Demilitarization.
2. Dissolution of the NSDAP, and expulsion of Nazis from public office.
3. Allied control over press and other information media.
4. No immediate decision on partition, but encouragement of decentralization.
5. Allied control of German educational system.
6. Subdivision of large estates.
7. Due regard for reparations claims of Allies.
8. Economic objectives:

    1) German economy should be maintained at the subsistence level.
    2) German economic power in Europe should be eliminated.

[27] Hull, *op. cit.*, p. 1606.
[28] Stimson, *On Active Service in Peace and War*, p. 569; see also pp. 567 ff.

3) The German economy should be so ordered that it would be dependent upon imports, thus making it impossible for Germany to begin a war.[29]

Secretary Stimson regarded even this revised State Department plan as too drastic and economically unsound.[30] Morgenthau voiced agreement with sections of the plan, and Harry Hopkins gave general approval with some reservations regarding phrasing. As no final agreement could be reached, the committee decided that each member would prepare a report of his views for the President.

Subsequent to this meeting the War Department drafted a memorandum for the President which argued that the population of modern Germany could not possibly be supported by agriculture alone, that "the sum total of the drastic political and economic steps proposed by the Treasury is an open confession of the bankruptcy of hope for a reasonable economic and political settlement of the causes of war." [31] Undersecretary of War McCloy endorsed the views of his chief. He described the Morgenthau Plan as "a program of the most severe character" which would bring about a state of impoverishment and disorder in Germany which would inflict an almost impossible role on the American occupying army. He said it was the natural instinct of army men to seek to establish order, but that this plan apparently would order them to encourage the opposite.[32]

The Cabinet Committee had not yet arrived at a final decision by the time of the Second Quebec Conference. Since the conference had been planned as chiefly a military planning meeting, neither Hull nor Stimson had expected any major political decisions to be made by Churchill and Roosevelt. Certainly they did not anticipate the endorsement of the Morgenthau Plan. Subsequent to the last meeting of the Cabinet Committee on September 9, Secretary Morgenthau drove to New York with the

[29] Paraphrased from Hull, *op. cit.*, pp. 1608-9.
[30] Stimson, *op. cit.*, p. 570.
[31] *Ibid.*, p. 579.
[32] *Forrestal Diaries* (ed. Walter Millis) (New York: Viking, 1951), pp. 11 f.

President. It was apparently during this drive that Roosevelt invited Morgenthau to attend the Quebec Conference.

At Quebec Morgenthau had the opportunity to present his plan to the Prime Minister and to defend his views without the presence of the Cabinet members who opposed him. Reportedly, Churchill's initial reaction to the plan was that it would leave England "chained to a dead body." He opposed it as economically and politically unsound. Morgenthau pointed out that the destruction of German productive capacity would free German overseas market areas for British trade, and he further offered England postwar credit of $6.5 billion. The President agreed that the United States would impose no restrictions on the use of this credit. Churchill capitulated and both he and Roosevelt initialed the Morgenthau Plan, thus accepting it as official Anglo-American policy.[33] The Quebec Conference went on to allot the occupation zones of Germany.

Both Hull and Stimson were shocked and angered by the Quebec endorsement of the Morgenthau Plan without consultations with the Cabinet. Hull wrote in his memoirs:

> This whole development at Quebec, I believe, angered me as much as anything that had happened during my career as Secretary of State. If the Morgenthau Plan leaked out, as it inevitably would—and shortly did—it might well mean a bitter-end German resistance that could cause the loss of thousands of American lives.[34]

On September 15 Hull received a memorandum from the President acknowledging that he had agreed to the Morgenthau Plan. Hull returned a memorandum opposing the decision. Shortly after this he visited the White House to tell the President personally that the Morgenthau Plan was "out of all reason," that, bluntly, it would condemn 40 per cent of the German population to death by starvation.

On September 21 the story of the acceptance of the plan was leaked to the press. Drew Pearson published an article strongly approving the plan and its acceptance. The reaction of the American press was almost unanimous: it violently opposed the plan

[33] William L. Neumann, *op. cit.*, p. 74.
[34] Hull, *op. cit.*, p. 1614.

and decried Roosevelt's endorsement of it. In Germany, Goebbels and the controlled Nazi press had a field day: "Morgenthau surpasses Clemenceau: forty million too many Germans! Roosevelt and Churchill agree at Quebec to the Jewish Murder Plan," and "Details of the Devilish Plan of Destruction: Morgenthau the Spokesman of World Judaism."[35] This, Goebbels said, was the answer: this was the ultimate meaning of Unconditional Surrender.

Roosevelt was shocked by the violence of the reaction. He telephoned Stimson and invited him to lunch on October 3. The President admitted to the Secretary of War that Henry Morgenthau had "pulled a boner." He insisted that he had had no intention of transforming Germany into a purely agrarian state, what he had intended was merely to prevent British bankruptcy after the war by removing the competition of the Ruhr. Stimson read passages of the plan to the President and reports that Roosevelt was "frankly staggered" by the magnitude of the measures he had agreed to. He could not believe that he had endorsed a plan to destroy the mines of the Saar and the Ruhr and for the conversion of Germany into a country "primarily agricultural and pastoral in its character." Stimson writes that evidently the President had signed the document "without much thought." He implored the President to rescind the endorsement, not to lower the high moral plane on which the war had until then been waged, not to adopt a policy which would impress world public opinion as blind vengeance.[36]

Hull submitted a State Department memorandum to the President on October 1 suggesting control of German trade and the conversion of war industries to peaceful production, allowing a standard of living in Germany which would preclude luxury but would not cause starvation.[37] The President did not formally or publicly repudiate the Morgenthau Plan, but he dissolved the Cabinet Committee and appointed Robert D. Murphy to serve with the rank of ambassador on Eisenhower's staff as political

[35] *Völkischer Beobachter*, Vienna ed., No. 268, Sept. 28, 1944, p. 1; *ibid.*, No. 271.

[36] Stimson, *op. cit.*, pp. 580-82.

[37] Hull, *op. cit.*, p. 1618.

adviser on German affairs. The Joint Chiefs of Staff proceeded to work out a plan for the administration of Germany in liaison with the State Department, and it was under this plan, JCS/1067, that the occupation of defeated Germany was ultimately launched.

Unofficially the Morgenthau Plan, although it had been initialed by the Prime Minister and the President at Quebec, was quietly jettisoned.[38] As far as German public opinion was concerned, however, the harm had already been done, the price in stiffened resistance still had to be paid.

Publicly, the President continued to hammer at the theme of total victory. In his annual Message to Congress on January 6, 1945, Roosevelt stated that the war must continue to be waged with persistent energy:

> Everything we are and have is at stake. Everything we are and have will be given. . . . We have no question of the cost. Our losses will be heavy. We and our Allies will go on fighting together to ultimate total victory.

He warned that German propaganda was seeking to divide the alliance by spreading poisonous rumors. He said that each of these rumors bears the same trademark—"Made in Germany": "We must resist this divisive propaganda—we must destroy it." [39]

Obliquely he defended himself against the press attack on the Morgenthau Plan. He reaffirmed the principles of the Atlantic Charter, admitting that the ideals it represented could not always be attained but warning that perfectionism could obstruct the path to peace no less than isolationism. No peace settlement could be perfect, but he extended the promise that the international organization which would be established at the conclusion of peace would be able to reform any flagrant injustices.

Yalta and JCS/1067

Three days after Roosevelt took the oath of office for the fourth time, he set out for the Crimean Conference. This meeting, known as the Yalta Conference, was the last of the wartime Big

[38] Churchill, never enthusiastic about the plan, was happy to see it abandoned.

[39] *War Messages of Franklin D. Roosevelt,* pp. 26-31.

Two or Big Three meetings and probably has become the most controversial. It was at Yalta that the final meaning was given to Unconditional Surrender.

The meeting opened on February 3, 1945. Prime Minister Churchill, Marshal Stalin, and President Roosevelt, each accompanied by his foreign secretary, chiefs of staff, and experts and advisers, met at Yalta in the Crimea to thresh out the questions that remained to be settled before the Allied occupation of Germany could begin. The war was racing to its close but many questions of immediate importance remained undecided.

Many subjects were discussed at Yalta and many reports have been written on the decisions taken there. The discussions and decisions which are of paramount concern to the student of Unconditional Surrender are perhaps the following five:

1. The joint communiqué issued at the close of the conference on February 11 called upon the German people to cease their hopeless resistance. It announced that the three powers had arrived at an agreement on "common policies and plans for enforcing the unconditional surrender terms which we shall impose together on Nazi German after German armed resistance has been finally crushed."

It announced that the Allies were determined to destroy German militarism and Nazism, that they would disarm and disband all German armed forces, break up the General Staff, eliminate or control all German industry which could be used for military purposes, punish war criminals swiftly and justly, exact reparations in kind for war damages, disband the Nazi party, and remove Nazi and militarist influences from German public life.

It announced that a plan had been agreed upon under which Germany would be divided into four zones of occupation, each to be under the administration of one of the Allies: Great Britain, the U.S.S.R., the United States, and France.

2. The question of the dismemberment of Germany came up once more at Yalta, but no final agreement could be reached and the question was reserved for a future peace conference. By the time of the Potsdam Conference in July, 1945, both the United States and Britain had decided against dismemberment, and so the plan was dropped.

3. Against the wishes of the Soviet Union, France was accorded a seat on the Allied Control Council. The seat of the Control Council was to be Berlin. The boundaries of occupation zones, as drafted by the European Advisory Commission, were accepted.

4. A commission was established to decide on the question of reparations. Its headquarters were to be in Moscow.

The Secret Protocol included a threefold reparations program: removals of equipment, machinery, rolling stock, raw materials, ships, etc.; annual deliveries from current German production; the use of German labor. The figure of $20 billion was agreed upon as a basis of discussion from which the commission might begin its study of the question.

5. The Soviet government suggested that the western Polish frontier be extended to the line of the Oder and Neisse Rivers to compensate for eastern losses to the U.S.S.R. Both Great Britain and the United States accepted the principle of compensation, but Churchill objected that the Soviet proposal was excessive. The official conclusion of the conference was that Poland should receive "substantial accessions of territory," but no definite line was accepted. By the convening of the Potsdam Conference, Polish authorities already occupied all land to the Oder-Neisse line, and all Germans had been forcibly expelled from territory east of the line.[40]

Sherwood, in *Roosevelt and Hopkins,* says of the Yalta Conference that Roosevelt's actions at Yalta reflected his basic formula: Unconditional Surrender. He was trying to preserve freedom of action, to postpone making specific plans for peace until after military victory had been achieved, until the Allies were in a better position to evaluate the political and economic situation within Germany.[41]

The decisions made at Yalta have been criticized on two

[40] Paraphrased; see "Toward the Peace," *op. cit.,* pp. 33 ff.; William L. Neumann, *op. cit.,* pp. 78-88; Leahy, *I Was There,* pp. 317-20. Details of the conference are also given in Edward R. Stettinius, Jr., *Roosevelt and the Russians: the Yalta Conference* (ed. Walter Johnson) (Garden City, N. Y.: Doubleday, 1949), pp. 39-68, 122-38, 255-66; and in James F. Byrnes, *Speaking Frankly* (New York: Harper, 1947), pp. 24-31.

[41] P. 862.

counts: because, it is argued, too many concessions were made to the Soviet Union and because the terms drafted for Germany were excessively harsh. For example, Admiral Leahy, who was Roosevelt's close adviser and friend as well as his personal chief of staff, described the Yalta decisions as a plan "to obliterate a once mighty nation," and he questioned whether this policy was not sowing dragon's teeth, whether the eighty million Germans would not somehow manage to survive to fight again in a war of vengeance. He feared, too, that the total destruction of German military power would make Russia the dominant power in Europe and thus breed future international disagreements.[42]

The decisions at Yalta were the implementation of Unconditional Surrender to the hilt. They echoed the theme that the Second World War was a moral war designed to teach a moral lesson: to punish aggression, that it must be fought to the point of total victory. Total victory, it became clear, implied the destruction of German sovereignty—that is, of the German state as it formerly had existed—and the unrelenting and total imposition on the German nation of the will of the victors. This was the meaning of Unconditional Surrender. This was the meaning that became clear in the official communiqué and in the secret protocols of the Yalta Conference.

The American implementation of the policy arrived at at Yalta is to be found in the program evolved by the Joint Chiefs of Staff to administer the United States Zone of Occupation of Germany, JCS/1067. This document, completed in April, 1945, was designed to guide General Eisenhower, the United States member of the Allied Control Council, and to act as a model for the other Allies to urge them to enforce similar programs in their respective zones of occupation.

This directive states that all rights and powers of the American Military Government derived from Germany's Unconditional Surrender, that the Commander in Chief was clothed with supreme legislative, executive, and judicial power, with the power to take all measures he might consider necessary to fulfill the objectives of maintaining orderly military government. The primary goal of the military government, aside from securing the safety

[42] Leahy, *op. cit.*, pp. 320-23.

of Allied troops, communications, and supply lines, was the apprehension of war criminals, the liberation of prisoners of war and of displaced persons, the protection of Allied property, the revocation of Nazi laws, the dissolution and abolition of the Nazi party and its subordinate organizations, and the purging of German courts of Nazi influence. The basic goal of the occupation was to demonstrate to the German people that the ruthlessness of the war had caused the chaos and misery in which they found themselves in 1945, that they themselves were responsible for the conditions. The directive stated: "Germany will not be occupied for the purpose of liberation but as a defeated enemy nation . . . the principal Allied objective is to prevent Germany from ever again becoming a threat to the peace of the world." [43]

All members of the NSDAP of more than nominal rank and all major militarists were to be removed from public office, from trade unions, from major industry and commerce, from finance, agriculture, education, press, publishing, etc. All military and paramilitary organizations were to be disbanded and disarmed and high-ranking personnel were to be interned. The German General Staff, the Officers' Corps, the Reserve Corps, and all military academies would be dissolved; all arms and ammunitions would be destroyed. War crimes suspects and all persons held to be a potential menace to occupation security would be interned until trial could be arranged. All German courts were to be temporarily closed until they could be purged of Nazi influence. The Gestapo and Security Police would be abolished; the normal police force would be retained but purged of Nazis. Schools would be closed until the textbooks and teaching and administrative staffs could be denazified. The military government would make every effort to preserve cultural monuments, art treasures, museums, and libraries; and freedom of speech, press, and worship were to be respected within the limitations imposed by denazification.

The directive ordered that no action was to be taken to raise

[43] *General Marshall's Report, The Winning of the War in Europe and the Pacific:* Biennial Report of the Chief of Staff of the U.S. Army, July 1, 1943-June 30, 1945 (published for War Department by Simon and Schuster, 1945), p. 195; the entire text of JCS/1067 is given on pp. 180-207.

German living standards to any degree higher than those in neighboring countries. The occupation forces could act only to prevent actual starvation, disease, and unrest which might endanger Allied troops. The economy would be controlled only to the extent necessary to achieve the basic objectives of the program. The Commander in Chief was ordered to take "no steps looking to the economic rehabilitation of Germany" or designed to strengthen the German economy. The production of iron, steel, chemicals, nonferrous metals, machine tools, radios, and electrical equipment, automobiles, heavy machinery, and parts would be prohibited. Production of light consumers' goods would be permitted; heavy industry would be converted to light industry wherever possible. The military government would control prices, wages, and foreign trade, permitting only those imports which were vitally essential and authorizing exports to Allied nations only.[44]

This, then, was the summary of the meaning of Unconditional Surrender as interpreted by the American Joint Chiefs of Staff and as communicated to the Commander in Chief who was to administer the United States Zone of Occupation in Germany. As the provisions regarding the German economy show, some of the philosophy of the Morgenthau Plan survived in JCS/1067. The plan itself and its extreme goal of the total deindustrialization of Germany, the conversion of Germany to an entirely agricultural and pastoral economy, had been abandoned. JCS/1067 permitted sufficient production to prevent starvation; light industries were to be encouraged. However, the concept that the German standard of living must be maintained at a level no higher than that of her poorest neighbor was retained. This concept was carried forward in the decision to fix the level of industry of Occupied Germany at a point which would maintain this relatively low standard of living and also prevent possible conversion to war production, but it was discovered that the population of Germany was too great to be supported under such a plan, that malnutrition and starvation did indeed result, and eventually the remnants of Morgenthauism were abandoned in the wake of the plan from which they had sprung.

[44] Paraphrased from *General Marshall's Report*, pp. 180-208.

THE SURRENDERS OF ITALY AND GERMANY

The meaning of Unconditional Surrender in theory was summarized in the Yalta program and in JCS/1067, but what was the meaning in practice? The first occasion to observe the actual application of the Casablanca Formula was in the case of Italy's surrender to the Western Allies in September, 1943. Let us examine briefly the nature of this surrender.

Immediately following the Anglo-American landing in Sicily on July 9, 1943, the Allies opened a propaganda offensive beamed from their radio station in Algiers designed to soften Italian morale and to induce the Italian government to capitulate. On July 16 President Roosevelt and Prime Minister Churchill issued a joint statement to the Italian people declaring that Italy's sole hope of survival lay in "honorable capitulation to the overwhelming power of the military forces of the United Nations." They urged the Italian people to consult their own self-respect and their own interests and to decide whether Italians shall die for Mussolini and Hitler—or live for Italy and civilization.[45]

On July 25 the Fascist Grand Council met and deposed Mussolini, King Victor Emmanuel accepted the Duce's resignation and assumed personal command of the Italian armed forces. Mussolini was interned and Marshal Badoglio was appointed prime minister. On July 27 the Fascist party was ordered dissolved, the act according unlimited powers to the Grand Council was rescinded, and martial law was proclaimed throughout Italy. The German command in Italy and the German government in Berlin prepared for an immediate Italian volte-face. Hitler anticipated an early Italian-Allied armistice.[46]

At precisely this juncture Franklin Roosevelt sounded the Leitmotif. In a radio address on July 28 he warned the Italian Fascists that they could not escape punishment by resigning from office. He announced: "Our terms to Italy are still the same as our terms to Germany and Japan—'Unconditional Surrender.'" He warned: "We will have no truck with Fascism in any way,

[45] *War Messages*, p. 76.

[46] Albert Kesselring, *Soldat bis zum Letzten Tag* (Bonn: Athenäum, 1953), pp. 232 ff.

shape or manner. We will permit no vestige of Fascism to remain."[47]

The hope for imminent Italian collapse subsided into uncertainty. General Eisenhower's aide, Navy Captain Harry Butcher, reports that Allied headquarters noted a stiffening of Italian resistance and tended to attribute this to "the hard-boiled attitude of the Prime Minister and the President, who publicly insisted upon 'Unconditional Surrender' as soon as Mussolini was out."[48]

On the following day General Eisenhower tried to offset the unfavorable impression by a conciliatory speech to the Italian people. He commended Italy on the deposition of Mussolini and extended the promise of a peace with honorable conditions. In reply to this, Marshal Badoglio sent General Castellano as his plenipotentiary to meet secretly with Eisenhower's chief of staff, Bedell Smith, in Lisbon on August 19. Smith informed Castellano that the Allies could accept only the unconditional surrender of Italy. He warned that still harsher terms would result from delay in capitulation and intimated that delay would incur the destruction of Rome and of Italian industry.[49]

Castellano returned to Rome to confer with Badoglio, who objected strongly to Unconditional Surrender; however, he felt that he had no alternative. On September 3 the Italian government signed a secret armistice agreement with the Allies. The agreement provided for the immediate cessation of hostilities by all Italian armed forces, for the release of United Nations prisoners of war, for the transfer to the Allies of all Italian aircraft and shipping, for Allied use of Italian ports, for the surrender of all Italian arms and ammunition, for the recall to Italy of all Italian forces serving beyond the Italian border, and for the disarmament, demobilization, and demilitarization of Italy under the direction of the Allied Commander in Chief. The document made no reference to Unconditional Surrender.[50] It was made public

[47] *War Messages,* p. 77.

[48] Butcher, *My Three Years with Eisenhower,* p. 386.

[49] Hankey, *Politics: Trials and Errors,* p. 44.

[50] *Documents on American Foreign Relations,* Vol. VI: July, 1943-June, 1944 (eds. Leland Goodrich and Marie Carroll) (Boston: World Peace Foundation, 1945), p. 161.

on September 8. On September 12 the German commander in Italy, Field Marshal Kesselring, declared martial law throughout Italy and prepared to defend the peninsula.

On September 20 a political representative of the Allied governments presented a document to Marshal Badoglio titled "The Unconditional Surrender of Italy." Badoglio protested that his plenipotentiary, General Castellano, had never signed an unconditional surrender instrument. He requested that the title of the document be changed. On September 29 he met with Eisenhower to state his case, to try to persuade him to have the phrase "Unconditional Surrender" deleted. He called the words humiliating to the Italian people. Eisenhower explained that he had no authority to alter the document, which had been drafted by the civilian authorities. He persuaded Badoglio to accept and sign the surrender, but he attempted to conciliate him and the Italian people by sending a subsequent letter in which he explained that, although Italy had surrendered unconditionally, she was now co-operating with the United Nations.

Badoglio continued to attempt to secure the deletion of the humiliating words. He wrote to the British Prime Minister and to the American President recapitulating the circumstances of the armistice negotiations, requesting that the words which had not been part of the original agreement be removed from the official document of surrender.[51]

The words remained, and with them the humiliation and the rancor. The days which passed proved vital to Field Marshal Kesselring, who was hurriedly consolidating German strength in Italy. The sense of betrayal which many Italians experienced undermined the enthusiasm of collaboration with the Allies and played into the hands of the German defenders. The battle for the Italian peninsula did not end in September, 1943. Kesselring's forces were not cut off and encircled. Instead, the Allies were forced to fight for every inch of Italy, suffering high losses until the very last weeks of the war.

[51] Hankey, *op. cit.*, p. 45. For a detailed discussion of the Italian surrender, see, especially, Paul Kecskemeti, *Strategic Surrender: The Politics of Victory and Defeat* (Stanford, Calif.: Stanford Univ. Press, 1958), pp. 71-118, 228-30.

It is impossible to say that Allied insistence on including the words "Unconditional Surrender" was the direct cause of the prolongation of the war in Italy. It is difficult to measure what precise effect this insistence had; however, it seems clear that some advantage accrued to the Germans by the Allied policy and by Italian disappointment. In any case those Americans most directly concerned with the cost of maintaining the demand for the unconditional surrender of Italy, the generals at the front, became the severest critics of the policy of continuing to insist on the unconditional surrender of Germany.

The Demands for Modification of the Policy of Unconditional Surrender

The events in Italy gave impetus to a demand which arose among Allied statesmen and American political and military leaders to mitigate or at least clarify the meaning of the Casablanca Formula. The demand for the unconditional surrender of the Axis enemy had by no means been universally popular in American and Allied official circles. Churchill had been only faintly cordial to the policy and Stalin had received the announcement of the Casablanca demand with coolness. Several American generals and indeed the American Secretary of State had opposed the policy from its inception. As the war moved toward its final stage, as signs of disintegration within Germany grew, opposition to Unconditional Surrender increased.

As early as August, 1943, Prime Minister Churchill noted evidence of disunity and war weariness within Germany. He confided to his foreign secretary that in the light of such evidence there was no need "for us to discourage this process by continually uttering the slogan 'Unconditional Surrender.' " He continued:

> As long as we do not have to commit ourselves to dealing with any particular new figure or government, our advantage is clear. We certainly do not want, if we can help it, to get them all fused together in a solid desperate block for whom there is no hope. I am sure you will agree with me that a gradual breakup in Germany must mean a weakening of their resistance, and consequently the saving of hundreds of thousands of British and American lives.[52]

[52] *Closing the Ring*, p. 663.

Later in the same year the question of modifying the Unconditional Surrender policy was raised by the Soviet government. Soviet Foreign Minister Molotov proposed to American Ambassador Harriman that the Allies issue a statement explaining the meaning of the phrase "Unconditional Surrender." Harriman reported the suggestion to Hull, who in turn prepared a memorandum for the President. Hull explained that he believed the intention of the Soviet government was not to propose milder peace terms for Germany but rather to eliminate the detrimental propaganda effects of the formula:

> As I understand it, the Soviet Government believes that some definition, however general and severe, of the conditions of surrender which will be imposed on enemy countries would deprive the enemy of this propaganda advantage and consequently weaken the morale of their armed forces and people.[53]

In reply to the Hull memorandum and his inquiry whether the President would approve American discussion of the question with Soviet and British representatives, Roosevelt replied: "Frankly I do not like the idea of conversation to define the idea Unconditional Surrender." He said that he believed the Allied agreement not to make peace without mutual consultation was sufficient. As for German public opinion, he suggested that his recent address in which he had promised that the German people would not be enslaved be announced to the German public. He repeated the anecdote about Grant and Lee at Appomattox, indicating that he still had an affection for his Casablanca phrase, and he explained that any prior announcement of Allied terms might give the Allies the appearance of weakness or inconsistency if they were later forced to modify the previously announced terms. In the light of this reply, Hull informed Ambassador Harriman that he must explain to Molotov that American policy remained unchanged, that the United States could not advocate a modification of the Casablanca Formula.

A few weeks after this reply the Soviet Union negotiated a peace settlement with Finland. The words "Unconditional Surrender" were involved in neither the negotiations nor the armi-

[53] Hull, *op. cit.*, p. 1573, memorandum of Jan. 14, 1944.

stice settlement. In his public statements Marshal Stalin carefully avoided any mention of the phrase and instead continued to distinguish carefully between National Socialism and the German people. He repeated consistently that the Red Army was fighting Hitlerism, not the German state or people.[54]

The next demand for a change or clarification of Unconditional Surrender came from within the United States. Early in 1944 the Joint Chiefs of Staff established a committee of intelligence officers with the duty of investigating the exact meaning of the term "Unconditional Surrender." On March 16, 1944, this committee recommended a joint Anglo-American declaration which would reaffirm the principle of Unconditional Surrender but would clarify the meaning of the phrase in such a way as to reassure the German public that, although Allied policy sought to prevent future German aggression, it did not seek to destroy the German state and that, although war criminals would be punished, the masses of the German people would not be subjected to inhuman treatment. The committee pointed out that the eventual co-operation of the German people would be an essential element of a lasting peace. President Roosevelt rejected the proposals of the committee, commenting: "We must seek to eliminate the word Reich and all that it stands for today." [55]

In the same month, perhaps inspired by the tenor of the Soviet-Finnish armistice, British Foreign Secretary Eden proposed a mitigation of the Unconditional Surrender formula in relation to the Axis satellite states. Halifax, the British Ambassador in Washington, gave Hull a cablegram from Eden dated March 17, 1944, in which the Foreign Secretary proposed that the satellite states be encouraged to withdraw from the war in return for Allied assurance of some sort of reward for defecting to the Allied cause. Soviet Ambassador Gromyko also presented a memorandum to Hull indicating his government's endorsement of the British plan. Hull forwarded the proposals to the President together with his own approval: "I think it would be advantageous now to free ourselves from the Moscow decision on Unconditional Surrender of Axis satellite states." [56]

[54] *Ibid.*, pp. 1574-75.
[55] Chamberlin, *op. cit.*, pp. 290-91.
[56] Hull, *op. cit.*, p. 1575.

The President replied that he thought it would be a mistake to abandon the policy of Unconditional Surrender or to make any prior exceptions. He pointed out that, although Italy had surrendered unconditionally, she had, nevertheless, been granted many privileges as a result of her post-Armistice co-operation with the Allies. He suggested that a similar settlement might be made with satellite states. Once again he referred back to the illustration of Grant and Lee and explained that, although the Confederate forces had surrendered unconditionally, Grant had displayed gallantry. This, he said, was the spirit he wished to see in Europe, "but it does not apply to Germany. Germany understands only one kind of language." He instructed his secretary of state to respond negatively to the British cablegram, adding: "The British Foreign Office has always been part of this and it is N.G. F.D.R." [57]

Hull was reluctant to forward the President's rejection of the proposal to the Allies. On the advice of his State Department aides he reopened the question with the President before sending his reply to England. He explained to Roosevelt that American refusal to consider the British suggestion might result in military disadvantage for the Red Army fighting in Eastern Europe. The President replied that he wanted, at all costs, to avoid giving the impression that the principle of Unconditional Surrender had been abandoned, warning that there was danger in commiting the Allies to prior exceptions. Hull, therefore, had no choice but to inform the British and Soviet governments that the United States opposed any "general departure from the principle of Unconditional Surrender." [58]

Nevertheless, both the British and the Soviet government continued to press for a modification of the principle in relation to the Axis satellites. On March 12 the three powers issued a joint declaration to the governments of Hungary, Rumania, and Bulgaria advising them that they still had it within their power, by withdrawing from the war and ceasing their co-operation with Germany, to shorten the European struggle, diminish their own ultimate sacrifices, and contribute to Allied victory. Eloquent

[57] *Ibid.*, p. 1576.
[58] *Ibid.*, p. 1577.

persuasion by Secretary Hull had secured Roosevelt's permission to omit the phrase "Unconditional Surrender" from this declaration even though the President continued to insist that the omission of the phrase was not to be construed as the abandonment of the principle of Unconditional Surrender. Perhaps silence on this point contributed to the result that a few months later Rumania and Bulgaria requested and were granted armistice agreements.[59]

The President's insistence that the principle of Unconditional Surrender be maintained had been aimed chiefly at the German problem. It was in regard to Germany that the new demands for clarification arose. In April, 1944, General Eisenhower, Allied commander in the European theater, requested that the policy of demanding the unconditional surrender of Germany be reconsidered. He suggested that the Allies issue an open declaration to the German people proclaiming the proposed peace terms. Both Eisenhower and his chief of staff, Bedell Smith, were convinced that the German government was exploiting the theme of Unconditional Surrender to bolster public morale. They suggested that Allied propaganda seek to counteract this by encouraging a possible German Badoglio to "undertake the necessary political steps for Unconditional Surrender." They proposed an Anglo-American-Soviet statement which would define Unconditional Surrender and guarantee a reasonable and orderly settlement in Germany following a surrender. They further proposed that the Commander in Chief on the Western Front be authorized to issue a statement calling for German surrender on clearly stated terms as soon as an Allied beachhead should be established following the proposed June invasion of the French coast. They warned that the failure to issue such a statement would neglect the opportunity of exploiting the crisis in Wehrmacht morale which would inevitably result from a successful Allied landing. Both Eisenhower's political adviser and the British policy adviser to SHAEF concurred in this view.[60]

Eisenhower's aide, Butcher, reports that there was a general feeling at SHAEF headquarters that the Unconditional Surrender

[59] *Ibid.*, pp. 1578-79.
[60] *Ibid.*, p. 1578.

formula had been adopted at Casablanca without a full realization of its ultimate implications. He wrote:

> Goebbels has made great capital with it to strengthen the morale of the German Army and people. Our psychological experts believe we would be wiser if we created a mood of acceptance of surrender in the German Army which would make possible a collapse of resistance similar to that which took place in Tunisia.

To this end he advocated the definition of Unconditional Surrender to be followed by a radio and pamphlet psychological offensive designed to make clear Allied war aims: demilitarization, denazification, punishment of war criminals, orderly transfers of population, establishment of freedom of religion and of the rights of trade unions. He stated that the staff at SHAEF favored a clear-cut statement in soldier's language to be issued by the Supreme Commander directly after successful Allied landings in Normandy.[61]

Eisenhower's official suggestion to delineate the Allied war aims was forwarded to Secretary Hull. Apparently during the months which followed there were frequent discussions between Hull and the President or between Undersecretary of State Stettinius and the President. Apparently both the Department of State and SHAEF brought pressure to bear to secure some clarification or modification of the Casablanca demand. Undersecretary Stettinius reported that during these months the President was "far from well" and that he was becoming increasingly difficult to deal with.[62] Perhaps for this reason, or perhaps because Roosevelt was still inwardly committed to the idea of Unconditional Surrender, no modification of the policy was achieved.

Despite this failure, in May the State Department prepared a draft declaration which it proposed to issue to the German people urging them to overthrow their Nazi leaders and end the senseless struggle. It stressed the overwhelming military superiority of the Allied forces, advised against the needless loss of life, and stated that the only hope for Germany lay in Unconditional Surrender. The draft made no specific promises regarding peace

[61] Butcher, *op. cit.*, p. 518.
[62] *Ibid.*

terms but it repeated past assurances that the Allies had no intention of destroying or enslaving the German people. On July 17 Roosevelt instructed Hull to withhold publication of this declaration until the Allied armies had made more substantial progress. Apparently he regarded the time as inopportune. It is interesting to note that this order was given to Hull three days before the July 20 assassination attempt against Hitler by the German resistance movement.[63]

On August 21 Hull forwarded to the President a message from SHAEF headquarters recommending the issuance of a joint Order of the Day by General Eisenhower, General Wilson, and Marshal Stalin calling on the Wehrmacht to surrender. SHAEF commented that the war was approaching its psychological climax and noted that there had been a slackening in the usually high morale of the German Army on the Western Front. Hull added his personal comment, that he saw no objection to the proposal, but once again the President replied that he did not think the time right for such an announcement.[64]

By November, 1944, Eisenhower himself advised against issuing an appeal for surrender because at that juncture the military situation was not favorable. His view was that the announcement must climax a successful military operation, otherwise it would be interpreted as a sign of weakness. By then Churchill, too, opposed the idea of a proclamation since it would have to be a joint declaration with the Soviet Union and the Soviet demand for the conscription of several million German men for forced labor in the U.S.S.R. had become well known in Germany.[65]

On November 21, at a press conference in Paris, General Eisenhower expressed his opinion that a German surrender was not then imminent. He said that, even though many Germans continued to fight only because of Gestapo terror, the control of the Gestapo was as firm as ever and so German resistance would probably continue until the end. He said that since Hitler's "leading gang of brigands has nothing to lose" and since they had

[63] Hull, *op. cit.*, p. 1581.
[64] *Ibid.*
[65] Butcher, *op. cit.*, pp. 710-11.

the power to compel the German people to continue to fight, the war would continue until the German power to resist was totally destroyed.[66]

In March, 1945, Eisenhower again predicted that the war would continue to the point of total destruction of German power to resist. When asked at a press conference how and with whom a surrender would be negotiated, he replied that he believed there would be no negotiated surrender, but that rather the Anglo-American forces and the Soviet forces would converge and assume control over all German territory, "and that will be unconditional surrender."[67] As a matter of fact, it was almost that way.

The Surrender of Germany

The Allied generals at SHAEF had wanted to issue a proclamation calling for German surrender after a bridgehead should have been established subsequent to the landings in Normandy. There is no question that the Allied operations in France took a heavy toll of German strength during the months following *Overlord.* By the end of August the Germans had suffered 200,000 casualties, killed and wounded, and had lost an equal number through capture by the Allies. In addition, they had suffered severe material losses: 1,300 tanks, 20,000 vehicles, 2,000 guns, and approximately 3,500 aircraft. The military situation on the Western Front approximated that of 1918, and yet surrender did not come.[68] Ever since the disaster at Stalingrad a number of military and political observers inside Germany had been thinking in terms of ending a militarily hopeless situation. With each major setback the ranks of those who hoped for peace swelled. A small hard core of anti-Nazis had opposed the war from its inception, and since 1939 had engaged in a long and discouraging series of negotiations with the Allies to attempt to end the war. Neither the despair of Nazi leaders nor the idealism of the opposition led to a successful negotiation of an armistice to the

[66] *New York Times,* Nov. 22, 1944, p. 5. See also Butcher, *op. cit.,* p. 706.

[67] *New York Times,* March 28, 1945, p. 4. See also Butcher, *op. cit.,* p. 784.

[68] Major General J. F. C. Fuller, *The Second World War: 1939-45* (New York: Duell, Sloan, Pearce, 1948), p. 331.

cessation of hostilities, until Western and Soviet troops converged on German soil.

The negotiations which culminated in the ultimate unconditional surrender of Germany in May, 1945, stemmed from two sources: the Vatican and Sweden. Although the surrender was not consummated until the final overrunning of Germany by the victorious Allied armies, the preliminary negotiations date back to 1942 and 1943. Strangely enough, it was within the SS that the seeds of capitulation first germinated. Although many anti-Nazi Germans had long wished to end the war, it was the chief of the Foreign Intelligence Service of the SS Security Service, Walter Schellenberg, who was to a large extent responsible for undertaking peace negotiations through the good offices of Swedish Count Bernadotte, and it was General Karl Wolff, commander of the SS and of the German police forces in Italy, who successfully undertook to contact Allied agents through the good offices of the Vatican. Let us take a brief look at these two cases.

Since the tense prewar period the Vatican had consistently used its political and moral influence for peace. The Pope and his aides had arranged a series of meetings between peace-minded Germans, primarily anti-Nazis, and English or American representatives. The Pope had corresponded with Roosevelt and with Ribbentrop and had conferred with Kesselring and Mark Clark in attempts to end the war or at least to mitigate its destruction. Papal action had rescued many Italians and others from SS and Gestapo prisons, and it was a papal envoy who had pleaded with Kesselring to declare Rome an open city to prevent its destruction by Allied bombs and artillery.[69]

The earlier attempts to achieve peace had ended in failure, but shortly before Christmas, 1943, SS General Wolff undertook a series of negotiations which culminated in the surrender of all German forces south of the Alps. At the end of 1943 Wolff confided to Weizsäcker, the German ambassador to the Holy See, that he believed Germany ought to end the war with the

[69] Kesselring had issued the order to save Rome before the intercession of the papal representative. The Vatican's action is mentioned as an indication of its attitude toward peace. See Konstantin Prinz von Bayern, *Der Papst* (Frankfurt: Ullstein, 1952), pp. 112-26, 149-60.

Western Allies in order to be able to defend Europe against the Soviets. He asked the ambassador to try to arrange an audience for him with the Pope. In May, 1944, a modest civilian was ushered into the private chambers of Pope Pius XII for a secret audience: Karl Wolff. The details of this conference have not been recorded but a Vatican official reports that the Pope, although regarding the Allied aim of Unconditional Surrender as an obstacle, agreed to use the influence of the church to arrange negotiations and in any case to assure a reasonable standard of subsistence for the German people in the postwar world.[70]

In February, 1945, the papal representative in Milan, Cardinal Schuster, told General Wolff that it was time for him to meet with Allied agents. The Cardinal reported that the Allies were anxious to avoid the destruction of the industries in North Italy and so were eager to arrange an armistice. Wolff flew to Berlin to confer with Himmler and Hitler and confided to Hitler his conviction that Germany must sue for peace. Apparently Hitler did not disapprove Wolff's mission; in any case he did not have him shot for defeatism, but neither did he give him any direct authorization to negotiate. In mid-February a British agent arrived in Italy to meet with Wolff and to arrange a meeting with higher Allied representatives in Switzerland.[71] Wolff said that he was prepared to negotiate the surrender but not the unconditional surrender of troops in Italy. The agent promised to bring Field Marshal Alexander's answer within a week. On March 9, at noon, Wolff in civilian clothes was in Zurich sitting opposite Allen Dulles, American OSS chief there. The negotiations proceeded in earnest; as a preliminary manifestation of good will Wolff agreed to order the release of certain Italian partisan leaders.

When he reported back to Hitler in Berlin, the SS General found the Führer enraged by his independent action. Once again he was fortunate to escape being shot. On returning to Italy he sent a deputy to secure Kesselring's permission to continue the negotiations and then met again with Dulles. Finally on April 29,

[70] *Ibid.*, p. 189.

[71] See also Allen W. Dulles, *Germany's Underground* (New York: Macmillan, 1947), pp. 38 ff.

1945, at the headquarters of British Field Marshal Alexander, General Wolff signed the document which provided for the capitulation of all German troops on the Southern Front.[72]

An interesting sidelight on the question of Wolff's negotiations is the indignation and suspicion they aroused in Moscow. It seems that when Field Marshal Alexander had informed the Combined Chiefs of Staff of the German interest in negotiations, they had authorized the discussions but had advised him to wait until the Soviet government could be informed. Molotov apparently insisted that Red Army delegates be allowed to sit in on the meetings with Wolff and when this was not arranged the Soviet government ordered that the negotiations be broken off. Stalin sent a sharp wire to Roosevelt, charging that the purpose of the German plan was to release troops from the Southern to the Eastern Front. He implied an accusation of Anglo-American bad faith. Reportedly the tone of the message "deeply offended Mr. Roosevelt."[73] The incident also stirred Roosevelt's suspicion that perhaps the entire incident had been planned deliberately by the SS to undermine Allied unity.[74]

The second center of gravity of peace attempts lay north of the Alps. As early as August, 1942, SS Foreign Intelligence Chief Schellenberg had approached Himmler to ask him in confidence: "In which drawer of your desk have you got your alternative solution for ending this war?"[75] Himmler's initial reaction was anger but he was persuaded by Schellenberg's arguments that, since Germany could no longer hope for strategic victory, the best hope lay in negotiating while German strength still constituted a powerful bargaining pawn. Himmler commented that any compromise solution was impossible as long as Ribbentrop remained foreign minister, and from that time on he sought to undermine Ribbentrop's influence with Hitler and to have him removed. At that phase of the war the two SS men hoped to achieve terms

[72] Konstantin von Bayern, *op. cit.*, pp. 195-200.

[73] Byrnes, *op. cit.*, p. 57.

[74] Leahy, *op. cit.*, pp. 333-36.

[75] Walter Schellenberg, *The Labyrinth: Memoirs of Walter Schellenberg* (New York: Harper, 1956), p. 309.

which would ensure at least the German borders of September, 1939. Himmler said that he would try to convince Hitler of the wisdom of their plan by Christmas.[76]

Before Christmas, 1942, Himmler fell into Hitler's temporary disfavor and so the plan to work for peace was delayed. Early in 1943 Schellenberg established contact with the British Consul General in Zurich, but once again delays ensued. Ribbentrop, still foreign minister, issued an order forbidding the political sector of the Secret Service from contacting enemy nationals. Schellenberg, however, continued his activities, making contact with Swiss, American, and Swedish representatives.[77] Each time the talks reached a crucial point requiring Himmler's action, Himmler wavered and delayed. Finally at the end of 1944 Himmler agreed to meet with a former president of Switzerland, Musy, and as a demonstration of good faith he arranged for the release of 1,200 Jews, who were sent across the border into Switzerland. Hitler learned of the discussions and the agreement and was furious. The talks were suspended.[78]

In February, 1945, the Swedish Count Bernadotte seized the initiative by announcing that he wished to come to Berlin to meet with Himmler. Although Hitler commented, "One cannot accomplish anything with this sort of nonsense in a total war," Bernadotte met with a number of SS and Foreign Office men including Kaltenbrunner and Ribbentrop. Once again Schellenberg tried to persuade Himmler to act to end the war. He proposed that Bernadotte fly directly to Eisenhower to arrange an immediate armistice, but again Himmler was dilatory. By the end of March the German military situation had deteriorated to the point where the SS chief realized that he must act, but apparently he was unable to determine whether to arrest or shoot the Führer. He did neither. He waited. On April 22 the military situation became critical. Hitler ordered four Waffen-SS Divisions to throw themselves into a suicide attack against the Red Army—a senseless measure. Himmler was finally impelled to act.

[76] *Ibid.*, p. 315.
[77] *Ibid.*, pp. 321-331, 343-48, 370-71.
[78] *Ibid.*, pp. 379-80.

He and Bernadotte agreed to contact Washington and London to communicate Himmler's desire to surrender to the Western Allies. Himmler still insisted: "It is not possible for us Germans, and especially it is not possible for me, to capitulate to the Russians." [79]

On April 26 Count Bernadotte received a reply from President Truman, stating that the German offer of surrender would be accepted only on condition that it included surrender to the U.S.S.R. as well as to the Western powers. The message instructed the German forces to cease resistance on all fronts and surrender in the field to local Allied commanders. "Should any resistance continue anywhere, the Allied attacks will be ruthlessly carried on until complete victory has been gained." [80]

Within Germany Hitler learned of Himmler's attempted negotiation and bitterly he named Admiral Doenitz instead of the SS chief as his successor. At the end of April Hitler committed suicide and Doenitz at once undertook to negotiate a surrender to the Allies.[81]

On May 4 SHAEF headquarters was informed that representatives of the Doenitz government would arrive to sign a surrender document. On the following day the German Admiral Hans Georg von Friedeburg arrived. When the Admiral said that he would like to discuss several points Eisenhower sent word to him that he could accept only surrender—total and unconditional—without discussion. Friedeburg maintained that he was not authorized to do this and was permitted to wire Doenitz, who replied that Colonel General Jodl was on his way to assist in negotiations. Eisenhower believed that the Germans were deliberately delaying the surrender in order to secure time to transfer as many troops as possible from the Eastern Front to the West so that as many Germans as possible could be spared Soviet capture. Eisenhower was angered by this and warned the German representatives that any further delay would compel him to close the entire Allied

[79] *Ibid.*, pp. 382-89, 396-99. See also Count Folke Bernadotte, *The Fall of the Curtain* (London: Cassell, 1945), pp. 55-58.

[80] Bernadotte, *op. cit.*, p. 61. See also Eisenhower, *Crusade in Europe*, p. 424.

[81] Bernadotte, *op. cit.*, p. 62. See also Schellenberg, *op. cit.*, pp. 401 ff.

front by force to prevent any additional German refugees from crossing behind the Western lines.[82]

A series of cables to and from Doenitz culminated in the fact that General Jodl signed the Instrument of Unconditional Surrender at 2:41 A.M. on May 7, 1945, surrender to become effective at midnight, May 8. After the signing General Eisenhower informed Jodl that he would be held personally responsible for German adherence to the terms of the document. Jodl said that he understood; he saluted and returned to Doenitz headquarters. On May 9 formal Four Power ceremonies of surrender were held in Berlin.

Eisenhower commented: "The German surrender on May 7 marked the accomplishment of the first and greatest Allied objective." [83] He was probably correct. The German government had surrendered unconditionally. The German Army had clearly been defeated in the field by the three major Allies. Representatives of Great Britain, the Soviet Union, and the United States met in Berlin to celebrate their victory and to launch a new era of German and of European history.

On May 11, 1945, the American War Department released a declaration stating the assumption of supreme authority in Germany by the governments of the United States, the U.S.S.R., the United Kingdom, and France. It proclaimed that the German armed forces had been completely defeated and had surrendered unconditionally, that Germany was thereby subject to any requirements which the Allied governments "now or hereafter" might impose. Germans were ordered to cease all hostilities, to evacuate all non-German territory, to surrender all weapons, aircraft, and ammunition, to furnish labor, plant facilities, information and records to the Allies on demand. Principal Nazi leaders and war criminals would be arrested, and the Allies would take whatever steps were deemed necessary to bring about the demilitarization and disarmament of Germany.[84] By this proclamation Unconditional Surrender was transformed into the Four

[82] Eisenhower, *op. cit.*, p. 426. See also Butcher, *op. cit.*, p. 827.
[83] Eisenhower, *op. cit.*, p. 428.
[84] *Documents on American Foreign Relations,* Vol. VII, pp. 217 ff.

Power Occupation of Germany and the Second World War gave way to the postwar period in Europe.

What were the over-all results of this policy of Unconditional Surrender? Had there been a workable alternative? What had been the effect of the formula on the wartime situation within Germany? Let us turn now to the German scene and try to evaluate the impact of Unconditional Surrender on Germany and on the Germans.

MILITARY CHRONOLOGY
of the
Second World War: 1939-1945

1939

1 September	German Wehrmacht crosses the Polish border
11 September	First major victory against the Polish Army
17 September	Red Army invades Eastern Poland
6 October	Destruction of last major force of Polish Army by Wehrmacht
12 October	Government General ordered for Poland
26 October	Wehrmacht turns over control of Poland to civilians
30 November	U.S.S.R. attacks Finland

1940

13 March	Peace between U.S.S.R. and Finland
9 April	German troops land in Denmark and Norway
10 May	Beginning of German campaign in West
14 May	Capitulation of Holland's Army
17 May	Pétain becomes head of French Vichy government
27 May	Capitulation of Belgian Army

28 May–4 June	Evacuation of BEF at Dunkirk
5 June	Beginning of the battle for France
9 June	Breakthrough of Wehrmacht on the Aisne
10 June	Italy declares war on Britain and France
14 June	Paris occupied by Wehrmacht
15 June	Breakthrough of the Maginot Line
16 June	Components of the Red Army occupy Baltic States
25 June	France signs armistice with Germany
3 July	English attack the French fleet near Oran
13 August	Beginning of air offensive against Britain: The Battle of Britain
13 September	Italy attacks Egypt
28 October	Beginning of Italian offensive in Greece
4 November	English troops land in Crete
9 December	English begin offensive against Italians in North Africa
1941	
11 February	First German troops land in Tripoli
12 February	General Rommel assumes command in North Africa
31 March	Afrika Korps begins offensive at Tobruk
6 April	German offensive against Yugoslavia and Greece
18 April	Armistice in Yugoslavia
21 April	Armistice in Greece
20 May	German airborne landing in Crete

22 June	German attack on U.S.S.R.: Operation Barbarossa
9 July	Wehrmacht takes Minsk
5 August	Germans take Smolensk
8 September	Germans reach Leningrad
26 September	Germans take Kiev
2 October	New German offensive on whole Eastern Front
7 November	German victory in Crimea
12 November	German Wehrmacht reaches Moscow
18 November	German offensive against Moscow begins; English counteroffensive in Libya begins
6 December	Failure of German offensive at Moscow; Red Army begins counteroffensive against German Army Group Center
7–8 December	Pearl Harbor: U.S. enters the war
19 December	Hitler assumes personal command of the Wehrmacht
1942	
21 January	Beginning of German offensive in North Africa
26 May	German-Italian forces attack at El Alamein
30 June	Rommel reaches El Alamein
1-25 July	German offensive in the East captures Sevastopol and Rostov
25 August	German Sixth Army reaches Stalingrad
17 October	German offensive against Stalingrad
23 October	English begin offensive at El Alamein
3 November	English Breakthrough at El Alamein

8 November	Allied landing in North Africa
13 November	Germans lose Tobruk
22 November	Stalingrad encircled
1943	
10 January	Beginning of Soviet offensive at Stalingrad
24 January	Unconditional Surrender announcement
30 January	Capitulation of German Sixth Army at Stalingrad
14 February	Germans withdraw at Rostov
9 March	Rommel relinquishes the command of the Afrika Korps
27 March	Germans lose Mareth Line in Southern Tunisia
12 May	Capitulation of Afrika Korps
10 July	Allied landing in Sicily
25 July	Overthrow of Mussolini government in Italy
3 August	Russians begin offensive against Army Group South
5 August	Broadening of Russian offensive against Army Group Center in the direction of Smolensk
17 August	Americans occupy Messina; end of the Sicilian campaign
22 August	Germans lose Kharkov
1 September	Beginning of Russian breakthrough between German Army Groups Center and South at Kiev
3 September	Secret signing of an armistice between Italy and the Allies
9 September	American landing at Salerno
1 October	Americans occupy Naples

6 October	Beginning of Russian winter offensive on the Black Sea
23 October	Russians encircle the Crimea
6 November	Fall of Kiev to Red Army; breakthrough toward the Pripet Marshes
24 December	Red Army begins offensive west of Kiev
1944	
14 January	Russian offensive against Army Group North
22 January	Allied landing at Anzio; bridgehead contained by Kesselring
4 March	Russian offensive against Army Group South
8/9 April	Soviets begin the reconquest of the Crimea, take Odessa
15 April	Red Army attack on Sevastopol
9 May	Fall of Sevastopol to the Red Army
11 May	Beginning of the Allied offensive on Rome
22 May	Allied breakthrough at Anzio
4 June	Americans capture Rome
6 June	Allied landings in Normandy: Operation Overlord; 82nd and 101st Airborne (U.S.), plus British airborne troops
22 June	Russian offensive against Army Group Center
26 June	Cherbourg falls to Allies; Red Army takes Vitebsk
3 July	Red Army takes Minsk
9 July	English capture Caen
13/14 July	Red Army begins offensive against Army Group North and Army Group North Ukraine

19 July	Germans lose Saint-Lô in Normandy
25 July	American breakthrough at Avranches
27 July	Beginning of a battle south of Warsaw
4 August	Americans take Florence
15 August	Lieutenant General Patch (U.S. Seventh Army) lands in Southern France
20 August	Beginning of Red Army offensive against South Ukraine
25 August	French troops take Paris
30/31 August	Germans lose oil fields at Ploesti; Bucharest falls
3 September	English occupy Brussels
10 September	Americans begin offensive in Apennines near Bologna
11 September	American First Army reaches the German border near Trier
10 October	Russian breakthrough south of Riga to the Baltic Sea
16 October	Red Army reaches East Prussia
19 October	Red Army takes Belgrade
23 October	Aachen falls to the Americans
8 November	Beginning of American offensive near Metz
22 November	French troops take Mulhouse and Belfort
3 December	Americans break through the Westwall near Saarlautern
16 December	Beginning of the German counteroffensive in Ardennes

1945	
3 January	Beginning of the Allied counteroffensive in Ardennes
12 January	Beginning of a Russian offensive on the Vistula
13 January	Beginning of Russian breakthrough in East Prussia
18 January	Wehrmacht evacuates Warsaw
23 January	Russians reach the Oder in Lower Silesia
16 February	German counteroffensive in Pomerania, southeast of Stettin
23 February	Beginning of American offensive near Cologne
7 March	Americans occupy Cologne
30 March	Russians occupy Danzig; Russians begin offensive against Vienna
12 April	Capitulation of Königsberg
13 April	Occupation of Vienna by the Russians; American troops reach the Elbe
16 April	Beginning of Red Army offensive against Berlin
19 April	English troops reach the Elbe at Dannenberg; American breakthrough at Bologna; Red Army on the Oder
20 April	Red Army tanks eight miles from Berlin
24 April	Berlin encircled
25 April	Meeting of American and Russian troops at Torgau on the Elbe
2 May	Berlin falls to First White Russian and First Ukrainian armies
3 May	End of the battle in northern Germany

4 May	American troops from Italy and South Germany meet at Brenner Pass
7 May	German Twelfth Army retreats across the Elbe; Unconditional Surrender instrument signed at Reims

CHAPTER 3

The Effects of the Policy of Unconditional Surrender on the Military Conduct of the War

Between the time of the Casablanca announcement and the final surrender of Germany the English and American political and military leaders who called for the mitigation or clarification of the demand for unconditional surrender contended that the formula would prolong the war and increase its intensity. Since the end of the Second World War the question of whether indeed the Casablanca Formula did lengthen the war and increase its cost has been debated in the memoirs of wartime soldiers and statesmen, in the commentaries of historians, and in the analyses of military writers. Final answers to such questions of historical speculation must be left to philosophers or to propagandists. The political scientist or historian must content himself with a more modest goal. This study will not attempt to prove that Unconditional Surrender did or did not prolong the war, was or was not directly responsible for increasing the intensity of German resistance, but will rather confine its aim to the collection and evaluation of available evidence and to the sketching of tentative, perhaps probable, conclusions. It will examine the testimony of both German and Allied military commanders and will consider the views of military historians on these two questions: (1) Did the Casablanca demand for unconditional surrender prolong the war beyond the point at which the German commanders had become convinced that victory was impossible, that peace was necessary? and (2) Did the Allied intention of achieving an unlimited war aim result in the use by both sides of unlimited means? Did, for example, the Allied aim of compelling the total submission of the enemy lead logically to the use of extreme methods of warfare such as saturation bombing? Did the German fear that Unconditional Surrender might imply the destruction of the German state and a doubtful future for the German people inspire fierce and uncompromising resistance?

Let us begin by examining the question of whether the demand prolonged the war.

THE EFFECT OF UNCONDITIONAL SURRENDER ON THE DURATION OF THE WAR

When Had Germany Lost the War?

The question of whether the policy of Unconditional Surrender prolonged the Second World War beyond the point of German military defeat implies certain other preliminary questions: What is the meaning of the word "defeat"? At what point in the war had German defeat become inevitable? At what point did a significant number of German generals recognize that defeat was inevitable? What sort of peace conditions might have been negotiated at this earlier date? Let us begin with the first question.

The term "strategic defeat" can be interpreted in three ways:

1. One can say that Germany had lost the war at the point that the German Wehrmacht had been so reduced in striking force that it was no longer potentially capable of destroying the Red Army and of repelling Anglo-American invasion forces, in other words, no longer capable of effecting a German military victory.

2. One can define military defeat as the reduction of German

power to the point where it was no longer able to prevent the ultimate invasion of the homeland by the Allies.

3. Or, in the narrowest sense, the term "defeat" could imply the total envelopment of the German Army, its total separation from its source of supply, or its dissolution on the field of battle in complete rout and disorganization. This sort of defeat would almost automatically result in unconditional surrender whether or not that had been the demand of the victor.

Let us examine the question of the points at which Germany arrived at the two preliminary or relative degrees of defeat: at what point did the Wehrmacht lose the opportunity of winning the war and, second, at what point did ultimate defeat become inevitable?

It can be argued that at no point in the war was German military victory a reasonable possibility, that the German Wehrmacht had never been in a position to compel the submission of its combined enemies, that the tremendous land mass and overwhelming superiority of manpower of the U.S.S.R. combined with the economic and technical potentiality of England and the United States had made strategic victory for Germany a hopeless goal from the outset. It is impossible to be sure whether ultimate German defeat was inherent in the basic power positions of the antagonists, but that question is purely academic.[1] From the point of view of policy what matters is not the actual point at which the German military position became hopeless but rather the point at which a significant proportion of the German military leaders became convinced of the hopelessness.

There was a segment of German military opinion which held from the outset that a German military victory was impossible. Before the outbreak of war, from 1936 through 1938, the chief of the General Staff, Colonel General Ludwig Beck, repeatedly warned against any movement toward war on the grounds that eventual defeat for Germany was inevitable.[2] In the summer of 1938, during the Czechoslovakian crisis the leading generals of

[1] The question of whether indeed Germany had ever been in a position to win the war is still debated by military authorities and former German military commanders.

[2] Wolfgang Foerster, *Ein General Kämpft gegen den Krieg,* pp. 29-32, 113 ff.

the German Army were unanimous in their opposition to war. A staff study prepared by Beck and his colleagues at that time warned clearly that Germany was not in a position to achieve military victory in a world war, that the manpower and production of the German Reich were not sufficient to compete with those of the British Empire, the Soviet Union, France, and probably also the United States.[3] At this time the German generals were so emphatic in their judgment that they threatened a general strike of generals in the event that Hitler should lead the country into war.[4] Beck himself resigned as chief of the General Staff in protest against Hitler's war policy. The attitude of the generals who remained continued to be skeptical regarding the ultimate outcome of a possible war. If war had come in 1938, it is impossible to conjecture what the generals might have done. The Munich Pact postponed war and gave Hitler a diplomatic and popular triumph. The generals who had warned of disaster were labeled defeatists and unrealistic pessimists.

By the time war actually broke out in September, 1939, the faith of the generals in their own judgment had been undermined and their prestige had been weakened. Many of them continued to believe in the inevitability of ultimate defeat, while others were carried along by the tide of amazing initial successes to an optimism regarding the final outcome. For example, Field Marshal Albert Kesselring believed that despite the obvious superiority of the Allied potential, their essential disunity might provide a slim possibility of German victory. If it were possible to encounter each of the Allies separately and in succession and if it would be possible to prevent American entry into the war, victory might be achieved.[5]

[3] *Ibid.*, pp. 116-19, also pp. 120, 122.

[4] *Ibid.*, p. 122.

[5] Interview with Field Marshal (ret.) Albert Kesselring, Bad Wiessee, July 22, 1958. In postwar retrospect Field Marshal Kesselring concluded that the ultimate defeat of the German Wehrmacht had been rendered inevitable by the failure of the Supreme Command to exploit the favorable strategic situation, and also by the tremendous political mistakes of the German government, such as the failure to evacuate and to conclude peace settlements with France and the Ukraine, the resort to measures contrary to international law, and the persecution of Jews. See also his account in *Gedanken zum Zweiten Weltkrieg* (Bonn: Athenäum Verlag, 1955), pp. 45-53, 123-29, 180-95.

According to General Warlimont,[6] opinion in the OKW [7] was even more optimistic. After Hitler's early successes the generals at headquarters apparently believed that eventual victory was fully possible.[8] Even though many of the other generals continued skeptical, their viewpoint was ineffective as long as a pivotal segment of military leadership believed in victory and as long as the masses of the German people were dazzled by early successes. No matter how clearly the generals who followed the views of Beck foresaw ultimate German defeat, it was a political and historical impossibility for a single segment of generals to attempt to end the war on any terms less than triumphant as long as the Wehrmacht continued to roll up victories.[9]

The initial German successes were impressive. In 1939 Poland succumbed after a campaign of six weeks. In April, 1940, the Wehrmacht occupied Denmark and Norway without serious resistance. In May the Germans rolled into Holland, where the Dutch Army was able to resist for only four days. At the end of May the Belgian Army capitulated and the BEF was forced to evacuate at Dunkirk. In June the battle for France began: Paris was occupied on June 14; the Maginot Line was broken on June 15; on June 25 the armistice with France was signed.

In August the Luftwaffe launched the air offensive against England, and in September the Italians attacked Egypt and Greece. Early in 1941 Rommel led the Afrika Korps to a series of triumphs, and in the spring Yugoslavia and Greece fell to German arms, and Crete was taken, primarily, by paratroop assault. Thus, within two years almost the entire European Continent had been transformed into a German fortress. *Operation Barbarossa*, the invasion of the Soviet Union, began in June, 1941. From July until the end of November victory followed victory: Minsk fell in July, Smolensk in August, Kiev in September, the

[6] The Deputy Chief of Staff of the Operations Staff of the OKW.

[7] OKW: Oberkommando der Wehrmacht: Supreme Command of the Armed Forces.

[8] Interview with General (ret.) Walter Warlimont, Rottach-Egern, Bavaria, July 25, 1958.

[9] This viewpoint has been expressed by many former German generals in postwar interviews and writings, including General (ret.) Hermann von Witzleben in an interview June 27, 1958, at Munich, Germany.

Wehrmacht swept through the Ukraine and the Crimea. In the north the Germans reached Leningrad. By November the final offensive against Moscow was under way.

Until this point, November, 1941, the Allies had not achieved a single strategic victory. In the East the Red Army was falling back along a thousand-mile front, literally millions of Russian prisoners had surrendered to the Germans, Soviet supplies were scarce and primitive in quality in comparison to German precision instruments. In the West, England stood alone.

Only then did the wave of counteroffensive begin. In Libya the English attacked the Afrika Korps, the Red Army assumed the offensive at Moscow, and the Japanese attack at Pearl Harbor brought the United States into the war. This was the first step in the turning of the tide, but still the Wehrmacht had suffered no strategic defeat. It remained a powerful weapon, perhaps still capable of destroying the Red Army.

The year 1942 brought renewed German offensives in North Africa and Russia. By July Rommel had reached El Alamein, within striking distance of the Egyptian border, threatening the Suez Canal. By August Sevastopol and Rostov had fallen to the Germans, and the German Sixth Army was preparing its offensive against Stalingrad.

In October the English launched a counteroffensive in Africa. On November 3 they broke through at El Alamein; on November 8 the Allies landed in North Africa; on November 13 Tobruk fell. In the East the Soviets began a counteroffensive on January 10, 1944. On January 30 the German Sixth Army capitulated at Stalingrad; in February Rostov fell. In March the Mareth Line in Southern Tunisia collapsed, and on May 12 the remnant of the Afrika Korps capitulated. The Western Allies prepared to invade Sicily and Italy. The Red Army was in a position to launch a general attack on all segments of the Eastern Front. The Wehrmacht, by no means shattered as a fighting force, was nevertheless in full retreat.

The Impact of Stalingrad

The loss of more than 200,000 men in the battle of Stalingrad was the most disastrous defeat on the field of battle in German history. It shattered the faith of overwhelming numbers of the German people, of many young officers and men of the German Wehrmacht, and of high-ranking troop commanders in the ability and integrity of the Supreme Commander and in the possibility of final German victory. The loss of the entire German Sixth Army created a gap on the Eastern Front that could never be filled. Among the twenty lost divisions had been some of the finest German troops of the Wehrmacht. Among the officers who fell or went into captivity were sons of many of the old military families of Germany.[10] The prestige of the Nazi regime had never sunk lower among the German people or in the army. It was clear to many that the Sixth Army had been sacrificed to a single man's stubbornness and blind fanaticism.

As early as November the chief of the General Staff, Colonel General Kurt Zeitzler, had urged Hitler to allow the evacuation of Stalingrad and the shortening of the Southeastern Front. Hitler had refused, shouting, "I won't retreat from the Volga."[11] By November 22 the Soviets had succeeded in encircling the German units at Stalingrad. The Red Army then concentrated its attack against Army Group B, the German unit nearest Stalingrad, and slowly pushed it farther to the west, isolating the forces at Stalingrad. Twenty German divisions and two Rumanian divisions, from 200,000 to 300,000 men, were enclosed in a pocket 25 miles wide and 12 miles deep. General Paulus, the commander, radioed for permission to fight his way out of the encirclement. Although Hitler at first agreed to this proposition, he changed his mind on the grounds of a promise by Reichsmarschall Goering to supply the encircled troops by air. Zeitzler warned that the air force would be required to deliver a minimum of three hundred tons of supplies daily and denied that Goering was in a position to meet this minimum. Goering insisted that he could do it and Hitler accepted Goering's promise.[12] Field Marshal von Manstein,

[10] Field Marshal (ret.) Fritz Erich von Manstein, *Verlorene Siege* (Bonn: Athenäum Verlag, 1955).

[11] General Werner Kreipe *et al.*, *The Fatal Decisions* (New York: Berkeley, 1958), p. 144.

[12] *Ibid.*, pp. 151-57. Field Marshal Kesselring differs somewhat with the interpretation of General Zeitzler. In a letter dated April, 1959, he reported to the author that in a conversation Goering had assured him that he had

the commander of the German force nearest Stalingrad, launched an all-out attack to attempt to break through to the encircled Sixth Army, but he lacked both manpower and tanks. He was halted within thirty miles of the pocket. Again at this juncture Hitler refused to allow Paulus to try to break out of the encirclement to join Manstein despite the pleas of both Manstein and Zeitzler.[13] Then, contrary to Hitler's specific orders, Manstein ordered Paulus to attempt to break out of the ring to the southwest, but for tactical reasons Paulus refused.[14]

By the beginning of January the Soviet offensive had reduced the pocket to about half its former size. Contrary to Goering's repeated promises, the air force had been able to drop only about a third of the necessary supplies. Each day ammunition, food, and medical supplies became scarcer. Casualties increased at such a rate that only the worst cases could be flown out. The physical strength of the troops declined, they suffered from undernourishment, thousands of them died from the cold. By the middle of January there were not even bandages to cover the wounds or warm shelter for the injured men. Still the Sixth Army continued to resist and, in compliance with the repeated orders of Hitler, Paulus rejected the Red Army's offers of surrender. At first the officers and men within the encirclement could not believe that Hitler would allow an entire army to be abandoned to the enemy. They continued to hope for relief and release. As the end of January approached, it became clear that relief would not come but also that by then they had no choice but to continue their resistance.

On January 24 Paulus reported that unified command was no longer possible. The 18,000 wounded men could not be cared for. There was no ammunition, almost no shelter. The Sixth Army suffered from increasing shortage of rolling stock, fuel, and men.[15] The entire 5th Infantry Division had been destroyed.

been in the position to deliver the promised 300 tons daily, but the over-all strategic situation changed drastically after he had given the promise. For example, the airfields within the pocket gradually became unusable.

[13] *Ibid.*, pp. 159-61.

[14] Manstein, *op. cit.*, p. 392.

[15] Manstein, *op. cit.*, p. 384; Hans Doerr (Maj. Gen. a.D.), *Der Feldzug nach Stalingrad* (Darmstadt: E. S. Miller & Son, 1955), pp. 114-16.

The last airfield by which supplies had been delivered and wounded evacuated had fallen.[16] On January 26 the Red Army succeeded in splitting the remnant of the German Sixth Army into two separate pockets. The Russians took the grain silos, canning factories, and the railroad station of Stalingrad South. On January 27 the southern German pocket was again split. The death struggle of the Sixth Army began. Between January 24 and February 2 more than 100,000 German men and officers fell. On January 30 Paulus, who had been made field marshal just a few days earlier, signed the capitulation. Of the more than 250,000 men who had been encircled in the pocket only 90,000 remained to enter Soviet prison camps.[17]

With the destruction of the German Sixth Army, morale on the Eastern Front appeared to be virtually shattered. Both Field Marshal von Manstein and General Zeitzler attempted to resign their commands.[18] Many of the generals on the Eastern Front demanded that Hitler relinquish his command of the Wehrmacht in favor of a reputable professional soldier. Hitler refused, and the army whispered of revolt.[19] Even men as unshakable as General Guderian regarded the disaster at Stalingrad as a national catastrophe and feared a grave crisis on the Eastern Front. "Morale had reached a low point both in the army and in the country." [20]

The repercussions extended to all German fronts. Lieutenant General Bodo Zimmermann, chief of operations to the commander on the Western Front, Field Marshal von Rundstedt, reported that Rundstedt had reacted to the fall of Stalingrad with shock and pessimism. He felt that continued attrition of German manpower and supplies in the East obviously implied a drain on the defense potential of the Western forces in the face of an anticipated Allied invasion.[21]

In the minds of many German generals, the time had come for

[16] Kurt von Tippelskirch, *Geschichte des Zweiten Weltkriegs* (Bonn: Athenäum Verlag, 1956), pp. 275-76.

[17] *Ibid.*, p. 276. See also Doerr, *op. cit.*, pp. 116-17.

[18] Kreipe *et al.*, *op. cit.*, pp. 176-77.

[19] Wilmot, *The Struggle for Europe*, p. 166.

[20] Heinz Guderian, *Erinnerungen eines Soldaten* (Heidelberg: Vowinckel, 1951), p. 284.

[21] Kreipe *et al.*, *op. cit.*, p. 187.

a political decision. Manstein believed that after the loss of the Sixth Army decisive German victory was no longer possible, that the most that could be hoped for was the prevention of total disaster. He believed that the remaining strength of the Wehrmacht should be employed to secure a compromise *remis* solution, that to this end the lines in the East should be shortened and the army should assume strong defensive positions. The successes of his operations following Stalingrad, including the capture of Kharkov, which prevented a serious Soviet breakthrough, could have provided the military framework for a political solution, had such a solution lain within the realm of possibility.[22]

Field Marshal Kesselring, German supreme commander in the Mediterranean area, agreed with the Manstein interpretation that after Stalingrad German victory was no longer possible but that early in 1943 the German war machine still held great potential. The entire homeland was still intact, full-scale enemy bombing had not yet begun, the raw materials and the industrial potential of most of Europe were at Germany's disposal, the German Wehrmacht stood deep in Russian territory. Sound military policy, including strengthening the submarine fleet, allocating a top priority to the Luftwaffe, and emphasis on new weapons such as the snorkel, the V-1's, and the V-2's would have made Germany a still-powerful enemy. Had the Allies wished to end the war on the basis of mutual interest, Germany would still have been, from her viewpoint, in a good bargaining position.[23]

A compromise solution at the beginning of 1943 would have been based on the recognition that German victory was no longer realizable, that the world's power situation had shifted permanently. The war had forced the United States to assume the status of great power and had reduced the status of France and undermined that of Great Britain. Germany, although she would have retained considerable strength from a 1943 remise, would have been overshadowed by the existent power of the United

[22] Manstein, *op. cit.*, pp. 397-98; Kreipe *et al.*, *op. cit.*, p. 178.

[23] Interview, F. M. Albert Kesselring, Bad Wiessee, Germany, July 22, 1958.

States and the potential power of the Soviet Union and by the slowly emerging powers of the Far East, China, and India.

The realization of the full import of the Stalingrad disaster came slowly to the German people. In November, when the encirclement was first forged by the Red Army, the hope of liberation was still strong. As the weeks passed and Manstein's attempt to relieve the Sixth Army failed, as the size of the pocket was gradually reduced, hope began to wane. All through January, 1943, the German public waited, their attention fixed on Stalingrad, and gradually the inevitability of disaster became clear. The shock of this terrible loss was profound. Germany shuddered under the realization of the destruction of an entire army in the field. Doubts, mistrust, and resentment spread, but the moment of the final struggle of the lost Sixth Army was also the precise moment of the Casablanca pronouncement. On the day that the pocket was split, January 24, the Western Allies proclaimed that they would accept nothing less than the unconditional surrender of Germany.

Some members of the anti-Nazi resistance movement insist that this proclamation disrupted their organization overnight. Wilmot says that the policy deterred many German officers from taking action against the Nazi government, that Kluge and Manstein, for example, now refused to implement their opposition to Hitler since the Allies seemed determined to destroy Germany. Apparently many officers believed that Hitler must be given another chance to try to accomplish another military miracle in order to prevent the destruction of Germany and compel the Allies to agree to honorable peace.[24] Jodl warned that there was now clearly no political solution possible, that there was only one way out—a fight to the finish—that capitulation under the Casablanca Formula would mean the end of the German nation.[25]

Whatever the cause, and probably there were many influencing factors, the generals did not revolt in January, 1943, the resistance leaders did not move to overthrow Hitler, and the German people not only renewed their dedication to the war but were soon fired by Goebbels if not with enthusiasm then at least with

[24] Wilmot, *op. cit.*, p. 166.
[25] *Ibid.*, p. 165.

determination for the all-out program he called Total War. After Stalingrad the war intensified and its cost in lives and destruction mounted.

The Next Crisis: Spring, 1943

Despite the successes of the German counteroffensive on the southern segment of the Eastern Front which re-established a firm line and prevented a strategic Soviet breakthrough after Stalingrad, the spring of 1943 brought serious reverses to the German cause. The front in North Africa, imperiled since Rommel's defeat at El Alamein and the loss of Tobruk in November, collapsed entirely in the spring. In March the Germans withdrew from Libya to the Mareth Line along the Tunisian border. Rommel, in poor health, relinquished his command. Despite tactical victories, the Germans could not hold the line; pressed from both the east and the west, the German and Italian forces were forced to withdraw. On May 12 the remnant of the German Army Group Tunis capitulated and Africa fell entirely to the Allies. The invasion of Sicily and Italy was imminent.

The losses in Africa deeply shook Italian morale; great numbers of Italian soldiers had surrendered with the Afrika Korps. Mussolini's government tottered. The Wehrmacht rushed seven German divisions into the Italian peninsula to bolster both defenses and morale, strength that was soon sorely missed on the Eastern Front.[26]

By May Rommel expressed pessimism about the ultimate outcome. In a conference with Hitler he pointed out that as many as thirty German U-boats were being lost each month, that the situation in the East and in Italy was menacing, and that even with the increased arms production resulting from the total labor mobilization policy, Germany could not possibly keep pace with the whole world.[27] Rommel reports:

> Hitler listened to it all with downcast eyes. . . . Suddenly he looked up and said that he, too, was aware that there was very little chance left of winning the war. But the West would conclude no

[26] Kreipe *et al., op. cit.,* p. 179.

[27] *The Rommel Papers* (ed. B. H. Liddell Hart) (New York: Harcourt, Brace, 1953), p. 427.

peace with him. . . . He had never wanted war with the West. But now the West would have their war—have it to the end.[28]

At this stage of the war Rommel himself no longer believed that Germany could achieve victory, but he still hoped that German strength was sufficient to persuade the Allies to "conclude a tolerable peace."[29] As the military situation deteriorated in late spring and summer, his conviction grew that a political solution was essential to Germany's salvation. In July he told his former Afrika Korps chief of staff, Lieutenant General Bayerlein, that his long-range aim was to achieve a "tolerable peace" by wearing down the enemy, making the Red Army pay for every mile of territory it gained by the full use of antitank guns and fighters and then launching a quick counteroffensive to achieve not victory but peace. In the West he hoped to be able to throw the Anglo-American invasion forces back into the sea and so dampen their enthusiasm for war and for Unconditional Surrender.[30] He confided to his family that from the summer of 1943 on he believed that Germany's future required the arrangement of a reasonable peace even against Hitler's will, that it would probably necessitate a coup d'état to overthrow the Hitler government. In Rommel's view such a solution was complicated by three stubborn factors: (1) a change of regime within Germany might produce a collapse of resistance on the Eastern Front which would allow the Red Army to flood into Central Europe; (2) the younger officers and men who were not informed about the full gravity of the situation and who still believed in the possibility of eventual victory would not understand the coup and would regard the older officers as traitors, might even lead a counterrevolt; and (3) the Western Allies could not be expected to give up their demand for unconditional surrender except under pressure. Rommel thought that a successful German repulsion of an invasion attempt might provide this pressure. In that event the Allies might fear either that the Soviets would be able to invade Germany alone and occupy the whole of Central Europe or else that the Germans might be able to retrieve their position on the

[28] *Ibid.*, pp. 427-28.
[29] *Ibid.*, p. 427.
[30] *Ibid.*, pp. 451-53.

Eastern Front and launch a new full-scale offensive there. He believed that Germany must exploit any occasion to force the enemy to accept a conditional peace.[31]

July to December, 1943

The occasion did not arise, and meanwhile during the summer and fall of 1943 Germany's military situation continued to deteriorate. Allied use of radar against German submarines gradually brought about the defeat of that weapon, especially in the Atlantic Theater. The Anglo-American air offensive against German cities began in July. In the attack on Hamburg on July 26, 1943, 55,000 civilians were killed. Early in July Allied troops landed in Sicily under cover of heavy naval and air support. The Italian Sixth Army was quickly overrun and the two combat-ready German divisions in Sicily could not repulse the invasion. Only with the arrival of two additional German divisions, rushed to their support, could the Axis defenders assume a delaying-action defense and so hold the island until the middle of August, but when the Americans took Messina on August 17 the German and Italian troops were evacuated to the mainland.

The Mussolini government, already deeply shaken by the losses in Africa, fell on July 25, and Marshal Badoglio formed a government whose first aim was to make peace. To prevent Italy's defection, Hitler rushed eight divisions commanded by Field Marshal Rommel into Northern Italy, but despite this the Italian government arranged a secret armistice with the Allied commanders in September, and the Italian fleet fled to Malta to capitulate. The American landing at Salerno followed, and by the first of October the Americans had reached Naples. Kesselring, the commander of German defense forces in Southern Italy,[32] was operating in at least partly hostile territory with inadequate fuel supply, with communications hampered by the destruction of roads and bridges, and under conditions of enemy air superior-

[31] *Ibid.*, p. 485.

[32] At the time that Rommel commanded eight divisions in Northern Italy, German forces in Italy had two commanders, Rommel in the North and Kesselring in the South. Rommel, however, was soon transferred to prepare defenses in the West and Kesselring became commander in chief in Italy.

ity; nevertheless, he was able to dig in and hold his line through the fall.[33]

Toward the end of January, 1944, the Allies launched a landing south of Rome at Anzio. The Germans were able to delay the exploitation of the landing long enough to be able to seal off the bridgehead. It was not until June that the Allies were able to take Rome. Nevertheless, despite the successes of the defense in Italy and the consequent high cost to the Allies, the war there was defensive and the long-range prospects for the Germans were not encouraging. The best of Kesselring's troops and much of his air power were steadily drained away to the critical Eastern Front.

In the East Hitler had ordered a renewed offensive by Army Group Center in the Orel area early in July, 1943, but the German tanks had run into such heavy Russian defensive positions that the attack had to be called off. Soviet Marshal Koniev referred to this abortive offensive as "the swan song of the German Panzer Divisions." [34] The attack was a failure, and the failure undermined the already ebbing strength of the Eastern Front. In August the Soviets began an offensive which pushed the Wehrmacht back slowly and with heavy losses throughout the winter. At many points the Germans were faced with manpower odds of from eight to twelve Russians to every German. The German manpower pool was running low, there were never sufficient replacements. The Red Army was beginning to profit from American Lend-Lease aid. By February, 1944, the Soviets had retaken the rich Donetz Basin and most of the fertile land of the Ukraine. By early spring a disastrous breakthrough threatened.

In December, 1943, a representative of the German resistance movement approached Rommel and asked his view of the military situation. Rommel saw no chance of German victory; militarily the war was already lost.[35] He warned the representative, however, that Hitler lived in a world of illusion, that he would

[33] For a full account of the military situation at this juncture see, especially, Kesselring, *Soldat bis zum Letzten Tag,* pp. 249 ff.

[34] Kreipe *et al., op. cit.,* p. 180.

[35] Brigadier Desmond Young, *Rommel: The Desert Fox* (New York: Harper, 1951), p. 197.

not consider making peace. Rommel appraised the situation as so grave that he agreed to co-operate with the resistance movement should he be unable to persuade Hitler to end the war.[36]

The months of 1943 had brought eventual German defeat within sight for those in a position to know and evaluate the military events. In the air war the new long-range American fighter had given the Allies superiority in the skies over Germany and enabled them to undertake around-the-clock strategic bombings of German cities. On the sea and under it the U-boat had been virtually routed and the Mediterranean had been reopened to Allied shipping. Wilmot reports that the German Wehrmacht had lost more than a million men, fallen or taken prisoner, during 1943, that by the end of 1943 the fatal casualties of the German Army had exceeded the German total of the entire First World War.[37] By the end of 1943, to those Germans who knew the facts, defeat was clearly in sight but peace was not.

Spring, 1944

On the Eastern Front the Red Army began a renewed offensive on all segments of the front, in the North, the South, and the Center. Hitler's uncompromising order permitting no withdrawal for strategic or even tactical purposes and no preparation of secondary defenses resulted in tragic losses and in the further undermining of Wehrmacht strength. In January and February a small-scale Stalingrad took place at Cherkassy: 54,000 men were encircled in a pocket. By the time the Führer permitted them to attempt to break out only 35,000 could be rescued.[38] All along the line Hitler ignored the primary rule of strategy in sacrificing strength for land. By spring the Seventeenth Army in the Crimea was virtually cut off. Kleist and Manstein were removed from command. By the middle of April the entire Crimea had been lost and Soviet strength was increasing with the help of Anglo-American aid. The Red Army was advancing into Rumania, the government in Bulgaria was overthrown, morale in

[36] *Ibid.*

[37] *Struggle for Europe,* p. 168.

[38] Hans Speidel, *Invasion 1944: ein Beitrag zu Rommels und des Reiches Schicksal* (Tübingen: Rainer Wunderlich Verlag, 1949), p. 23.

Hungary and Finland was tottering. Politically Germany stood virtually alone. A new Soviet offensive was anticipated in the East and a full-scale Anglo-American invasion was anticipated in the West.

Hitler welcomed the Allied invasion, or at least officially he said that he did. On March 20, 1944, he addressed the commanders of the Wehrmacht in the West and predicted that the Allied landing would last no more than a few hours, that the Anglo-American troops would be repulsed with heavy casualties, and that morale in both England and America would be dealt a crushing blow. His long-range predictions were still more optimistic. He said that the invasion failure would result in the defeat of Roosevelt in the November election and that "with luck" Roosevelt would end his days in jail somewhere. He counted on discouragement and war weariness to help him persuade the American and English people to make peace.[39]

The Wehrmacht generals were not so optimistic and the anti-Nazi resistance leaders were not so naïve, although they too hoped for peace. Hans Bernd Gisevius reports that General Beck believed that by March, 1944, German defeat was clearly imminent and that many of the leading generals were then ready to break with the Hitler government in order to prevent further senseless loss of lives. However, they were not ready to surrender unconditionally and on that account they withheld their support from any attempt to overthrow the regime. Beck hoped that at this juncture the Allies might be willing to relax their demand for unconditional surrender or at least modify it by a generous interpretation. He wanted to discover whether the Allies truly desired a constructive solution in Germany or whether they had become prisoners of their own policy,[40] and to this end he sent Gisevius as an agent to Switzerland to meet with Allen Dulles, the American intelligence representative there. Dulles, interested and sympathetic, received no encouragement from his government.[41]

At Supreme Wehrmacht headquarters in the West, where the

[39] *Rommel Papers*, pp. 465-66.

[40] Hans Bernd Gisevius, *To the Bitter End* (London: Jonathan Cape, 1948), p. 475.

[41] *Ibid.*, pp. 475-78, and Dulles, *Germany's Underground*, p. 141.

generals prepared to meet the inevitable Allied attack, pessimism prevailed. Among the high-ranking officers close to Rommel there was apparent unanimity. Speidel, Rommel's chief of staff, states that all thoughts were turned to saving the Reich by ending the war, if possible, by first overthrowing Hitler. He writes that Rommel's views were clear: he adhered to the Moltke principle of the ethical duty of a soldier, the duty of humanity over obedience, the duty to prevent the destruction of his own people.[42] Rommel held that his first duty was obedience to God, his first responsibility was for the fate of his nation. By March, 1944, Rommel, Speidel and Blumentritt, the Chief of Operations, were in agreement: the war must be ended. They conferred with Field Marshal von Rundstedt to sound out his views and found them in accord with their own, and so they began to plan for an armistice.[43]

This pessimism was grounded on the facts of the military situation. The Anglo-American air forces had controlled the air space over France since early spring, 1944. By the time of the invasion the major French railroad lines had been so thoroughly bombed that they were useless to the Germans as supply lines. The roads were also under constant attack and many bridges had been destroyed so that truck supply lines were hard pressed and irregular.[44] During the landings on June 6 the Allies were able to support their ground forces with about 25,000 planes, while the defending German Luftwaffe in the West had only about 500, of which only 90 bombers and 70 fighters were in flying condition when the attack occurred.[45]

On the ground in the West the Germans had fifty-nine divisions of which eight were in Holland and Belgium and more than half were merely training divisions. Of the field divisions only ten were armored. In the invasion area along the Normandy coast were only six divisions, three of these in the Cherbourg peninsula, two along the 40-mile stretch between Cherbourg and Caen, and one between Caen and the Seine. General Blumen-

[42] Speidel, *op. cit.*, p. 86.
[43] Liddell Hart, *The Other Side of the Hill*, pp. 269-70.
[44] Speidel, *op. cit.*, p. 56.
[45] *Ibid.*

tritt states that the Wehrmacht did not anticipate an invasion on the western side of the Cherbourg peninsula and so that area was only lightly defended.[46]

Throughout the spring Rundstedt and Rommel tried to bolster the coast defenses but they were hampered by shortages of supply, of manpower reserves, and by the continual interference of Hitler. No troops could be moved without Hitler's express permission. He permitted the commanders in the field no operational freedom, he ordered the ground to be held inch by inch.[47] The German command situation in the West was somewhat unorthodox. Rundstedt was the Commander in Chief West, but Rommel exercised a more or less independent command of the coastal defenses from Denmark to the Pyrenees. Neither general had independent powers of command, since all orders had to be confirmed by the OKW and Hitler. SS troops in the West were under the direct command of Himmler in all matters regarding security and the Organization Todt was virtually autonomous.[48]

Against this rather flimsy and hampered defense the Allies had approximately forty to forty-five British divisions and twenty to twenty-five American divisions, including motorized, tank, and airborne troops. Their equipment was excellent and abundant. Their air cover and naval superiority gave them a virtual pipeline across the Channel and in turn prevented the Germans from carrying out reconnaissance flights over England. In addition, the Allies could profit from the sabotage and intelligence activities of the French underground.[49]

Small wonder that by early June the German generals in the West had prepared their armistice plans.[50] Liddell Hart reports that he had asked Rundstedt whether at any stage after the landing he had been hopeful of repulsing it, and that he had replied:

> Not after the first few days. The Allied Air Forces paralysed all movement by day, and made it difficult even at night. They had smashed the bridges over the Loire as well as over the Seine, shutting

[46] Liddell Hart, *op. cit.*, pp. 247-48.
[47] Speidel, *op. cit.*, p. 42.
[48] *Ibid.*, pp. 43-44.
[49] *Ibid.*, pp. 35-37.
[50] *Ibid.*, p. 91.

off the whole area. These factors greatly delayed the concentration of reserves there—they took three or four times longer to reach the front than we had reckoned.[51]

Rommel had only three Panzer divisions for his entire front, a number greatly inferior to those of the invading forces. Rundstedt called this "a very light punch with which to counter a powerful invasion." [52]

Rommel's estimate of the military situation was deeply pessimistic. On June 11 he confided to Admiral Ruge that he found the outlook hopeless. Ruge gave his opinion that Hitler ought to resign or commit suicide so that peace negotiations could begin. Rommel answered:

> I know that man. He will neither resign nor kill himself. He will fight, without the least regard for the German people, until there isn't a house left standing in Germany.[53]

On June 12 Rommel sent a brutally frank "Military Estimate of the Situation" to OKW headquarters. He said that enemy strength was increasing faster than he could bring up reserves, that the enemy had complete control of the battle area and up to sixty miles behind the front, that enemy airpower prevented virtually all transport and even troop movements by day while the enemy could move freely. The Anglo-American forces were well supplied with numerous new weapons, while the German supplies were constantly being destroyed in transport or were simply not available. "Our position is becoming increasingly difficult. I request that the Führer be informed of this." [54]

By the second week, when it became clear that the order to defend the beaches and throw the enemy back into the sea could not be carried out, Rundstedt and Rommel determined to withdraw their troops to a line behind the Orne or along the Seine, which could be more easily supplied and would allow for defense in depth. They asked Hitler to come to France for an urgent conference and on June 17 Hitler and Jodl met with the two

[51] *Op. cit.*, p. 253.
[52] *Ibid.*, p. 249.
[53] Young, *op. cit.*, p. 181.
[54] *Ibid.*

West Front field marshals at Margival near Soissons. The front commanders warned that the situation was hopeless, that despite almost superhuman efforts of both officers and men, despite fighting to the last breath, the coastal divisions had not been able to hold back the waves of enemy troops supported by overwhelming air and sea superiority and lavishly supplied with first-class equipment. Rommel warned that an Allied beachhead was an established fact, that there was imminent danger of a breakthrough at Avranches, followed by a mobile attack against Paris which would eventually threaten the German homeland. He warned against the further senseless waste of men and matériel in attempting to hold the present line.[55] Rundstedt supported Rommel's view. Hitler was adamant. The line must be held. The field marshals tentatively mentioned the possibility of contacting the Allied commanders to discuss the possibility of an armistice. Hitler was furious. The conference ended abruptly in a most unfriendly atmosphere.[56]

Shortly after that the situation grew still more critical. When Keitel telephoned Rundstedt for a report on the situation and asked the Field Marshal what ought to be done, Rundstedt replied, "End the war! What else can you do?"[57] On June 26 Cherbourg fell to the Americans and a breakthrough threatened. On June 28 both Rundstedt and Rommel received sharp orders to appear at Berchtesgaden headquarters. In an interview with Hitler on June 29 both urged him to end the war. Hitler expressed firm confidence in the new miracle weapon (presumably the V-1 or V-2), which was under design, and refused to hear of surrender proposals. Rommel then took up the matter with OKW Chief Keitel, warning him that Hitler's notion of total victory was absurd, that total defeat was the more likely prospect. He implored Keitel to help end the war in the West so that the Eastern Front could be held and so that Germany could be saved from the chaos of total air destruction. Keitel admitted, "Even I know that there is no more to be done," but he resigned

[55] Accounts of this meeting are given in *The Other Side of the Hill*, pp. 254 and 60-61; Young, *op. cit.*, pp. 181-83; Speidel, *op. cit.*, pp. 114-18.

[56] Young, *op. cit.*, pp. 182-83, and Speidel, *op. cit.*, pp. 128 ff.

[57] Liddell Hart, *op. cit.*, p. 255.

himself to Hitler's stubbornness.[58] Hitler removed Rundstedt as commander in chief and appointed Field Marshal von Kluge in his place.

By the beginning of July a new British offensive threatened Caen. The German Army on the Western Front had lost more than 100,000 officers and men during the first month of fighting and had received only 8,395 replacements.[59] Caen fell on July 9. On the same day Rommel estimated that the Invasion Front could be held a maximum of two to three weeks. On July 13, 14, and 15 Rommel made a tour of the front, conferring with commanders of all ranks including SS Generals Dietrich and Hauser. All the front officers to whom he spoke were in agreement on the hopelessness of the situation and would, he felt, offer no opposition to armistice negotiations.[60]

On July 15 Rommel made a last attempt to convince Hitler of the gravity of the situation. He prepared a report for the Führer's headquarters detailing the crisis: the situation was worsening from day to day, the Wehrmacht was losing 2,500 to 3,000 men each day and there were few replacements, the enemy had overwhelming material superiority, 225 German tanks had been lost and only 17 had been replaced, supply deliveries were hampered by tactical air attacks. Although the troops were fighting heroically, a breakthrough in the immediate future was inevitable. He therefore begged Hitler to estimate the political consequences of the military situation.[61] Two days later, before he had a chance to send the report, he was seriously injured and removed from the front.

On July 21 Field Marshal von Kluge forwarded the Rommel report together with his comment that the two weeks he had spent on the Western Front had convinced him that Rommel's estimate of the situation was unfortunately right. He said that, although he had come to the front with the intention of making

[58] Speidel, *op. cit.*, pp. 128-29.

[59] Young, *op. cit.*, p. 183. For details of campaign see Friedrich Hayn, *Die Invasion: von Cotentin bis Falaise* (Heidelberg: Scharnhorst Buchkameradschaft der Soldaten, 1954), especially pp. 53-89.

[60] Speidel, *op. cit.*, pp. 133-36.

[61] Young, *op. cit.*, pp. 187-88; *Rommel Papers*, pp. 486-87.

a stand at any price, he now realized that the overstrained front was bound to collapse.[62]

At the end of July the breakthrough came at Avranches. The Allies had achieved an open plain and were in a position to push toward Paris. Kluge, removed from command, took his own life, leaving a letter in which he warned Hitler:

> Make up your mind to end the war. The German people have borne such untold suffering that it is time to put an end to this frightfulness. There must be ways to attain this end, and above all, to prevent the Reich from falling under the Bolshevist heel.[63]

There is little question that the Western Front generals wanted to end the war, if possible by persuading the Chief of State to "take the political consequences," that is, to resign or commit suicide, since it was obvious to everyone that the Allies would not negotiate with him or with any leading Nazi. If this was not possible—and it became clear that it was not—then Hitler would have to be ignored or removed. Either the front generals would have to open direct negotiations with the Allied field commanders for local surrender of their troops or a Putsch would have to overthrow the Hitler government in order to make a general settlement possible. To prepare for either eventuality, General Speidel and Infantry General Karl Heinrich von Stülpnagel prepared a draft armistice agreement which they hoped to arrange with Eisenhower and Montgomery. The plan provided for the German evacuation of the Western Theater and withdrawal behind the Westwall in return for the immediate termination of the Allied bombing of German cities. In the East the front was to be shortened and held. Hitler and his top aides would be arrested and tried by a German court; the Nazi party would be removed from power and abolished; the German people would be informed of the true political and military situation. Later a final peace settlement could be arranged.[64]

Obviously the arrangement of such an armistice would have required a change of Allied policy. What was envisioned by the

[62] *Rommel Papers*, p. 189.
[63] Liddell Hart, *The Other Side of the Hill*, p. 260n.
[64] Speidel, *op. cit.*, pp. 91-93.

Western Front generals was a traditional armistice agreement and ultimately a negotiated peace, not Unconditional Surrender. Speidel and other military men have written of the tremendous psychological conflict involved in the decision of a general officer to commit an act that under normal conditions would be treason, the decision to disobey and betray his chief of state, his commander in chief, to surrender in the face of clear orders to fight on. In the German Army in 1944 the conflict was not simply between the obvious danger of the destruction of the German nation and the useless waste of lives and the alternative of disobedience in order to preserve lives and the state. The decision was gravely complicated by the Allied insistence on Unconditional Surrender. Speidel states that this formula posed a psychological barrier which the civil courage of the soldier found it difficult to overcome.[65] The soldiers of the resistance movement and many of the nonpolitical, purely professional soldiers hoped desperately that a sense of enlightened self-interest would ultimately persuade the Anglo-American statesmen to amend their policy, but in this they were mistaken.

The anti-Nazi leaders in Berlin had tried since the early days of the war to win some assurance from the Western Allies that a successful overthrow of the Nazi government would meet with a favorable response from London and Washington. Since the Casablanca announcement the agents of the group had again and again sought some encouragement to believe that the formula of Unconditional Surrender would be softened in the event of an anti-Nazi coup d'état, but each such attempt had ended in failure. In the next chapter we shall examine in detail the effect of this failure on the fate of the German resistance movement: key soldiers, especially, refused to co-operate in a plan to overthrow Hitler unless the plan would spare Germany the destruction they believed to be inherent in Unconditional Surrender.

On June 3, 1944, just six weeks before the actual assassination attempt of July 20, some of the leading members of the anti-Nazi conspiracy had met in Potsdam to receive the report of their agent, Adam von Trott zu Solz, on his final attempt to win some

[65] *Ibid.*, p. 31.

concession or commitment from the English and Americans regarding a peace settlement. Trott reported that he had received only one answer—Unconditional Surrender. On hearing this final rebuff, Field Marshal von Witzleben, one of the chief conspirators, jumped to his feet shaking with excitement. "Now," he said, "no honorable man can lead the German people into such a situation." The conspiracy could very well have disintegrated entirely over this point had not General Beck remained firm: for moral reasons the crimes of the Nazi government must be stopped, regardless of the consequences.[66] Count Claus von Stauffenberg, the officer slated to carry out the assassination, was uncompromising, and so the fateful *Operation Walküre* was launched and ran its tragic course.

Had the plan succeeded, had Hitler actually been assassinated, and had the leaders of the plot succeeded in establishing effective control in Berlin, there is little question that they would have taken steps to end the war immediately. On the Western Front Field Marshal von Kluge was prepared, in the event of a successful coup, to order immediate cessation of V-1 attacks on England and to establish contact with the Allied field commanders to arrange an armistice.[67] The new Cabinet would certainly have continued to seek a mitigation of the Unconditional Surrender policy, and it is conceivable that Allied refusal to compromise on the question might have resulted in the continuation of hostilities as long as possible even by a resistance government in order to prevent the overrunning of Central Europe by Soviet troops.

Such questions are highly speculative. The plot did not succeed. Certainly a major factor in the failure was the refusal to participate in the plan by certain key military figures. Reportedly a major reason for the refusal of these generals to act was the Allied insistence on unconditional surrender. This insistence had caused even Witzleben to throw up his hands in dismay. It was an insurmountable barrier of conscience for many field and staff commanders.

[66] The scene is described in a letter by Baron Hermann von Lünick to Pater Max Pribilla, dated Jan. 19, 1950. Lünick attended the meeting.

[67] Liddell Hart, *The Other Side of the Hill*, p. 272.

The majority of German military leaders on all fronts were convinced after the breakthrough at Avranches that the war was lost, that continued resistance was senseless, that further destruction and sacrifice of lives was irresponsible, and yet they were trapped in a war that was senseless. From sheer lack of alternative they continued to fight. The war did not end in July, 1944, nor did it become less costly in the battle-filled months that stretched on until May, 1945.

The Battle in the East: Summer, 1944

In June, 1944, on the third anniversary of the launching of *Operation Barbarossa,* the German invasion of the U.S.S.R., the Red Army began its full-scale offensive. The attack came between Bobruisk and Vitebsk against the bow of Army Group Center on the east side of the Dnieper. Within two weeks it had rolled the Germans back along Napoleon's invasion route as far as Minsk, destroying twenty-eight German divisions with the loss of 350,000 men, a greater loss than at Stalingrad. The Red Army was then in a position to push ahead into East Prussia and along the Vistula to cut off the German forces in the Baltic, and also to penetrate south into the Balkans to begin rolling up the German forces there and to reap the political benefits military conquest would bring in its wake. By late July the Soviets were advancing along a 600-mile front at the rate of 440 miles in fifty-two days.

This fresh disaster was the result of a miscalculation and of Hitler's now tragically familiar "no retreat!" order. During the winter, 1943-44, Army Group Center had repelled a succession of Soviet attacks, but the successes had been bought at the price of sacrificing irreplaceable reserves and of weakening certain sectors of the front by deploying troops to the sectors under attack.

In the middle of June Field Marshal Busch, commander of Army Group Center, conferred with Zeitzler, chief of the Army General Staff, on possible Soviet moves. They anticipated that the main enemy attack would come in the Ukraine, that only a secondary attack would be aimed against Army Group Center.[68] One Panzer army was, therefore, transferred to the Ukraine. This left Busch with only thirty-eight divisions and virtually no reserves to cover a bow-shaped front about 700 miles long. Army Group Center had only forty pilots while the enemy had marshaled 4,500 planes against that sector.[69]

The Soviet attack was aimed at five sectors of the front. Its goal was to force five wedges into the German front and to split the defenders into small isolated groups which could be encircled and destroyed or captured, the German's own "Keil und Kessel"—wedge and encircle—tactic. On the first day the Red Army succeeded in breaking through at Vitebsk. The German Third Panzer Army was split in two and Vitebsk cut off. In consequence, a whole German corps was trapped and taken prisoner. The Ninth Army, also encircled, fought its way out of the envelopment, but not without severe losses. The Soviet breakthrough on the northern sector of the front threatened to cut off Army Group North. By July the Germans had suffered such losses and had so few reserves with which to replace them that they were throwing only regiments and battalions against whole Soviet armies.[70] In mid-July the German Army in the Ukraine suffered the worst defeat yet with a loss of almost thirty divisions. The Red Army pushed forward almost 250 miles closer to the German border.[71] Certainly in the East, as in the West, the end was in sight.

Hitler raged. Himmler accused the front commanders of defeatism and sabotage.[72] Zeitzler was removed as chief of the General Staff and replaced by Guderian. Guderian suggested an immediate shortening of the front. Characteristically Hitler refused to permit this, but a Soviet breakthrough in the area of the Pripet Marshes compelled the shortening. To fill the gap on

[68] "Zum Zusammenbruch der Heeresgruppe Mitte im Sommer, 1944," *Vierteljahrshefte für Zeitgeschichte,* Vol. III, 1955, No. 3, p. 321.

[69] *Ibid.,* pp. 320, 322.

[70] Kurt Assmann, *Deutsche Schicksalsjahre: Historische Bilder aus dem Zweiten Weltkrieg und Seiner Vorgeschichte* (Wiesbaden: Brockhaus, 1951), p. 448; see also pp. 445 ff.

[71] *Ibid.,* p. 449.

[72] "Zusammenbruch," pp. 317-18.

this front troops were deployed from Rumania, and this caused the almost immediate collapse of the Rumanian Front. Rumania switched sides, and the Red Army was in a position to pour into Central Europe along the southern route.[73]

By the end of July, 1944, there was little doubt that the Wehrmacht had been defeated in the field on both Eastern and Western Fronts. On both fronts the enemy had achieved strategic breakthroughs. The situation in the East approached collapse. Generals on both fronts talked about the inevitability of defeat, of the necessity to make peace. Everywhere the front was receding in the direction of the German borders; it had already reached the border in East Prussia. Only desperation, the stubbornness of Hitler, and the absence of an alternative kept the German Army fighting. The war was over, and yet its cost and bloodshed continued for nine more months.

!

The Cost of Desperation: The Ardennes Offensive

The war was irretrievably lost. The only possible goal of a German offensive in the West was not victory but a chance for an acceptable peace settlement. In retrospect the thought of a German offensive in the winter of 1944-45 seems fantastic and impossible. The German Army in the West had been retreating steadily since the American breakthrough at Avranches in July. In mid-August General Patch had led an American landing in Southern France; on August 25 Paris had fallen; in September the British took Brussels and the Americans reached the German frontier; in October and November the Allies took Aachen and began rolling up German forces in Alsace and Lorraine; on December 3 American troops penetrated the Westwall, the famous Siegfried Line. On December 16 the Germans began their counteroffensive with a strength and vigor which amazed everyone and terrified some, but which represented the last-ditch energy of desperation, doomed to fail but not without tragic cost to themselves and to the Allies.

The offensive had been planned at a secret meeting of the front commanders with Colonel General Jodl on November 3, 1944. Jodl had announced the plan as an "unalterable decision"

[73] See Liddell Hart, *The Other Side of the Hill*, pp. 67-70.

of the Führer.[74] The attack was to be launched from behind the Westwall against the thin and extensive line of enemy forces in the Ardennes. The Allies had suffered heavy losses through their fall offensive, the December weather would offer favorable cover for German ground moves by keeping the Allied air forces grounded, and the element of surprise would favor the German strike. By marshaling all available strength the Germans would be able to commit twenty-eight to thirty divisions to the offensive, including the Sixth SS Panzer Army, the Fifth Panzer Army, and the Seventh Army. Their aim would be to seize the bridgeheads on the Meuse and push toward Antwerp, hoping to cut major Allied forces from their source of supply, to capture supply depots, and to isolate and defeat thirty Allied divisions.[75]

The opening phase of the attack, December 16 to 19, was more successful than even the German commanders had hoped, but the Allies recovered quickly from the initial surprise and began to bring up reserves by the third and fourth day. By the 20th the Allies were threatening the flank of the Seventh Army and by the 24th the German advance had been halted. Unexpected Allied resistance at Bastogne forced the Germans to weaken their attack on the Meuse by redeploying troops. By the 25th the Allies had begun a counteroffensive. The weather had cleared and once again Allied airpower could offer tactical support. Rundstedt proposed a swift withdrawal to a shortened line but again Hitler refused, until on January 13 a new Soviet offensive on the Eastern Front compelled a diversion of troops from the West. On January 25 the German Front was withdrawn: the Ardennes phase was completed. The war, now on German territory, was entering its final weeks.

The Views of German Generals

Let us examine some of the available comments of German generals on the effect of Unconditional Surrender on the duration of the war. Shortly after the war ended Liddell Hart interviewed many of the leading German military figures and found them in agreement on the futility of having pursued the war beyond

[74] Kreipe *et al.*, *op. cit.*, p. 232.
[75] *Ibid.*, pp. 233-34.

summer, 1944, and certainly beyond the failure of the Ardennes offensive:

> They were tied to their posts by Hitler's policy, and Himmler's police, but they were praying for release. Throughout the last nine months of the war they spent much of their time discussing ways and means of getting in touch with the Allies to arrange a surrender.
>
> All to whom I talked dwelt on the effect of the Allies "unconditional surrender" policy in prolonging the war. They told me that but for this they and their troops—the factor that was more important—would have been ready to surrender sooner, separately or collectively. "Black-listening" to the Allies' radio service was widespread. But the Allied propaganda never said anything positive about the peace conditions in the way of encouraging them to give up the struggle. Its silence on the subject was so marked that it tended to confirm what Nazi propaganda told them of the dire fate in store for them if they surrendered.[76]

Statements by some of the German field marshals tend to support this generalization.

Field Marshal Albert Kesselring said that at the time the Casablanca Formula was announced he was too busy with activities on his front to be able to discuss the pronouncement with his colleagues, and so he cannot speak of a general reaction but, as he recalls it, his own immediate judgment was that the demand would prolong the war. When asked whether, in retrospect, he now believes that this was the effect of the policy, he answered, "Absolutely." He expressed the view that after the defeats at Stalingrad and in North Africa a German victory was no longer possible; after the stabilization of the Invasion Front in Normandy defeat was inevitable. A Western policy based on the desire to arrange a reasonable peace, a policy in which the German people could have confidence, could have brought about an earlier end to the war.

Kesselring's view on what would have constituted a reasonable settlement included the end of the Nazi government, restoration of prewar boundaries, and German payment of reparations to restore war damages and to help revive the European economy.

[76] *Op. cit.*, p. 304.

Continuation of the war to the point of total defeat caused needless loss of life and a dangerous degree of material destruction and social disorganization and has had disastrous moral as well as political and economic effects.[77]

Field Marshal Fritz Erich von Manstein said that the Allied demand "naturally lengthened the war. This was the surest means to weld the Germans to the Hitler regime." In his view it would have been conceivable for the military leaders to end the war earlier by means of a coup d'état against Hitler *only* if there had been a previous assurance of acceptable conditions. Although such an agreement between German generals and the Allied governments would have been complicated by the memory of the promise of the Fourteen Points and the actuality of the Versailles Treaty, he thought that a reasonable settlement could have been constructed on the basis of a mutual desire to establish a stable economic, political and social order in Europe founded on justice and reason. Manstein held that a demand for unconditional surrender works as propaganda for both sides in a war: it sharpens hatred against the enemy who is shown as unworthy of negotiation, but it also stiffens the opposition of the enemy.[78]

The reaction of Field Marshal Erwin Rommel to the Unconditional Surrender formula is not clear, but his view that the war was hopeless dates back to spring, 1943. His aides and comrades on the Western Front knew of his belief that the war must be ended, with Hitler's co-operation or without it. His major fear was that the prolongation of the war would bring the Red Army closer and closer to the heart of Europe, that eventually Communism might sweep through Europe and destroy all the Western powers. Shortly before his death, when he was recovering from his wound at home in July, 1944, he told his son Manfred that

> our enemy in the East is so terrible that every other consideration has to give way before it. If he succeeds in overrunning Europe, even only temporarily, it will be the end of everything which has made life appear worth living.[79]

[77] Interview with the author at Bad Wiessee, July, 1958.
[78] Letter to the author dated June 2, 1953.
[79] *Rommel Papers,* p. 502. See also Young, *op. cit.,* p. 200.

He once told Admiral Ruge that it would be better for Germany to end the war as a British dominion rather than "see Germany ruined by going on with this hopeless war." [80]

It is clear that Field Marshal Erwin von Witzleben more than shared Rommel's view. He was at the very center of the anti-Nazi conspiracy which planned the assassination attempt of July 20, 1944, and he paid for his convictions with his life in August, 1944—strangled with piano wire suspended from meat-hooks.[81] His will to overthrow the Nazi regime and to seek an end to the war was unequivocal, and yet like many of the conspirators he continually urged that an agreement be sought with the Western Allies to gain mitigation of the insistence on Unconditional Surrender. Again and again emissaries of the resistance movement contacted Allied representatives, and again and again they met with an adamant "No!" The last no, in June, 1944, had proved almost too much for Witzleben. He reacted violently and would have opposed any further action had he not been persuaded by Beck that what was at stake was not German survival but German honor. Not all the military leaders were able to make this decision.

General Günther Blumentritt belongs to the group of generals who believed from the outset that a German war against both East and West would be hopeless. He felt that there was a decisive difference in the attitude of the German generals in the Second World War from that of 1914: in 1939 there had been no enthusiasm for the war, the generals were hesitant and pessimistic from the beginning, and they would have been happy to seek peace in 1939 or 1940 or 1941 if the question of war or peace had been theirs to decide. In a dictatorship, however, only the dictator formulates policy, and the military leaders are bound by their oath and by the obedience expected of soldiers to carry out orders, not to defy official policy.

From 1943 on the situation was further complicated by the fact that the Anglo-American governments had promised the Soviets

[80] Young, *op. cit.*, p. 181.

[81] The trials and executions are described in many works including Constantine FitzGibbon, *20 July* (New York: Norton, 1956), pp. 214-16. The author viewed the film of the trial at a private showing in Munich in 1948.

not to make a separate peace with Germany. This implied that peace would have to be made simultaneously in the East and the West, a fact which might mean that the entire German Army on the Eastern Front, approximately eight million men, might fall into Soviet hands as prisoners of war. The policies formulated by the Big Three conferences gradually made clear that the Allied war aim was "Germania delenda est." Naturally this sharpened German resistance.[82]

The German generals wanted peace, but neither at the expense of the destruction of their country nor at the price of seeing Europe overrun by Communism. Blumentritt feared that during the war the Western Allies had a false appraisal of Bolshevism. The Germans had lived closer to the Soviet Union, they had been aware of the menace of world communism since 1917. Allied policy forced them to continue the war long after they knew it to be hopeless, in the hope that perhaps the Western powers would realize before it was too late the dangers to Europe inherent in their policy.[83]

General Heinz Guderian was even more outspoken:

> The demand for "unconditional surrender" certainly contributed to the destruction of every hope in Germany for a reasonable peace. This was true not only for the Wehrmacht and for the Generals, but also for the whole people.[84]

After the Casablanca Conference, he states, the Germans knew that no generosity was to be expected from the Allies. Guderian maintains that the softness of Allied—especially of the United States—policy to the U.S.S.R. during the war was disastrous. He describes Roosevelt, the father of Unconditional Surrender, as "the gravedigger not only of Germany but also of Europe" and asserts that the entire civilized world, not just Germany, has had to pay for Roosevelt's naïve wartime policy. He continues:

> Roosevelt underestimated Russia, Bolshevism, and Stalin. The Americans came to Germany in the belief that Russia was governed by only

[82] Letter to the author dated Marburg, March 1, 1950.
[83] Letter of April 18, 1950.
[84] Letter by General Guderian to the author dated Dietramzell, March 28, 1950.

"another form of democracy" than in the U.S.A. They believed in an understanding with Stalin and Russia. They found themselves in fundamental error. In Russia the government is no democracy but a total dictatorship. Not to have realized this was the greatest mistake of Roosevelt. With the destruction of Germany, Europe was deprived of the dam against Bolshevism. . . . The destruction of Germany certainly removed a competitor but it created the powerful Soviet bloc with which the United States must deal. The question of whether this policy was correct seems to me not difficult to answer.[85]

In his book General Guderian uses even stronger language. He devotes several pages to a discussion of Unconditional Surrender. He writes:

The effect of this brutal formula on the German nation and, above all, on the Army was great. The soldiers, at least, were convinced from now on that our enemies had decided on the utter destruction of Germany, that they were no longer fighting—as Allied propaganda at that time alleged—against Hitler and so-called Nazism, but against their efficient, and therefore dangerous, rivals for the trade of the world.[86]

He holds that drastic peace measures, such as the large-scale transfer of population from East Prussia which he terms "atrocious" and "unjust," were inherent or at least implied in the demand for unconditional surrender.[87] It was, therefore, not amazing that he drew the conclusion that the war had to be pursued to its fatal conclusion, that no compromise could be considered.

The former chief of the General Staff, General Franz Halder, was separated from his post in 1942 and after that time he lived in seclusion in Bavaria. Although he kept in constant contact with the anti-Nazi resistance group through couriers, his observation of the effect of the Unconditional Surrender policy was limited by his seclusion. However, he wrote that in the contacts he had in Southern Bavaria he frequently encountered the argument that it was senseless to plan a coup d'état against Hitler and to try to sue for peace in the light of the demand for unconditional

[85] *Ibid.*

[86] General Heinz Guderian, *Panzer Leader* (New York: Dutton, 1952), p. 284; see also pp. 285-87.

[87] *Ibid.*

surrender: ". . . the same frightful fate awaited us with or without Hitler. . . . The only thing to do was hold out until the end." He recalls that Goebbels and the Nazi press made great use of the slogan. Unconditional Surrender gave them "a powerful propaganda weapon in their demand to hold out." [88]

General Alfred Jodl left behind some notes on the anti-Hitler plot of July 20, 1944, in which he refers to Unconditional Surrender. He states that he, too, had been convinced, long before July, 1944, that the war was already lost, but that he had seen no way out: "Had not our Opponents called for the destruction of Germany and not that of the Nazi regime? Could one change this fate by the elimination of Hitler?" Jodl thought not. Despite the inevitable loss of men and material which resulted from pursuing the war until May, 1945, he drew the conclusion that "the road to the bitter end" was the better choice.[89]

Admiral Erich Raeder expressed an evaluation almost identical with that of General Jodl. Although he states that he believes fully that the aims of the Beck-Goerdeler group had been to replace a bad German government, he doubts that there had ever been a reasonable prospect for success on the latter count because of the Allied insistence on unconditional surrender.[90]

General Hasso von Manteuffel has given a great deal of attention to the question of the significance of the Unconditional Surrender policy. In the postwar years he has met regularly with a group of former comrades to discuss the mistakes of the war, both Allied and German, and there is no question that he and his group consider Unconditional Surrender as one of the mistakes, a boomerang which resulted in sacrifices of lives during the final months of the war which "*were entirely unnecessary because* Germany had conclusively lost the war with the breakthrough at Avranches in July, 1944: and every single human life is too expensive!" He continues:

> The proclamation was so frightful—in the original sense of that word—because unconditional surrender judged an entire people! So

[88] Letter to the author dated Königstein, March 22, 1950.

[89] From notes left behind by General Jodl in Nürnberg, 1946, and supplied and guaranteed authentic by his widow, Luise Jodl.

[90] Erich Raeder, *My Life* (Annapolis: U.S. Naval Institute, 1960), p. 380.

we realized that the result of this foolish demand was that we must fight to the bitter end with a courage of desperation. . . . Without the spiritual morale of the Front . . . The demand certainly *lengthened the war.* . . . Without this our resistance fighters would have acted earlier . . . and probably would have been able to contact the "other side" which, it must be mentioned, never gave the slightest sign when or how one might get in touch with them.

He states that the Goebbels radio continually warned the Germans, both the civilians on the home front and the soldiers, of the fate that awaited them if they should let their efforts slacken, that in the event of defeat the entire nation would be punished, not just the soldiers but also the old people and the children would be exposed to unrestrained vengeance. This fear of punishment goaded workers as well as soldiers to the limits of endurance. During the closing years of the war men, women, and even children worked in unbelievably difficult circumstances, despite shortages of living quarters, lack of sleep, insufficient food, clothing, and consumers' goods, they continued to produce so that the front troops would be supplied.

The threat of inhuman punishment kindled renewed diligence in these people. . . . The demand for Unconditional Surrender welded workers and soldiers together in a way which amazed me.

He said that soldiers at the front often told him that they had only begun to want to fight after they learned of the demand for unconditional surrender. It is only in terms of this courage of desperation that he can account for the success of his troops in the Ardennes offensive in the sixth year of a war already clearly lost: his army was able to penetrate the American lines deeply and then withdraw back over the Rhine without being annihilated or imprisoned despite the overwhelming superiority of enemy forces. This, he concluded, was one of the costs of the policy of Unconditional Surrender.[91]

General Hans Speidel admits[92] that the original draft of his book, *Invasion 1944,* contained a somewhat sharper view of the policy of Unconditional Surrender than that which appears in

[91] Letter to the author dated March 12, 1950.
[92] Letter to the author dated Freudenstadt, March 13, 1950.

the published version in which he states that the dilemma of the German soldier, torn between his traditional role as unpolitical and his moral consciousness and civil courage, was complicated by the Allied demand for unconditional surrender, "a formula that posed a barrier that was especially difficult psychologically for soldiers to overcome." [93]

In his book he indicates clearly that he had believed the war hopeless by spring of 1944: "it was clear that Germany could no longer win." [94] He deplored Hitler's senseless orders to occupy space in Russia rather than defeat the Red Army and to stand fast rather than effect necessary withdrawals. Speidel was one of the generals on the Western Front who were instrumental in drawing up plans to surrender to the Western Allies in June, 1944. He was appointed by Rommel to the staff which was to have negotiated with the Allies to arrange an armistice.[95] His book leaves very little doubt that he believed the war should have been ended at the latest after the Avranches breakthrough, but ended by a conventional armistice and not by unconditional surrender.

General Walter Warlimont described the demand for unconditional surrender as a knife which sharpened Germany's will to resist. If the Germans did not understand the meaning of Unconditional Surrender they received an object lesson in the surrender of Italy in September, 1943; Warlimont said that the treatment of Italy, despite the Allied offer of cobelligerency status, was a shock to German officers, who then began to realize that Unconditional Surrender really meant Unconditional Surrender. In the final months of fighting the Nazi government used the fear of Unconditional Surrender to exhort the troops to new enthusiasm and courage, and so it served to increase the severity of German resistance. However, he is cautious about suggesting an alternative policy. A propaganda offensive which had offered a settlement in terms of a program like the Fourteen Points would have been met with skepticism by the German public and would not have shortened the war. He also points out that as long as

[93] Speidel, *op. cit.*, p. 31.
[94] *Ibid.*, pp. 20 ff; see also, pp. 69, 77-81, 88-93.
[95] *Ibid.*, pp. 91-93.

Hitler and the Nazi party remained in power no compromise would have been thinkable, a dictatorship cannot compromise and cannot admit defeat. The only feasible alternative would have lain in the Allied encouragement of a resistance movement, and in Allied concentration on separating the German people from Hitler.[96]

General Siegfried Westphal is another of the generals who considered a war against three great powers a hopeless cause: "The world was simply too big. A German victory against such tremendous odds . . . in manpower, raw materials and industrial capacity, was quite out of the question." [97] He, too, states that many soldiers had always opposed the war, that all through its course they desired peace:

> . . . and this did not make it easy for them to do their duty, yet as soldiers they had no choice *but* to do their duty. After the Casablanca Declaration, in which it was announced that only unconditional surrender on Germany's part would be acceptable to the Allied governments, even those who were fully informed concerning the true situation saw no alternative to fighting on until the bitter end.[98]

Only a few, he said, were willing to risk rebellion under such conditions.

General Hermann von Witzleben, cousin of the late Field Marshal, expressed the views of resistance generals: the war was always hopeless, Germany's geopolitical position does not permit her to fight on two fronts, a fact known to military analysts since 1914. Hitler's only possible hope lay in blitzkrieg, sudden, mobile war ended by an equally sudden armistice and peace, and until 1940, until the Battle of Britain, it seemed as though he might carry it off. The anti-Nazis, however, did not want to see a German victory because this would have meant the triumph of Hitler in Europe and would have consolidated the hold of the party on Germany. Their aim was to end the war as quickly as possible, preferably on the basis of compromise.

[96] These views were expressed in an interview with the author in Rottach-Egern, Bavaria, July 25, 1958.

[97] Kreipe *et al., op. cit.,* p. 269.

[98] *Ibid.*

After the first victories the people were intoxicated with success and hypnotized by Hitler's military genius; they would not have accepted any action by the generals which robbed them of their hoped-for victory. Therefore, the resistance movement had to wait until the proper psychological moment, until the people and younger officers had begun to learn the truth: that the hope of final victory was illusory. For this they had first to experience severe defeats in the field: El Alamein, Stalingrad, Avranches. The resistance leaders continued to hope that when the time came to act the Western powers would amend their Unconditional Surrender policy. That they did not, Witzleben maintains, certainly shook the morale of the group and perhaps weakened its hand.[99]

Two German admirals have expressed their views on Unconditional Surrender. Admiral Karl Doenitz states unequivocally that, even though he considered the German military situation hopeless in the summer of 1943, he did not confide his pessimism to Hitler or suggest that the government sue for peace. "My conviction that the attitude adopted by our opponents precluded the possibility of any peace by negotiation led me . . . to regard such a statement as useless."[100] By 1944, when many German generals subscribed to the idea that Germany should seek to make peace with the West so that all remaining German power could be concentrated against the Red Army, Doenitz criticized his colleagues as unrealistic and said that the essential political prerequisites to such a move were lacking. Doenitz concludes that the Casablanca Formula implied that "in the event of our submitting we should have no rights whatever, but would be wholly at the mercy of our enemies, and of what that meant, some idea can be gathered from Stalin's demand at the Teheran Conference, for four million Germans to serve as forced labor in the U.S.S.R."[101] It seems clear, then, that Doenitz, too, regarded the Allied demand for unconditional surrender as an impregnable barrier to peace at a date earlier than May, 1945.

[99] In an interview with the author in Munich, June 25, 1958.

[100] Karl Doenitz, *Memoirs: Ten Years and Twenty Days* (trans. R. H. Stevens) (Cleveland: World Publishers, 1960), p. 307.

[101] *Ibid.*, pp. 307-8.

THE VIEWS OF OTHERS

Fabian von Schlabrendorff, one of the earliest spokesmen of the anti-Nazi resistance, was in touch with many German military leaders of all ranks and with civilians as well. As an agent of the underground he was in an excellent position to evaluate the fluctuations in morale, to measure the effect of the Casablanca announcement. He divides the reaction into three categories—the Nazis, the anti-Nazis, and the non-Nazis:

1. To the Nazis the pronouncement was a stimulant: after Casablanca they knew that there would be no pardon for them, that they were fighting for their existence, and so they fought with doubled strength.
2. To the anti-Nazi group the slogan was a painful one. It did not weaken their political opposition to Hitler and his regime, but it convinced many that any active resistance in the face of Allied determination to destroy Germany was useless, that the only practical course lay in passive resistance; they would merely wait to act until the Hitler government had collapsed.
3. The great mass of the people were neither pro- nor anti-Nazi. At first they tended to regard the war as Hitler's enterprise, and they made a distinction in their minds between the cause of National Socialism and that of Germany. This had to end with the demand for Unconditional Surrender since the Allies refused to distinguish between Nazism and Germany.

Schlabrendorff states that he is convinced that the policy of Unconditional Surrender had

an exclusively negative effect on the various groups of the German people. On the other hand, the prospect of an honorable peace with honorable conditions—with the borders of the year 1938—would have dealt a death blow to National Socialism in Germany forever.[102]

Albrecht von Kessel, another survivor of the resistance movement, endorses this view. He states that as early as 1943 the underground leaders had worked out a program for peace which they tried to persuade Allied statesmen to accept: the boundaries of 1938; trials of leading Nazis in German courts; an end to German occupation of foreign territories; and the construction

[102] Letter to the author dated Wiesbaden, April 8, 1950.

of a European federation. He feels that had the Allies accepted such a program many non-German Europeans would have supported it in the interest of a rationalized European economy. If an over-all peace settlement of this nature could not be arranged, then the resistance, especially such men as Stauffenberg and Goerdeler, would support the plan of total armistice arrangements through diplomatic channels, for example, by negotiating directly with the Danish King for the evacuation of Denmark on a *quid pro quo* basis.[103] In Kessel's opinion it would have been wiser for the Allies to have agreed to arrange a cease fire with an anti-Nazi successor government, in the event of the successful overthrow of Hitler, to allow the German Wehrmacht to withdraw to the German borders, and to postpone a final peace settlement until the passions of war had cooled. The strength of the resistance movement had consolidated by the end of 1942; early 1943, after the Stalingrad disaster, was a propitious moment for peace, but at exactly that moment came the Casablanca announcement, and the prospects of peace vanished.

Most of the German military historians of the Second World War have commented on the effect of the Unconditional Surrender policy. The consensus of the German writers is that the demand for unconditional surrender was at the very least psychologically unwise because it stiffened the will to resist of the troops and, therefore, sharply increased the cost of Allied victory. It also undermined the strength of the anti-Nazi resistance forces and so in two ways seems to have contributed to the lengthening of the war.[104]

Several Allied military leaders and war historians have contributed to the appraisal of Unconditional Surrender. Admiral Leahy gives no full or vehement argument on the subject, but he writes that during the course of the war "there were occasions when it might have been advantageous to accept conditional surrender in some areas, but we were not permitted to do it." [105]

[103] Interview with the author in Washington, D. C., April, 1957, and June 5, 1957.

[104] See especially Herbert A. Quint, Die Wendepunkte des Krieges (Stuttgart: Steingrüben Verlag, *c.* 1950), p. 191.

[105] *Op. cit.*, p. 145.

In February, 1945, General Eisenhower, Allied Commander in Chief of the European Theater, told a press conference his views on the military effect of the demand for unconditional surrender: "If you were given two choices—one to mount the scaffold and the other to charge twenty bayonets, you might as well charge twenty bayonets." [106]

General Albert C. Wedemeyer devoted considerable attention to Unconditional Surrender in his book. As early as the Casablanca Conference, when he first learned of the President's intention to demand unconditional surrender, he advised against it on the grounds that it would "weld all the Germans together." [107] Later he wrote that the Allied demand for unconditional surrender had increased the enemy's will to resist and had compelled even the anti-Nazis in Germany to go on fighting to save their country. He quotes the early Chinese strategist Sun Tze-wu: "Soldiers when in desperate straits lose the sense of fear. If there is no place of refuge, they will stand firm. . . . Do not press a desperate foe too hard." [108] Wedemeyer feels that it was a mistake of Allied policy to make no distinction between Hitler and the anti-Nazis, in spite of the reports of British and American intelligence agents of the size and importance of the resistance forces in Germany: ". . . we forced all Germans to fight to the last under a regime most of them hated. They had no alternative." [109] He concludes that certain errors in strategic planning plus the doctrine of Unconditional Surrender "certainly lengthened the war by a full year." [110]

Sir John Slessor, RAF marshal, is less definite in his views or more restrained in their expression. In his discussion of the exploitation of airpower over the European Continent he considers the possibility that Germany might have been forced to surrender by the intelligent use of airpower alone, without the need for a land-sea invasion. He concludes:

[106] Quoted in R. E. Dupuy: *Men of West Point* (New York: Sloane, 1952), p. 324.

[107] *Wedemeyer Reports!*, p. 186.

[108] *Ibid.*, p. 95.

[109] *Ibid.*, p. 96.

[110] *Ibid.*, p. 169.

In retrospect, I am now not at all sure we could not have done it, had it not been for the unconditional surrender policy, and had our political warfare been more alert when we first knew of the generals' plot against Hitler; but I certainly did not think so at the time.[111]

Slessor was also present at the meetings of the Joint Chiefs at Casablanca, but he writes that he does not recall a discussion of the Casablanca Formula at these sessions. He states:

It is by no means certain that, had we been consulted, we should have foreseen its implications and advised against it, though that is not impossible. But as far as I remember the use of the words in the President's address to the Press Conference on the 24th made no particular impact on our minds at the time—any more than they seem to have done on the minds of the War Cabinet when considering Mr. Churchill's message. That the actual influence of that phrase on the outcome of the war, and particularly on the bomber offensive, was unfortunate I have no doubt. It is difficult to believe that any subsequent explanations putting its meaning in a less unpalatable form, had any effect in countering its value to Goebbels in stiffening German resistance—to which was added later in the war the preposterous Morgenthau plan for the "deindustrialization" of Germany.[112]

Marshal Slessor warns that the effect of the Unconditional Surrender demand cannot be precisely measured and should not be overrated. He does not go so far as to describe it as "one of the most disastrous decisions of the war," but he concludes that "its effect . . . was unfortunate." [113]

H. C. O'Neill is the author of a concise history of the Second World War in which he strongly criticized the lack of political foresight and wisdom of the United States strategy; however, he does not share the opinion that the Unconditional Surrender demand lengthened the war. His conclusion is that the formula was intended as an act of defiance at a stage of the war where Allied morale needed encouragement, "that it sounds well but is meaningless, since no surrender can be entirely unconditional." [114] From

[111] *The Central Blue* (New York: Praeger, 1957), p. 434.

[112] *Ibid.*, pp. 447-48.

[113] "Grand Strategy and the Second World War," *The Listener*, Vol. LVI, No. 1443 (Nov. 22, 1956), p. 839.

[114] H. C. O'Neill (Strategicus), *A Short History of the Second World War* (New York: Praeger, 1950), p. 289; see also, pp. 159, 285 ff.

the fact of the July 20 attempt against Hitler he deduces that the Allied demand for unconditional surrender did not deter the resistance leaders from their efforts to overthrow Hitler and end the war, a logical deduction. It is possible that at the time of writing the book, in 1950, the details of the effect of Unconditional Surrender on the operations of the resistance movement were not yet accessible.

Dupuy and Dupuy, American military historians, consider the effect of the Unconditional Surrender demand at some length. They conclude:

> It was during the final months of the [Ardennes] campaign that the consequences of our "unconditional surrender" policy became distressingly clear. A negotiated peace any time after January 1945 would not in any way have reduced the value of the lesson of complete and utter defeat which had been inflicted on the Germans. It would have saved thousands of lives on both sides. And the continuity of a government carried on by those responsible German elements already in covert opposition to Hitler might well have precluded any opportunity for the Russians to establish a separate East German government. Fortunately we learned this lesson and avoided the evils of "unconditional surrender" in the case of Japan.[115]

They point out the use made of the Unconditional Surrender threat by the Nazi press long after the military situation had become patently hopeless to prod the Germans to further resistance. Even in the final weeks of the war Nazi fanaticism "fed by the terror of the 'unconditional surrender' fiat of the Allies, was still rampant."[116] They attribute the "ten bloody days" of the battle of Berlin entirely to the Unconditional Surrender Formula.[117]

The views of Dupuy and Dupuy on Unconditional Surrender can be summarized in this statement:

> Ringing well as a slogan of unlimited defiance, it yet closed the door upon any negotiated peace; hence it induced in all German minds the despairing fury of the cornered rat.[118]

[115] *Military Heritage of America* (New York: McGraw-Hill, 1956), p. 562.
[116] *Ibid.*, p. 557.
[117] *Ibid.*, p. 518.
[118] *Ibid.*, p. 466.

In *The Struggle for Europe* Chester Wilmot writes that by proclaiming the demand for unconditional surrender the Western Allies

> denied themselves any freedom of diplomatic manoeuvre and denied the German people any avenue of escape from Hitler. . . . After Casablanca Goebbels had delivered into his hands a propaganda weapon of incalculable power. The Nazis were now able to command conviction when they said to the Nation, "It is you, as well as we, that they want to destroy." [119]

Desmond Young is still more emphatic. Apparently quoting Fuller he writes that the Allies were not free to negotiate a peace settlement with the resistance leaders because of the "putrifying albatross" of Unconditional Surrender:

> Clamped on by their own choice at Casablanca, it "whipped the Germans together under the Swastika," strengthened Hitler, prolonged the war and cost many thousands of British and American lives.[120]

Perhaps the strongest criticism of Unconditional Surrender has been made by Major General J. F. C. Fuller in *The Second World War*. He estimates that the war had reached its climacteric following the battle of Stalingrad and the collapse of the Afrika Korps; that by spring, 1943, the initiative of war had passed to the Allies. He says that at this point the Western Allies ought to have determined the sort of peace they wanted to conclude and seized the psychological advantage by announcing their terms. Obviously the terms would not have included Hitler, but they might have comprised a settlement which would appeal to the German people and to the anti-Nazis in particular. Had such terms been announced, Fuller estimates that the July, 1944, attempted assassination of Hitler might have occurred a full year earlier and might very well have been successful. "Had this happened, then *National Socialism would have been* destroyed by the will of the German people, and replaced by the ideals of the Atlantic Charter." [121]

[119] P. 123.
[120] *Op. cit.*, p. 198.
[121] J. F. C. Fuller, *The Second World War: 1939-45*, p. 258. (Italics are in the original text.)

Instead, the American President and the British Prime Minister announced their war aim as Unconditional Surrender. "Henceforth these two words were to hang like a putrifying albatross around the necks of America and Britain."[122] Fuller continues:

What did these two words imply? First, that because no great power could with dignity or honour to itself, its history, its people and their posterity comply with them, the war must be fought to the point of annihilation. Therefore, it would take upon itself a religious character and bring to life again all the horrors of the wars of religion. For Germany it was to become a question of salvation or damnation. Secondly, once victory had been won, the balance of power within Europe and between European nations would be irrevocably smashed. Russia would be left the greatest military power in Europe, and, therefore, would dominate Europe. Consequently, the peace these words predicted was the replacement of Nazi tyranny by an even more barbaric despotism.[123]

He further said that unconditional surrender could mean only victory or annihilation to every German: "Therefore, unconditional surrender crippled opposition to Hitler within Germany and, like a blood transfusion, gave two years of further life to the war."[124]

In discussing the Italian surrender Fuller is again vehement against the Unconditional Surrender demand. He asserts that

this foolishness, conceived by President Roosevelt and Mr. Churchill at Casablanca, trapped the British and Americans into tactically the most absurd and strategically the most senseless campaign of the whole war. Unconditional Surrender transformed the "soft underbelly" into a crocodile's back; prolonged the war; wrecked Italy; and wasted thousands of American and British lives.[125]

He described conditions on the German Eastern Front and in the war generally as "desperate in the extreme" by August, 1944. The Red Army stood on the border of East Prussia; in France the Allies had broken out of their beachhead; in Italy Kesselring had withdrawn from Florence.

[122] *Ibid.*
[123] *Ibid.*, p. 259.
[124] *Ibid.*, p. 275.
[125] *Ibid.*, p. 265.

Total collapse seemed imminent, total collapse was expected and predicted; yet hedged in by unconditional surrender, total collapse meant total ruin. Therefore, the war continued.[126]

By August 25 General Eisenhower was of the opinion that the military situation had reached that of 1918,[127] but there was no German request for an armistice. Fuller concludes:

> The reason for this was that, whereas in 1918 President Wilson's Fourteen Points offered a fire escape to the beaten Germans, in 1945 (*sic*) President Roosevelt's Unconditional Surrender offered nothing less than total incineration . . . no effect was missed to stimulate German resistance.[128]

After the failure of the last desperate gamble of the Ardennes offensive, the Germans had certainly lost the war. Fuller contends that "in a sane war" hostilities would have ended then, "but because of unconditional surrender the war was far from being sane. Gagged by this idiotic slogan, the Western Allies could offer no terms, however severe." Consequently, he concluded, Hitler was permitted to achieve his ultimate war aim: chaos.[129]

The eminent military analyst Captain Basil Liddell Hart has given a great deal of attention to the subject of Unconditional Surrender. His opposition to the phrase dates back to 1943. In July, 1943, he prepared a memorandum in which he wrote:

> A good slogan . . . is not necessarily identical with good strategy and policy. . . . When, in war, the opponents are beginning to wilt, a rigid demand for unconditional surrender has a natural tendency to stiffen their resistance, and may even cement an incipient crack. This elementary truth was pointed out in the first classic work on the art of war, that of the Chinese master-strategist Sun Tzu, in 500 B.C.
>
> "Honorable capitulation" is a more reassuring and, therefore, more inviting formula, while just as flexible.[130]

[126] *Ibid.*, p. 311.

[127] *Supreme Commander's Report*, p. 64, as quoted by General J. F. C. Fuller, *op. cit.*

[128] Fuller, *op. cit.*, p. 331.

[129] *Ibid.*, p. 355.

[130] Unpublished memorandum, "The Background to 'Unconditional Surrender,'" dated July 31, 1943. See also Liddell Hart, *The Defence of the West*, pp. 52-61.

By the middle of 1943 Captain Liddell Hart regarded the war as virtually won by the Allies, won, that is, in the essential strategic sense: Germany's power to attack had been crippled. From that point on the German Wehrmacht would be on the defensive. Therefore, he pointed out, the enemy "might well be glad to make peace on the terms we defined on entering the war, or on any terms, indeed, that did not involve his complete downfall." [131] He believed that a coup d'état by the military leaders in Germany was a very real possibility, but he pointed out that

> no inducement is created by the uncompromising demand for "unconditional surrender." . . . Those who have the power to achieve such a coup d'état will be aware that it is bound for the moment to weaken their country's resistance to invasion, and will thus want specific assurances as to the conditions of peace before they are likely to make the attempt.[132]

He concluded:

> Insistence on "unconditional surrender" thus aids the hostile regime in keeping control of its people, and convincing them that they have no alternative than to sink or swim with the regime. The effect tends to be like that of a frightened crowd pressing down a passage towards a barred gate—more effective in suffocating the leading ranks of the crowd than in breaking open the gate. Beyond this is the question whether people who feel themselves the target of an unlimited attack with an unlimited object—i.e., an unconditional surrender that provides no safeguards against their maltreatment when submission has rendered them completely helpless—will not be inclined to rally to the regime, tyranny though it is, which at least organizes their defence. In such an impasse, the failure to make clear any limitation of the object may blunt the edge of the bombing weapon.[133]

After the war Liddell Hart concluded that it may well be that "Unconditional Surrender" was the most expensive of all phrases and of all policies. The phrase "sounded so simple and neat, ruling out all argument by the losing side, but proved a source of worse complications than it was intended to avoid." He be-

[131] Unpublished memorandum, "A Reflection on Strategy and Policy—and Humanity—in relation to the Past and the Present," dated July 3, 1943.
[132] *Ibid.*
[133] *Ibid.*

lieves that it prolonged the war "far beyond its likely end" and thus greatly added to the cost in lives and material, and that the great devastation of such a prolonged and intensified war destroyed the European balance of power by making Russia "top dog" on the Continent.[134]

The Military Cost of Unconditional Surrender

Since all the German military authorities who were in a position to form a judgment on the question have not expressed their views on the effect of Unconditional Surrender, one cannot speak of a consensus except in a limited sense. However, of those who have published their evaluation or have contributed letters or interviews to this study, the overwhelming majority of generals and military analysts, both Allied and German, seem agreed that Unconditional Surrender did prolong the war. All the German generals who had contact with the anti-Nazi movement emphasized the unfortunate effect of the policy on the anti-Hitler plot. The British and American writers who discuss the German anti-Nazi movement in greatest detail seem to share this emphasis.

The consensus of the military writers whose views have been presented overwhelmingly supports the view that Unconditional Surrender lengthened the war and added to its cost. The estimates as to when the war might have ended range from January, 1943, immediately after the Stalingrad disaster, to January, 1945, after the Ardennes failure. All these estimates assume that a negotiated peace would have presupposed the overthrow of Hitler and the elimination of National Socialism in Germany. The comments of the German generals make it clear that they would have regarded as reasonable a peace which provided for the payment of reparations to the states they had occupied, the punishment of war criminals, and disarmament. War aims which transcended these traditional ones would probably have met with opposition. The desirability of attaining such far-reaching aims as, for example, total occupation of the German state by the four Allied powers, total reorganization of the German economy, social order, and educational system, and

[134] Unpublished memorandum, "The High Cost of 'Unconditional Surrender,'" dated Nov. 21, 1947, p. 1.

total control of German communications media in order to change the German way of life, to demilitarize, denazify, and democratize the German people must be weighed against the costs of achieving them. One of the costs, by no means the only one, seems to have been the continuation of the war beyond the point at which Germany had lost it. Other costs will be examined in the next chapter.

In other words, had the Allies been willing to accept peace terms more conventional than those anticipated by Big Three wartime conferences, peace might have been concluded in January, 1943, in July, 1943, in January or July, 1944, or most certainly in January, 1945. The saving in lives alone would have been impressive. By way of illustration, the battle casualties of the United States Army and Army Air Corps in the Atlantic Theater were as follows: [135]

January to June, 1943	20,671 dead and wounded
July to December, 1943	39,546 dead and wounded
January to June, 1944	117,903 dead and wounded
July to December, 1944	360,486 dead and wounded
January to May, 1945	222,360 dead and wounded

This means that had the war in Europe ended in January, 1945, following the Ardennes offensive, the United States would have saved 222,360 casualties; had it ended in July, 1944, after the Avranches breakthrough, 582,846 would have been saved; peace in January, 1944, would have prevented 700,749 United States casualties; in July, 1943, more than 740,000, and in January, 1943, after Stalingrad, more than 760,000.

This, of course, gives no indication of British, French, Soviet, and German losses. The German losses, military and civilian, killed and missing for the entire Second World War amounted to approximately four million.[136] Certainly the highest proportion of German casualties, especially of civilian casualties, occurred in the final years of the war. Precise statistics are still not avail-

[135] Department of the Army, *Army Battle Casualties and Non-battle Deaths in World War II*, Final Report, Dec. 7, 1941–Dec. 21, 1946, p. 6.

[136] Professor Percy Schramm of the University of Göttingen has made this estimate, but he indicates that it is only an approximation. Many records have been destroyed.

able, but the implication of the cost in lives of the last year or two of the war is clear. To indicate that the last years of the war were costly is not tantamount to proof that the cost was excessive or not worthwhile, but it does offer one standard by which to measure the goals attained by the war's continuance to its ultimate end.

It is contended that the demand for unconditional surrender intensified the war by stiffening German resistance and by inspiring the German soldiers and civilian workers with the courage and staying power of desperation. The American Generals Eisenhower and Wedemeyer and British Air Marshal Slessor, all of whom were in a position to observe the cost and course of the war in Europe, point to the stiffening of German resistance after the demand for unconditional surrender.

This is an entirely different contention than that the demand lengthened the war, although some authorities make both contentions. The charge against Unconditional Surrender as a prime factor in lengthening the war is a charge against a policy of no compromise, as a war aim of pursuing hostilities to the point of final destruction of German power, of refusal to negotiate. It implies that the Western Allies should have maintained a more flexible general policy, a more moderate war aim. The charge that the Casablanca Formula stiffened resistance is essentially a charge against Unconditional Surrender as propaganda. Even had the Allies maintained the war aim of "a fight to the finish," they could have avoided the phrase "Unconditional Surrender," an ominous phrase which played into the hands of the Goebbels propaganda machine.

The complaint against Unconditional Surrender as poor propaganda involves two separate elements: the simple implication that soldiers faced with no alternative except the destruction of their country will fight with desperation, and the more profound charge that an announcement of an unlimited objective in war will produce unlimited warfare, that a demand for unconditional surrender will compel the enemy to harness his entire economy, his full strength to resist, and in the modern world will inevitably produce Total War. Let us examine both of these aspects of the question briefly.

There is no question that Goebbels and Hitler exploited the phrase "Unconditional Surrender" to lash the Germans to continued resistance. Goebbels described the Allied demand as "a world-historical tomfoolery of the first order," and admitted:

> I should never have been able to think up so rousing a slogan. If our Western enemies tell us: we won't deal with you, our only aim is to destroy you . . . how can any German, whether he likes it or not, do anything but fight on with all his strength? [137]

Hans Fritsche, a prominent Nazi radio commentator, made frequent use of the Unconditional Surrender slogan. He warned his listeners that capitulation meant a "Super Versailles," a peace which promised only retribution and devastation.[138]

Hitler played upon the fear of Unconditional Surrender to inspire the German troops in the defense of Rome after the Allies had made their costly landing at Anzio. In January, 1944, in an Order of the Day titled "The Battle for Rome," he exhorted the troops:

> The Battle must be waged with holy hatred toward a foe who is fighting a merciless war of extermination against the German people, who considers every means justified, and who without any higher ethical purpose aims only at annihilating Germany and thereby the culture of Europe.[139]

In September, 1944, when the Wehrmacht was compelled to evacuate France and fall back to the Westwall, the morale of the troops dropped sharply. The "Commissars" of the National Socialist Leadership Corps, officers and noncommissioned officers chosen for their party loyalty and for their persuasive powers, were rushed to the Western Front to attempt to bolster the faltering morale of the retreating Germans. Again and again these commissars used the threat of unconditional surrender to inspire the soldiers with the terror of what total defeat would

[137] Quoted from Wilfred von Oven, "Mit Goebbels bis zum Ende" (Buenos Aires: Dürer Verlag, 1949), Vol. I, p. 204, in *Unconditional Surrender,* Wiener Library Bulletin.

[138] Quoted in the Wiener Library article from *Hier Spricht Hans Fritsche* (Zurich, 1948), p. 210.

[139] Unpublished "Order of the Day" supplied by a former German general officer.

mean for Germany and for their families.[140] The amazing degree of success achieved by this beaten army in the Ardennes offensive in December, 1944, is a measure of the effectiveness of their propaganda. Manteuffel, Field Commander of the German Fifth Panzer Army which figured prominently in the Ardennes campaign, underlined the fear of Unconditional Surrender as a major factor in the high morale of his officers and men.[141]

Liddell Hart reports that the slow Allied advance throughout the fall of 1944 was due in no small measure to the stubbornness of German resistance, and that this stubbornness was to a great degree due to the fear of Unconditional Surrender. The German Army at this point was seriously outnumbered by the Allies and its supplies and air cover in no way compared to those of the Anglo-American forces. He states that many of the German prisoners taken during these months were "poor specimens, and ardent Nazis were rare among them. But these low-grade troops fought harder than high-grade troops had done earlier. They were stiffened by the courage of desperation." He concludes: "That desperation was due to the absence of any gleam of hope in the Allies' ominously bare demand for unconditional surrender." [142]

The degree of desperation of a beaten army which continues to fight and to win battles and to take a significant toll in lives and material is not something which can be measured in statistics. Its existence cannot be scientifically demonstrated, but, nevertheless, it is a factor which military writers and the commanders of troops have traditionally taken into account. It is a factor which many commanders and writers have pointed to as one of the costs of Unconditional Surrender.

THE QUESTION OF TOTAL WAR

The Second World War was the first major European and international encounter in the modern period, that is, since the re-

[140] Obtained from an interview with a former German general officer who prefers not to be quoted; July, 1957.
[141] See Kreipe *et al.*, *op. cit.*, p. 243.
[142] "The High Cost of Unconditional Surrender," p. 4.

ligious wars of the seventeenth century, which was ended by the unconditional surrender of the defeated powers. It was also the first war which was officially described by the belligerents as "Total War." Historically it is interesting to note the sequence of events that brought these two phenomena into being in modern war.

Throughout the month of December, 1942, the attention of the German public had been riveted on Stalingrad. With horror the realization had grown that the entire Sixth Army, more than 200,000 men, were trapped and isolated in the Stalingrad pocket, that they were going to be abandoned to their fate by the Commander in Chief, that 200,000 German troops would be annihilated or led into Soviet imprisonment. When at the end of January the blow fell, the horror mounted and morale, civilian and military, collapsed. Faith in Hitler as commander in chief and in the eventuality of German victory ebbed.

It was to this shocked and saddened German public that Roosevelt and Churchill announced their demand for unconditional surrender. It was from this same public on January 30 and on February 18, 1943, that Paul Joseph Goebbels, the Nazi Propaganda Minister, demanded the acceptance of Total War.

On January 30, 1943, just six days after the Casablanca announcement, Goebbels addressed the Berlin public at the Sportspalast. He thundered: "The word surrender does not exist in our vocabulary!" [143] He said that the renewed "Bolshevik winter offensive is a trumpet-call to the German nation for Total War."[144] He called upon the German people not to be taken in by the Allied propaganda bluff but instead to rally the entire force of the nation to meet the extraordinary dangers of the military situation. He warned that since the enemies of Germany were fighting to enslave the German nation the war had become an urgent struggle for national preservation in which no sacrifice could be too great.[145]

[143] *Deutschland im Kampf,* a publication of the Reichs Propaganda Ministry, ed. by A. J. Berndt (Berlin: Verlagsanstalt Otto Stollberg, 1943, No. 81/82, January, 1943), p. 59.

[144] *Ibid.,* p. 63.

[145] *Ibid.,* pp. 64-65.

In a second speech, on February 18, he elaborated his program of Total War. Warning of the danger of Bolshevism inherent in the deeply serious situation following the disaster at Stalingrad, he proclaimed Total War as the "command of the hour." [146] The time for velvet gloves was past! The entire people, regardless of class or sex or profession, was now part of the war. There could be no luxuries, no food delicacies, no fashionable dress salons, no waste of manpower or raw materials, of heat or light. The workday in all industries must be lengthened, more manpower must be diverted either to the front or to direct war industries; even within the government no bureaucratic nonsense would be tolerated. Space on the railroads would be rationed; there would be no unnecessary amusements; women would be drafted for industry. The enemy, he declared, believed that the German people had lost the hope of victory, but this was not true. "I ask you," he concluded, "do you want Total War?" The multithousand-voiced answer thundered "Ja!" [147]

In the Second World War not only Hitler and Goebbels accepted this total view of the aims and methods of warfare; in some areas the Allies endorsed it more enthusiastically than the Germans.[148] Liddell Hart points out that only the British manual of warfare, and later the American, advocated the use of airpower against civilian targets. The Germans held to the more conservative view that airpower was an auxiliary weapon to augment land movements. He maintains that the Germans resorted to bombing civilian targets only in support of ground troops or as retaliation measures: Rotterdam and Warsaw were bombed in conjunction with troop movements on those cities and London was raided only after six successive RAF raids on Berlin.[149]

Apparently both the totalitarian dictatorship in Germany and the democratic governments of Great Britain and the United States viewed the Second World War as a departure in both aims and methods from traditional warfare, a war *sui generis.*

[146] *Ibid.*
[147] *Ibid.*, No. 83/84 (February, 1943), pp. 91-104.
[148] Liddell Hart, *Defense of the West*, p. 316.
[149] *Ibid.*, p. 318.

To the extent that Germany's war policy was directed by the generals rather than by Hitler and the party it tended to be more conservative in scope than that waged by the Western democracies. Liddell Hart holds that the German military leadership viewed war dispassionately, from the viewpoint of professional soldiers.[150] Like that older professional soldier, Sherman, they saw the wisdom of viewing destruction in war as only a means to an end, a means that must be carefully restricted. In the democracies there were certainly also professional soldiers who pointed to the wisdom of limiting warfare against civilian targets. This is revealed in the debates among the Anglo-American generals about strategic air warfare. There was by no means unanimity among Western strategists concerning the efficacy or morality of saturation bombing, for example, any more than there was on the question of Unconditional Surrender but in both cases the advocates of the extreme position held the day: the Allies adhered to the strategy of pursuing an unlimited objective with unlimited means.

One explanation of this development might lie in the nature of the modern democratic state. Liddell Hart has examined this possibility, and he concludes that in the vast modern democratic society a large "volume of emotional pressure" arises, especially in time of crisis, which "too often overwhelms reason and drives the leaders to extremes—in order to keep their lead,"[151] and such pressure can lead to excesses in means as well as in ends.

Totalitarian governments, although ostensibly dedicated to the fulfillment of rigid ideological programs such as the establishment of a classless society, the proletarian revolution, or the creation of a New Order in Europe, can prove more flexible in meeting changing situations. For example, when Hitler became aware of the basically changed strategic situation on the Eastern Front after Stalingrad, when it became clear even to him that Germany had been forced on the defensive, he quickly revised his political line. When his armies had been advancing victoriously he had called for a New Order under the leadership of the Germanic peoples. As German victories gave way to disasters, as

[150] *Ibid.*, p. 319.
[151] *Ibid.*, p. 319.

the Wehrmacht was forced to withdraw step by step along its invasion route, Hitler and Goebbels said less and less about racism or German Lebensraum and more and more about the defense of European freedom against Bolshevism. He understood the popular terror of a Russian invasion, he knew that even anti-Nazis in Germany and throughout Europe would be forced to support him as the only possible barrier against a Soviet flood.[152]

Democratic governments seem less able to maneuver this freely in the policy field, perhaps for the obvious reason that democratic governments cannot manipulate public opinion as quickly and completely as can their totalitarian rivals. In a democratic society it takes a long and moralistic propaganda campaign to arouse public opinion to war fever; once this fever has been aroused, once war has been proclaimed for absolute moral purposes, it is difficult to stem the tide. A dictatorship can proclaim an immediate about-face, a reversal of all its former propaganda as the U.S.S.R. did in making its pact with Nazi Germany in 1939 and, at the risk of appearing cynical to critical observers, follow a policy dictated by a rational appraisal of changing national interest. The democracies seem to become tied to policies dictated by sentimentality and governed by emotion.[153] They seem to have had a greater tendency to confuse ends and means.

However, there is no question that in the Second World War both the dictatorships and the Western democracies pursued Total War. For Germany Total War meant:

1. The full utilization of manpower. This required the drafting for armed service and for the labor force of every capable man and woman and of many adolescents, both Germans and citizens of occupied areas. It resulted in the dislocation of families: small children often had to be evacuated from cities to escape air raids, most of the men were in uniform, the women in industrial centers, the adolescents in youth camps or in labor service. Many men returned from the front to find their former residences destroyed and their families scattered throughout Germany. It

[152] See Fuller, *op. cit.*, pp. 274-75.

[153] See, for example, Nathaniel Peffer's discussion of this in "The United States and China: The Politics of Sentimentality," *Columbia University Forum*, Vol. II, No. 2 (Winter, 1959), pp. 28-34.

caused the dislocation of entire peoples: the German-speaking Russians of the Volga region, for example, were uprooted and transferred to Germany as the Wehrmacht retreated because to leave them behind would have meant to abandon them to Soviet reprisals for collaboration with the Germans. In addition, workers from Russia, Poland, the Balkans, and from the West were recruited to work in German factories, on the land, or as servants in German homes to release housewives for war labor. The number of displaced persons in Germany in 1945 is evidence of the degree of upheaval.

2. The full mobilization of the economy. Not only manpower but also raw materials, food, factories, transportation, and utilities had to be controlled and rationed or allocated in direct proportion to their importance to war production. Luxuries of production and of service were eliminated.[154]

3. Increased power for government and party agencies and for the political police, accompanied by increased tension, suspicion, and terror. The number of political arrests rose, and with a mounting sense of desperation the excesses of the Gestapo and Deathshead SS increased. Shortages of food, medication, and heat were especially acute in the prisons and concentration camps, since they had no priority status; deaths from starvation, disease, and execution reached a peak in the final two years of the war.[155]

4. For Germany the Allied pursuit of Total War meant the devastation of German cities by saturation bombing. Launched after Casablanca, the Anglo-American around-the-clock raids on civilian targets reached a climax during the final months of the war. By May, 1945, cities like Cologne and Würzburg had been approximately 75 per cent destroyed; Aachen, Münster, and Kassel were 65 per cent destroyed; Dortmund, Essen, and Hamburg were about 50 per cent destroyed as a result of air attacks.[156] The bombings meant not only interruption of production, a crisis

[154] For details of the effect of total war see, especially, Max Seydewitz, *Civil Life in Wartime Germany* (New York: Viking, 1945), pp. 241 ff.

[155] There are few adequate statistics for such questions.

[156] *Germany Reports* (Bonn: Press and Information Office, German Federal Republic, 1953), p. 179.

in housing, and forced relocation of inhabitants, but also a major cultural loss and serious social upheaval.

In brief, Total War led to the disruption of family life, increased terror and demoralization, and the devastation of cities. For the Allies it meant a costly last-ditch struggle against a desperate enemy, and victory, when it came, meant the conquest of the shattered remnants of Central Europe, its cities, its economy, and its morale reduced to rubble. "Better a desert than a country ruled by heretics."

Unconditional Surrender and Total War

War, said Clausewitz, is an instrument of policy, "it must necessarily bear its character, it must measure with its scale." The character of a war, the degree of force to be employed, the extent of the military commitment will depend upon the nature and gravity of the political goal.[157] Where the political objective is unlimited, that is, where the aim is Unconditional Surrender, it follows logically that the means used to achieve this end may have to be unlimited. To compel a powerful enemy to accept unconditional surrender will require every weapon in the arsenal, and the enemy in turn will be forced to resort to the most desperate form of warfare to resist. In this sense there is an inherent logical link between a demand for unconditional surrender and the proclamation and practice of total war.

Modern technology and the modern mass society seem to have conceived the phenomenon of Total War. The Casablanca demand for unconditional surrender seems to have heralded its birth. The cost in added intensity of resistance, in lives of political prisoners, and in the unmeasurable factors of social cohesion, moral values, and cultural monuments can only be guessed.

[157] Clausewitz, *On War,* pp. 121-23.

CHAPTER 4

The Effect of the Policy of Unconditional Surrender on the German Anti-Nazi Resistance Movement: 1943-1944

The demand for the unconditional surrender of Germany announced at the Casablanca Conference in January, 1943, initiated a development that culminated in the signing of the instruments of surrender at Reims and at Berlin in May, 1945. The policy of Unconditional Surrender was the product of a confluence of events and of forces. The personality and the political views of President Roosevelt, the exigencies of the Three-Power Coalition, the split regarding war aims in domestic American political circles, the "win the war first" attitude that prevailed among American military and political leaders, and the general tendency in the United States to think of war and peace in terms of absolute moral values—these and many other psychological and historical factors shaped and gave impetus to the policy of Unconditional Surrender. Despite pressure from British and Soviet leaders and from American generals and Cabinet members, the policy of Unconditional Surrender remained the official war aim of the United Nations until the end of the Second World War.

We have examined the military effects of this policy on the enemy, the reactions it provoked "on the other side of the hill." Let us now turn our attention to the political effects within Germany. Did Unconditional Surrender tend to demoralize the German people and to divide them from Hitler and his party or did it, rather, unite popular German resistance against an absolute and unmeasurable demand? What effect did the policy of Unconditional Surrender have on the unity and the resolution of the anti-Nazi forces within Germany? To what extent did it influence the attitude of military leaders regarding the possible overthrow of Hitler? Perhaps no final answer can ever be obtained to these questions; certainly it is not the intent of this inquiry to expound a final answer, but in this chapter we shall pose the questions and try to present and evaluate some of the facts and concepts which may lead in the direction of answers.

It is not a simple matter to evaluate the effect of the policy of Unconditional Surrender on the German anti-Nazi movement chiefly because most of the leaders of that movement were executed by the Gestapo and because only fragmentary documentation of the nature and aims of the movement has survived. However, by now the existence of such a movement within Germany has been documented, the size and scope of the groups which composed it are known. It is not necessary for the analyst of Unconditional Surrender to examine the history of the German resistance in detail; nevertheless, certain questions concerning it necessarily arise out of the consideration of whether Allied open or covert encouragement of the anti-Nazi forces within Germany might have provided a workable alternative to the demand for unconditional surrender:

1. Did the size and efficacy of the resistance warrant recognition by the Allies? Was the group merely a small clique of disgruntled militarists and reactionaries or did it represent broad segments of German society? What resonance did it have among the masses of the German people?
2. What were the political and social aims of the group? Would the Germany which might have resulted from a suc-

cessful overthrow of Hitler have been the sort desired by the Allied governments?

3. Did the resistance leaders formulate serious and workable plans for the overthrow of the Nazi regime? Did they intend to end the war after a successful revolt?
4. Did the resistance leaders attempt to negotiate with the Allied governments during the war? If so, what seems to have been the effect of the policy of Unconditional Surrender on these negotiations and on the morale and efficacy of the resistance?

Let us examine these questions in order.

THE SIZE AND EFFICACY OF THE RESISTANCE MOVEMENT

The Size and Influence of the Resistance Movement

Immediately following the attempt to assassinate Hitler on July 20, 1944, the official evaluation of the event by both American and British leaders was simply that high officials in the German Reich were murdering each other as a consequence of the desperation of Germany's military situation.[1] For several years following the close of the Second World War the American government continued to espouse the view that the plot against Hitler had been the work of a small clique of military leaders motivated only by a desire to end the war in order to preserve what little German strength remained in 1944, that the group had no resonance among the German people and no genuine anti-Nazi political or moral motivation. The existence of a widespread anti-Nazi resistance movement was denied, the profound political and spiritual implications of the movement were ignored, and reports concerning it were suppressed.[2] Allied admission during the war of the existence of a large-scale anti-Nazi movement within Germany might have threatened the moral basis

[1] Dulles, *Germany's Underground,* pp. 172 ff; Rothfels, *The German Opposition to Hitler,* pp. 145 ff.

[2] See, especially, Rothfels, *op. cit.,* pp. 20-22, and Louis P. Lochner, *Always the Unexpected* (New York: Macmillan, 1956), pp. 294 f.

of Total War pursued to the achievement of Unconditional Surrender. It could have invalidated punitive peace plans based on the assumption of the total guilt of the German people for the acts and the program of the Nazi party. For these and other reasons, the extent and even the existence of the resistance was denied, both during the war and in the immediate postwar years.

Within recent years, however, many of the facts and the implications of the German opposition movement have come to light as the result of the publication of memoirs, of documents, and of monographs. By now there is little question that the German anti-Nazi movement comprised more than a small clique of disgruntled military leaders. The actual assassination attempt of July 20, 1944, was implemented by the military segment of the movement, but civilians of many facets of German society and of varying political beliefs had contributed to the plans which preceded the explosion of the bomb. In Professor Rothfels' words, the military group formed the spearhead of the resistance movement, but it was not its body or soul. The movement was far broader than that.[3]

Some indication of the size of the conspiracy that planned the overthrow of the Nazi government can be gained from the number of trials and executions that followed the unsuccessful bomb attempt of July 20, 1944. According to Rothfels, approximately 7,000 Germans were arrested following the assassination attempt, and of that number more than 4,980 "were shot, hanged, or tortured to death." [4] He quotes German naval documents which had fallen into British hands to the effect that of the total number of persons executed only about 700 were officers of the army, navy, or air force.[5] These figures lead to two conclusions: (1) the number of people involved in the plot eliminates the charge that the conspiracy was the work of a small clique; (2) that the

[3] Rothfels, *op. cit.*, p. 84.

[4] *Ibid.*, p. 9.

[5] *Ibid.*, p. 10. The Bishop of Chichester cites a still higher figure as the total number of Germans executed following the July, 1944, attempt. He maintains that a total of approximately 20,000 men and women were executed in the wake of July 20. "The Background of the Hitler Plot," *The Contemporary Review*, September, 1945, pp. 203-8. He cites as his source *The Annual Register* for 1944.

military element, though proportionately large, did not dominate the group numerically.[6]

The arrests and executions involved men and women from many levels of German society, representing many shades of political opinion. The military officers involved included such men as former Chief of the General Staff Beck and former Commander of the Afrika Korps Rommel, and also scores of young lieutenants and captains on all fronts who felt that more than military considerations were involved in the decision to end the war and end the Nazi government. The civilian ranks of the movement were filled by former civil servants and diplomats, by the leaders of pre-1933 political parties, by the leadership and by rank-and-file members of the former Free Trade-Union Movement, by professional men and women, and by clergymen and laymen of both Protestant and Catholic confessions.

The resistance had cells and representatives spread throughout the ministries of the government in the major cities of Germany. The major commands of the army and of the police had been infiltrated and in each case the commanding general was a party to the plot. The major public services such as gas supply and radio were included in the plan as were other key industries.[7]

In addition to the group of soldiers and civilians who planned and executed the specific assassination attempt of July 20 there were other groups, not specifically associated with the plot, who nevertheless must be included in an appraisal of the anti-Nazi forces within Germany. The actual details of the assassination attempt were the secret of a small cadre but the spirit of resistance radiated throughout a wider circle of the German population. For example, Paul Maerker, a leader of the Trade-Union movement before the Nazi era, estimated that approximately 125,000 workers, that is, about 3 per cent of the total 1933 membership of the Free Trade-Unions, were active members of the anti-Nazi movement.[8] There was an anti-Nazi cell among the

[6] It should be remembered that many resistance leaders who were in the armed forces during the war were not professional soldiers but civilians who had been drafted.

[7] Rothfels, *op. cit.*, especially pp. 98 ff.

[8] Three per cent does not seem a high proportion, but the need for absolute secrecy necessarily kept the number of active oppositionists small.

workers of each major factory which maintained continual contact with similar cells in other factories and other cities. These cells were directed by a group of former Trade-Union leaders.[9]

The existence of the Gestapo and of the more than seventy concentration camps throughout Germany were eloquent testimony to the persistent if silent opposition of at least a segment of the people. Almost no foreigners were interned prior to the outbreak of war in 1939, and the Jews accounted for only one element of the prisoners. It is estimated that between 1933 and 1938 from 500,000 to 600,000 German men and women were confined to concentration camps for political reasons, in other words, for anti-Nazi beliefs or activities. Between 1933 and 1938 approximately 12,000 persons were executed for political crimes, and Gestapo files reveal that more than 2,000,000 Germans were listed as politically unreliable.[10] Even allowing for miscarriages of justice, which were certainly frequent in the Nazi special courts, these figures indicate a high degree of disaffection among the German people, and an undercurrent of popular anti-Nazi feeling upon which an organized underground could build.

In the broader sense the "resistance movement" included many private citizens who took no direct political action but resisted the regime by sheltering political or racial refugees or by opposing laws and programs of the government which they considered immoral. For example, an estimated five thousand Jews were able to survive the Nazi regime and the war sheltered secretly in the homes of individual Berliners.[11] Many prominent persons used their influence and their wealth to aid the escape of Jews and of others in danger of arrest. Otto Kiep of the Foreign Office and Elisabeth von Thadden, headmistress of a private school for girls, were only two of this group.[12] Both Catholic and Protestant clergymen opposed the Nazi-sponsored program of euthanasia in church hospitals and asylums, and many Christian leaders of both faiths courageously spoke out against the regime when it infringed on human rights or encouraged violation of the moral

[9] Rothfels, *op. cit.*, pp. 97-98, see also pp. 98-100.

[10] *Ibid.*, pp. 13 f.

[11] *Ibid.*, p. 34. See also Ruth Andreas-Friedrich, *Berlin Underground* (New York: Holt, 1947).

[12] Rothfels, *op. cit.*, p. 30.

code. Churches which before the war had been attended chiefly by women, children, and very old men began to be filled with young men and especially with officers in uniform. Luther's hymn, "A Mighty Fortress Is Our God," became a symbol of silent moral protest against the regime.[13]

The word "resistance" embraces three degrees of commitment: (1) the private citizen who was not organized into a group but took political action when his moral or religious views demanded it; (2) political groups which held meetings, maintained secret contact, and made plans for the new Germany which would follow the Hitler regime; and (3) the inner cadre which conspired actively to overthrow the Nazi government, to establish a new government, and to end the war. This group as a whole formed an active and a latent force within Nazi Germany. It represented political and moral factors that required consideration by the planners of policy and of strategy regarding Germany during the Second World War. This resistance included front commanders and front soldiers, workers in the war production plants and on the Home Front; it therefore had military significance. This group was a nucleus which could provide the political, moral, and cultural leadership for a postwar Germany, and so it also had long-range diplomatic and historical significance.

The movement was sizable. However, what was its significance? Who were the people who made up the resistance movement and what were the goals and the programs that motivated them? The group was worthy of consideration in formulating Allied policy, but was it worthy of recognition, of encouragement? Let us inquire into the composition and nature of the active elements of the movement.

Components of the Resistance Movement

The following brief analysis of the nature of the resistance against National Socialism within Germany is by no means a history of that movement. The story of the membership, aims, and activities of the various elements of this resistance has gradually become a matter of historical record, although many of the

[13] *Ibid.*, p. 34. See also Bishop of Chichester, *op. cit.*

details are still in doubt. From the point of view of American and Allied policy formation, one basic question was whether these groups were genuinely anti-Nazi, whether they opposed the Nazi regime on the basis of sincere moral and political convictions, or whether they were simply defeatists or disgruntled militarists, disappointed in Hitler only because he had failed to win the war. From this point of view only, let us examine some representative segments of the movement.

Youth

The square in front of the main entrance to the University of Munich is now called "Geschwister Scholl Platz" in honor of the sister and brother, Sophie and Hans Scholl, who led a student movement at the university and who were executed by the Nazi government in 1943. The Scholls have become famous in Germany as a symbol of the resistance of university students. Together with Munich philosophy professor, Kurt Huber, the Scholls had organized a group of Catholic students which devoted itself to a campaign of underground propaganda against the regime. The group published and distributed pamphlets which attacked the Nazis on moral and religious grounds. They were in contact with Catholic youth groups at other universities, with Bavarian Catholic publishers and intellectuals, and with individual clergymen. Their activities were discovered by the Gestapo and, in consequence, nine members of the group, including the Scholls and Professor Huber, were executed.[14]

Many of the survivors of the Scholl movement joined "the Edelweiss," a widespread underground youth movement which had branches in many cities, at several universities, and within the Hitler Youth organization. In one small city as many as 30 per cent of the Hitler Youth were secret members of the Edelweiss. As early as 1939 the Gestapo had estimated that at least two thousand young people were members of this underground.[15]

[14] The details of the Scholl movement are given in many books, such as Rothfels, *op. cit.*, pp. 11-12; Dulles, *op. cit.*, pp. 120-22; Annedore Leber, *Das Gewissen Steht Auf* (Berlin: Mosaik-Verlag, 1954), pp. 7-11, 22-24, and others.

[15] Rothfels, *op. cit.*, p. 12.

Overt opposition, open revolt was impossible in a nation supervised by an efficient secret police, but secret meetings, even secret publications, and a silent spiritual opposition were possible. After the execution of the Scholls, policemen on their early rounds in Munich frequently found the words "The spirit lives!" painted on the sides of buildings or on fences.[16] The words were efficiently erased by midday, only to reappear on another wall, another fence the following morning. The spirit was not so easily erased.

Throughout the Nazi period approximately 25 per cent of the students at German universities consistently refused to become members of the National Socialist student organization, even though this refusal automatically entailed political suspicion and reduced the chances of professional success following graduation.[17]

In Nazi Germany an organized rebellion of the youth was not possible, and certainly it should not be forgotten that many of the most ardent and uncritical supporters of the regime came from the ranks of the youth. The party spared no effort and no expense to win the youth to their cause and to keep them loyal to Hitler and his aims. Nevertheless, a substantial minority was able to resist the propaganda and the bribery, perhaps because of family influence or religious training. It took moral courage and intellectual independence to resist the appeal of the Nazi slogans in the days of intoxicating enthusiasm following Hitler's early triumphs. Gestapo files reveal the extent of the resistance: an entire concentration camp at Neuwied was maintained especially for the confinement of teen-age boys.[18] It was a minority of the youth which continued to resist, but a minority which must have been morally and spiritually stronger than the majority which capitulated. These young people formed a moral elite which should well have been considered by Allied policy. It was an elite to provide leaders in the postwar Germany, an elite to give resonance and support to the government which might have been established by the older leaders of the resistance.

[16] *Ibid.*, pp. 11-12.
[17] *Ibid.*, p. 35.
[18] *Ibid.*, p. 14.

Intellectuals: the Inner Emigration

Perhaps no group has been as widely or as sharply criticized as the intellectuals who remained within Germany during the Nazi regime and the war, but who maintained that they were spiritually opposed to the regime. They have been criticized for cowardice, for opportunism, for lack of intellectual integrity, for submitting to censorship, for failure to oppose the inhumanity and the monstrous nonsense of Nazi ideology, and finally, for hypocrisy in their claim of spiritual, inner opposition. Why did they remain in a Germany dominated by a criminal government? Why, if they remained, did they allow their silence to condone the acts of that government? How, if they were silent, can they claim to have been in opposition?

A full answer to these questions lies beyond the scope of a study of Unconditional Surrender and must be sought in the monographs on the resistance movement or in the memoirs or works of members of the Inner Emigration. Perhaps the questions cannot be answered satisfactorily; however, the evaluation of the degree of opposition to National Socialism within Germany must take into account the existence of a group which called itself the Inner Emigration and must reckon with the latent moral support such a group would be likely to accord to more active branches of the resistance.

The Church

Ever since the earliest days of the Nazi regime, the Nazi party leaders had recognized that the Christian Church, both Catholic and Protestant, constituted one of the major enemies of National Socialism within Germany. Many of the original high-ranking Nazis were violently anti-Christian and anticlerical, and much of the early terror and many of the first restrictive laws were directed against organized Christianity. Religious publications were forced to curtail their circulation because of an alleged paper shortage. Hitler Youth meetings, which young people were compelled to attend, were scheduled for the same hours as church services or as church youth meetings; the government confiscated monasteries, church-run hospitals, and seminaries for secular use; priests and pastors were spied upon, threatened, and arrested. The total number of clergymen, including nuns and monks, who were executed or who died in confinement is not known, but in one camp alone, Dachau, more than a thousand Catholic priests died or were executed.[19] Lay leaders of church youth groups or of such organizations as Catholic Action were automatically regarded as enemies of the regime. As early as the June, 1934, purge the Berlin Catholic Action leader was shot at the order of Gestapo Chief Reinhard Heydrich.[20]

From 1933 until the end of Nazism in 1945 many thousands of Germans stood before judges of the notorious People's Courts to be sentenced to prison, concentration camps, or to death simply as Christians.[21] The Christian churches formed an important link in the chain of resistance. Their organization and their facilities often provided the means for communication among the many separate underground groups. Their teachings provided a common ethic upon which men and women of many shades of political opinion could agree. The moral strength of clergymen and Christian laymen inspired respect even in previously anticlerical circles, and this spirit of respect and of co-operation which was born under Nazi persecution made possible new political alignments, new compromises. Formerly anticlerical Socialists or Trade-Unionists learned to respect and to like Christians, and conservatives; the conservatives learned to think in terms of the human and social needs of workers. The Christian opposition, then, was more than simply the churches. It was the spirit of the whole resistance movement.

The Kreisau Circle

Count Helmuth von Moltke was the leader of a group of oppositionists which derived its name from his estate in Silesia—Kreisau. The group included young and socially minded aristocrats such as Count Peter Yorck von Wartenburg, Count Fritz-

[19] Probably a comparable number of Protestant pastors also were arrested and executed but the figure is not given in the source: Walter Adolph, *Im Schatten des Galgens* (Berlin: Morus Verlag, 1953), pp. 50 f.

[20] *Ibid.*, p. 10.

[21] See, for example, Helmuth James Graf von Moltke, *Letzte Briefe* (Berlin: Henssel Verlag, 1950), p. 56.

Dietlof von der Schulenburg, Count Ulrich Wilhelm Schwerin von Schwanenfeld, and Adam von Trott zu Solz. It included also representatives of both church confessions such as the Jesuit Father Delp and Protestant Pastors Harald Poelchau and Eugen Gerstenmaier, educational leaders, members of the government and of the army, and representatives of the free trade unions and the Christian Trade-Union Movement.

The Kreisau program, which was not so much a political ideology as a broad moral attitude, comprised the following points, among others:

1. It emphasized the importance of Christian influence in culture and education. Even its Socialist members agreed that the schools of the post-Nazi period should offer education that would be Christian in character and emphasis.
2. The former spirit of nationalism should be transcended by a more modern supranationalism to be achieved through the creation of a federation of European states which would preserve local cultural autonomy but would eliminate tariffs and trade barriers to render an intra-European war unlikely.
3. Within Germany the rule of law would be re-established, limiting the power of the government and guaranteeing to the citizens freedom of conscience and human dignity.
4. War crimes and criminal acts by the Nazi hierarchy should be punished with strict regard for legal judicial procedure and without the spirit of vengeance. Moltke believed that unjust or peremptory trials would create bitterness and cynicism; he advocated that international war crimes be tried by a court composed of victor, vanquished, and neutral judges.
5. Although the social views of the Kreisau Circle were considered radical by the older and more conservative resistance leaders, the Circle believed strongly in personal freedom and totally rejected any form of totalitarianism. The group accepted the principle of free enterprise but proposed the elimination of cartels and monopolies. They endorsed thoroughgoing social reform, but they rejected violence and revolution and accepted the conservative principles of

property, family, religion, and law. The young aristocrats of this circle accepted and proposed to implement the ancient conservative principle: *noblesse oblige.*[22]

The young men of Kreisau were neither "radical" nor "conservative" in the old, doctrinaire sense of these words. In a new sense they were both: radical-conservatives. To a great extent the Kreisau Circle formed the theoretical segment of the resistance movement.

The Trade-Unions

The leaders of the former free trade-unions were the automatic enemies of the Nazi government. One of the first acts of the Nazis after coming to power was to outlaw the Free Trade-Union Movement and to arrest its most influential leaders. Many trade-unionists were confined in concentration camps throughout the Nazi period, others were able to escape abroad. Still others were released after specific prison or camp terms and were drawn into the activities of the resistance movement. Some of the most prominent trade-unionists became respected leaders of the resistance.[23]

One of these was Wilhelm Leuschner, former chairman of the German Social Democratic Trade-Unions. Leuschner was arrested in 1933 and spent two years in a concentration camp. After his release he established a small factory in a suburb of Berlin. He began to hire former trade-union associates as workers and supervisors in his factory, and before long his plant became the nucleus and nerve center of the trade-union resistance movement. His salesmen were in contact with other opposition cells throughout Germany, and Leuschner himself became the respected friend of General Beck, a frequent visitor to his factory, and of other members of the conservative and Christian opposition. The cadre of the underground planned to appoint Leuschner vice-chancellor of the interim government which would be established in the event of the successful over-

[22] See, especially, Rothfels, *op. cit.*, pp. 118-22, and FitzGibbon, *20 July*, pp. 84 ff, 223-46. Also Zimmermann and Jacobsen (eds.), *20, Juli 1944*, pp. 33 ff.

[23] See also Leber, *op. cit.*, pp. 67-100.

throw of the Nazi regime.[24] He was executed by the Gestapo following the unsuccessful assassination attempt of July 20, 1944.[25]

Catholics and anticlerical but also anti-Communist trade-unionists of both the left wing and right wing made common cause with one another and with the more conservative elements of the resistance. Social Democrats who had once condemned the General Staff as dangerous militarists became the fast friends and wholehearted admirers of Beck, former chief of the General Staff, and many who had once preached class warfare consulted with Count Moltke and many other anti-Nazi aristocrats. In many cases genuine friendships developed between men of divergent social backgrounds and opposing political views. This led to the serious reappraisal of former values, and in many cases to the realization that the social and political ideas and categories of the pre-Nazi era had lost validity.

Perhaps the true significance of the trade-unionist support of the resistance lay not simply in the opposition of these groups to Hitler. That was self-evident, almost inevitable. Perhaps much greater significance lay in the new spirit of co-operation and compromise that developed on all sides. Socialists tended gradually to become more tolerant of organized religion and less class-conscious. On the other hand, many aristocrats, churchmen, and army officers learned to like and to respect the trade-unionists and Socialists with whom they worked against a common danger, with whom they mutually risked their lives. The willingness of Leuschner to serve in a common enterprise with General Staff officers and other conservatives reveals the degree to which a new synthesis of political and social thinking had replaced the doctrinaire concepts of the past.

This very co-operation, this synthesis, was a major political factor which merited consideration by those who planned policy in regard to postwar Germany. Surely a resistance movement composed of so many diverse elements and including a nucleus

[24] Gerhard Ritter, *Goerdeler und die Deutsche Widerstandsbewegung* (Stuttgart: Deutsche Verlag Anstalt, 1955), pp. 601-2. See also Leber, *op. cit.*, pp. 97 ff, and Rothfels, *op. cit.*, pp. 92 f.

[25] Leber, *op. cit.*, p. 97.

of trade-unionists could not be described accurately as a reactionary clique. The word "reactionary" seems reactionary in this context.

The Government

One of the first acts of the new Nazi government in 1933 was to remove from office all civil servants who were classified as "non-Aryan" or were known and outspoken opponents of the NSDAP. Key posts in civil service, and especially in the Ministry of the Interior, were filled by Nazi party members and each branch of the middle and lower bureaucracy was brought under the control of a cell of the party.[26] However, even after its accession to power, the Nazi party remained a minority group. According to its own theory, the party was to form an elite which was not permitted to exceed approximately 10 per cent of the general German population.[27] The leadership within the NSDAP was still smaller,[28] and so it was inevitable that many government posts, in fact the majority, had to remain in the hands of non-Nazis and even of silent anti-Nazis.

In 1939, of the approximately one and a half million civil servants in the German administration fewer than 30 per cent were members of the party. Of this number only about 8 per cent were of the party leadership, 7 per cent belonged to the SA (Storm Troopers), and 1 per cent to the SS.[29]

Since the Nazis concentrated on infiltrating the Ministry or the Interior and the fields of economics, information, and education, such ministries as War and Foreign Affairs were left relatively free of Nazi control. In these ministries especially the higher ranks of the bureaucracy contained very few party members.[30] It was in these departments that the nucleus of opposition developed. Bernhard von Bülow, the Secretary of State for

[26] Franz Neumann, *Behemoth* (London: Oxford Univ. Press, 1942), pp. 379-82.

[27] *Ibid.*, p. 82.

[28] Approximately 500,000 party members filled the posts of district leader, subdistrict leader, local leader, cell leader, and block leader. This can be considered the NSDAP hierarchy. *Ibid.*

[29] *Ibid.*, p. 379.

[30] *Ibid.*, p. 370.

Foreign Affairs, during the early years of the regime strove to prevent party infiltration of the Foreign Office [31] and was in a large measure successful. Many of the men later exposed as leading members of the anti-Hitler plot came from the Ministry of Foreign Affairs: Ulrich von Hassell, German ambassador to Rome until 1937; Ernst von Weizsäcker, Bülow's successor as secretary of state for foreign affairs and later ambassador to the Vatican; Erich Kordt, Weizsäcker's liaison officer to Ribbentrop; his brother Theodor, German chargé d'affaires in London who handled secret negotiations on behalf of the opposition movement with the British Foreign Office; Otto Kiep, former consul general in New York; Adam von Trott zu Solz, writer and member of Count Moltke's Kreisau Circle, who joined the Foreign Office as a cover for anti-Nazi activities; [32] Albrecht von Kessel, personal aide of Weizsäcker and his liaison officer of the Foreign Office resistance cell to the War Ministry; and of course many others.[33]

Government officials from other ministries also were involved in the resistance. Dr. Hjalmar Schacht was in contact with General Beck as early as 1936 in an attempt to co-ordinate military and civilian resistance in the hope of planning a coup d'état against Hitler.[34] Johannes Popitz, Prussian Finance Minister, was a member of the Wednesday Society [35] whose purpose, although overtly only cultural and philosophical, was the planning of intellectual resistance against Nazism. Although Popitz was not fully trusted by the other resistance leaders because he was a Nazi party member, he is credited with saving the lives of many individuals scheduled for arrest.[36]

Perhaps the best-known leader of the resistance to be recruited from government circles was Carl Friedrich Goerdeler, who served as mayor of Leipzig until he resigned in 1936 in protest against anti-Semitic demonstrations in his city. After that he became

[31] Rothfels, *op. cit.*, pp. 55 f.

[32] *Ibid.*, pp. 135 ff.

[33] More details about Foreign Office resistance are given, for example, in Ulrich von Hassell's, *Vom Anderen Deutschland* (Zurich: Atlantis Verlag, 1946).

[34] Rothfels, *op. cit.*, p. 57.

[35] Dulles, *op. cit.*, p. 27.

[36] *Ibid.*, pp. 90 f.

adviser to the Robert Bosch industries in Stuttgart and gradually assumed a leading position in underground opposition to the Nazis.[37] Goerdeler personally contacted the leaders of all segments of the opposition movement: businessmen, trade-unionists, Socialists, intellectuals, church leaders, aristocrats, government members, and the military. He maintained contact with friends abroad, in England, France, Sweden, Belgium, and in the United States; before the war he traveled incessantly and spoke freely and openly against the menace of National Socialism. It was he who became the leading theorist of the opposition; he drafted a proposed post-Nazi constitution, proposed peace terms, suggested a Cabinet for the interim between the overthrow of the Nazis and new elections. Although he was regarded as too conservative by many younger conspirators,[38] he was respected by all branches of the resistance for his sincere idealism, for his courage, and for his boundless energy. He was tried with many of the other key conspirators and executed by the Nazis in February, 1945.

Many civil servants and high government officials continued to maintain that party politics were not the proper concern of the bureaucracy, that loyalty to the state required loyalty to the government in power. Others preferred to concern themselves more with their personal lives or with their career advancement than with political opposition.

Despite this, the genuine anti-Nazi element within the government was sizable. This group was able to exploit its access to information, its contacts abroad, and its power to aid victims of the regime, to cover its anti-Nazi activities, and to plan realistically for the overthrow of Hitler, for the establishment of an anti-Nazi government, and for the negotiation of peace with the Allies. Together with the army, the government circles formed a large and significant element of the nucleus of the opposition.

The Army

The tradition of noninterference in political matters was even stronger in the German Army than in the German bureaucracy.

[37] *Ibid.*, pp. 85 ff. See also Ritter, *op. cit.*, in its entirety.

[38] See, for example, Rothfels, *op. cit.*, pp. 108 ff., and Leber, *op. cit.*, pp. 146 ff.

Contrary to the myth prevalent in the United States and elsewhere that the General Staff was the real directing force of German, and especially of Nazi German, policy, the German Army and its General Staff had never formulated policy for the German state. It had less influence than ever over the government under Hitler. Despite efforts by the Nazi party to infiltrate and dominate the officer corps, the army as a whole remained non-Nazi. No party activities were permitted among the troops and army recruits were not subjected to ideological indoctrination.[39]

By 1937 the civilian anti-Nazi circles began to talk about "the generals" because by then it was clear that no peaceful or legal change of government would be possible. If Hitler was to be overthrown, force would be required, and in an increasingly totalitarian state the only force independent of the party lay in the army. Colonel General Ludwig Beck, Chief of the General Staff from 1935 to 1939, was an early and sincere opponent of National Socialism. A deeply religious man, Beck opposed both the aims and the methods of the regime. As a military man he believed that Hitler's aggressive foreign policy would lead Germany into war and ultimately to disaster. Again and again he warned Hitler that he would turn all Europe against Germany, but his warnings were ignored and ridiculed. In 1939, when Hitler violated the Munich Pact which he had signed only a few months previously, Beck resigned in protest.[40] In retirement he became a key figure of the resistance movement, remaining in touch with army circles through his successor, General Halder, and evolving a system of liaison with all the various branches of the resistance. He exerted such moral influence and leadership that he was ultimately slated for the post of chief of state in the interim government to be established by the resistance after the overthrow of Hitler.[41] He was a prime mover in the unsuccessful assassination attempt against Hitler on July 20, 1944; he took his own life after the failure of that attempt.

It is impossible to mention here all or even a substantial number of the Wehrmacht officers who were members of the resist-

[39] Rothfels, *op. cit.*, p. 67.
[40] Foerster, Ein General Kämpft gegen den Krieg, pp. 24 ff.
[41] Ritter, *op. cit.*, pp. 602 f.

ance movement or even of those who participated actively in the plot of July 20. An official SS report lists approximately seven hundred officers who were executed as the result of implication in that attempt.[42] Countless other officers survived the failure of the plot and the subsequent terror. Fabian von Schlabrendorff gives a full account of Wehrmacht resistance in his work *Offiziere gegen Hitler,*[43] and the many other monographs on the opposition also emphasize the role of the army in all active plans to overthrow the Nazi government.

The army opposition circles included men of all ranks on all fronts of the war.[44] At the center of the movement, in addition to Beck, were garrison commanders such as Field Marshal Erwin von Witzleben, commanding officer of the Berlin garrison, and General von Brockdorff, of the Potsdam garrison, whose cooperation was vital to the success of any plan to arrest or assassinate Hitler. It would have been their duty to occupy the capital, to arrest members of the government, and to disarm the Gestapo and SS troops. Colonel Count Claus Schenk von Stauffenberg, the General Staff officer who after a serious injury was appointed Chief of Staff of the Home Army, was an uncompromising member of the resistance. It was Stauffenberg who carried the bomb to Hitler's staff meeting on July 20. He was executed in the courtyard of the War Ministry following the failure of the plot.

On the Western Front the opposition was represented by such men as General Count Heinrich von Stülpnagel, Commander of Paris, who participated fully in the activities of July 20 by arresting all leading Nazis and SS leaders within his command, and who paid for his actions with his life in August, 1944; by General Alexander von Falkenhausen, Military Commander of Belgium; Field Marshal Erwin Rommel and his adjutant and aide, General Hans Speidel and General Günther Blumentritt; and by Field Marshal Günther von Kluge. On the Eastern Front there were several centers of opposition but perhaps the best known is that led by Major General Henning von Tresckow, Chief of Staff of the Second Army, who had been responsible for a brilliant with-

[42] Quoted by Rothfels, *op. cit.,* p. 10, N.1.

[43] Edited by Gero von Schultze-Gavernitz (Zurich, 1947).

[44] It included many who were not professional soldiers but were in service only during the war.

drawal on the Central Russian Front in 1943. Tresckow's ordnance officer, Fabian von Schlabrendorff, and one of his company commanders, Count Fritz-Dietlof von der Schulenburg, acted as liaison between the resistance group on the Eastern Front and the other cells of resistance. Tresckow took his own life following the plot failure; Count Schulenburg was executed; Schlabrendorff was imprisoned and then released upon the Nazi collapse in 1945.

It cannot be contended that the Wehrmacht as a whole constituted an unequivocal opponent of the regime, certainly not enough commanders of key garrisons participated in the July 20 plot to make the assassination attempt successful. Of the officers who refused to join the opposition perhaps the two following were typical:

General Heinz Guderian, the famous Panzer commander, refused unequivocally to participate in the plot. He regarded the oath of loyalty to Hitler as morally binding. He would not violate it. He could not encourage fellow officers to violate it.[45] Although he was favorably impressed with the plans for postwar social reform of the Beck-Goerdeler group and although he had full confidence in the character and integrity of the opposition leaders, he felt that the plans to overthrow Hitler were impractical. Too few troop commanders were committed to the action, and the eventuality of public resistance and of possible civil war had been overlooked. He writes that, although the evils of the Nazi regime were "plain even to me," he could not endorse a plan which he believed would lead his nation to ultimate disaster. For Guderian, as for many other Wehrmacht leaders, the Allied policy of Unconditional Surrender was as an absolute barrier to any action which would undermine German military resistance and lead to total defeat at the hands of an enemy who demanded Germany's destruction.[46] He had two long and sympathetic discussions with Goerdeler, but he could not be persuaded to join the plans; instead, he urged that the group abandon their intent. Failing in this, he agreed to keep silent and in this he kept his word.[47]

[45] General Heinz Guderian, *Erinnerungen eines Soldaten*, pp. 300-1.
[46] *Ibid.*, p. 301.
[47] *Ibid.*

Colonel General Alfred Jodl, chief of the Operations Staff of the OKW, also had been informed of the work and aims of the resistance movement, and he too refused to align himself with the opposition. In a postwar evaluation he emphasized his respect for the motives and the integrity of Beck and Witzleben and other resistance leaders, but he restated his belief that the overthrow of Hitler at a critical stage of the war would have led to disaster.[48] In the first place, he contended that the brutalities of the SS and the Gestapo were unknown to the general public and even to the majority of Wehrmacht officers, therefore, a coup d'état by the resistance leaders would not be understood and might lead to civil war. Although by 1944 most high-ranking officers considered ultimate defeat inevitable, less well-informed younger officers and the public might attribute the defeat subsequent to a successful revolt to a "stab in the back" by a disloyal army. Jodl states that the policy of Unconditional Surrender had been the decisive element in his thinking. Had the Underground been able to arrive at a firm agreement with the Western Allies for a negotiated peace they might have won popular support for their position. If the enemy had demanded the overthrow of Hitler instead of the destruction of Germany, General Jodl states that he and many of his colleagues might have supported the plot; in such a case they would have been able to justify their act historically to the German people. Since the Western Allies had offered no such assurance or even encouragement, Jodl could not bring himself to support the resistance.[49]

The leaders of the civilian facets of the resistance were often impatient with the army. Ambassador von Hassell referred to some generals as "hopeless Sergeant Majors" and Kaiser, the trade-unionist, compared contemporary Wehrmacht leaders unfavorably with Scharnhorst, Gneisenau, and other morally courageous German soldiers of the past.[50] There is no question that many high-ranking officers wavered, hesitated, and compromised

[48] The Jodl *Memorandum* is presented in full in Appendix B.

[49] These views were expressed by Colonel General Alfred Jodl in a memorandum written in his cell in Nürnberg, supplied to the author by his widow, Luise Jodl.

[50] Rothfels, *op. cit.*, pp. 70 f.

concerning the moral and political issues involved. However, there is also no question that a core of German officers were unhesitant and courageous in their commitment, that hundreds of them were shot, hanged, or garroted in the days and months of terror which followed July 20, 1944.

THE PLANS OF THE RESISTANCE LEADERS

The Political Aims of the Anti-Nazi Opposition

Although the resistance movement embraced widely divergent groups which espoused widely divergent political views, all the non-Communist elements of the resistance were able to agree on certain broad principles. An interim program to form the basis for ruling Germany after a successful overthrow of Hitler was drafted by the Beck-Goerdeler cadre and was accepted in principle by many segments of the opposition. This program included the following major points:

1. The Nazi party would be outlawed and high-ranking Nazis would be removed from office. The most dangerous party leaders would be arrested.
2. The SS and Gestapo would be interned. Concentration camps would be taken over by the army, guards disarmed, commanders arrested, inmates screened, and released if they had been political prisoners.
3. Political meetings and mass demonstrations would be temporarily banned; Nazi party medals and uniforms would be forbidden.
4. All party property would be confiscated by the state, and party welfare activities would be absorbed by local government.
5. Those accused of war crimes would be interned for later trial under due process of law.
6. The major immediate goal of the new interim government would be the re-establishment of lawful government. A new constitution would be drafted which would provide for the rule of law, for the protection of individual liberties, and for an independent judiciary.

7. The interim government would include all shades of political opinion from monarchist to Socialist. Communists would be excluded.

This government would serve until peace could be arranged and until the danger of a Nazi counterrevolution was past, and then free elections would be held. All groups agreed that the new government must accept modern social principles, that victims of the Nazi regime must receive compensation, that education must be made available to citizens of all economic and social levels, and that the Free Trade-Unions should be re-established and strengthened. The details of these programs were to be decided after the interim period.[51]

The Beck-Goerdeler group drafted several lists of Cabinet members slated to assume control in Germany after a successful coup. These lists show that, although leadership of the interim government would be in the hands of conservatives, the parties of the left would also have been represented. In most of the drafts the political representation was about as follows: [52]

Chief of State	Conservative (Beck or Rommel)
Chancellor	Conservative (Goerdeler)
Vice-Chancellor	Trade-Unionist (Leuschner)
Deputy Vice-Chancellor ..	Catholic Trade-Unionist
Foreign Affairs	Conservative (Hassell)
Interior	Social Democrat
War	Wehrmacht Officer
Reconstruction	Catholic Trade-Unionist

The government which would have resulted from a successful overthrow of Hitler would have been predominantly conservative but it would certainly not have been the tool of a small clique of reactionary militarists. The Ministry of the Interior, including police, would have been in the hands of the Socialists and three posts would have been held by trade-unionists. In addition, even the most conservative of the oppositionists were so socially minded that, for example, they would probably have

[51] The plans are to be found in full in Ritter, *op. cit.*, pp. 567 f, and pp. 553 ff. See also Hassell, *op. cit.*, pp. 377 ff; Zimmermann and Jacobsen (eds.), *20, Juli 1944*, pp. 40 ff.

[52] Ritter, *op. cit.*, pp. 601-3, and Rothfels, *op. cit.*, p. 96.

been considered left of center had they expressed their views in the United States.

The Plans of the Resistance Movement to Overthrow Hitler

The many attempts of the anti-Nazi leaders to remove Hitler from office have been well recorded and need not be repeated here in detail; however, a brief summary of these attempts is essential to demonstrate the seriousness of the intentions of the opposition. The earliest of the plans dates back to the Sudetenland crisis in September, 1938. On that occasion the Beck-Goerdeler group hoped to use the threat of war as an occasion to arrest Hitler. Secretary of State for Foreign Affairs Baron Ernst von Weizsäcker, sent a secret message to the British government through the German chargé d'affaires in London, Theodor Kordt, requesting the British to take a strong stand against Hitler's demands for the Sudetenland. The opposition leaders believed that British refusal to compromise would precipitate a political crisis in Germany, that the Chief of the General Staff could then act with popular support in removing Hitler to prevent a war. The General Staff accordingly prepared the orders for the troop movements which would follow upon the arrest of Hitler. The date for the action was set for December 29. On September 28 Chamberlain and Daladier agreed to meet with Hitler at Munich. The first concrete plan ended in failure.[53]

From the outbreak of the war until July, 1944, there were at least six attempts against Hitler's power, including plans to shoot him, arrest him, and blow up his plane. In 1943 Fabian von Schlabrendorff placed a concealed bomb aboard the Führer's plane, but the bomb failed to explode; General von Tresckow and a group of his fellow officers on the Eastern Front determined to shoot Hitler on sight, but Hitler failed to revisit their headquarters. The conspirators decided that a more elaborate plan was needed.

Late in 1943 Colonel Count Claus von Stauffenberg conceived a new plan. A new infantry uniform with new equipment had

[53] See, especially, Rothfels, *op. cit.*, p. 61.

been designed for the Eastern Front which would be demonstrated for Hitler at his East Prussian headquarters. Since Goering and Himmler would also be present at this demonstration, it would present an excellent opportunity for a Putsch. Stauffenberg designed a plan which seemed foolproof: the officer in charge of the demonstration would carry a sufficient quantity of high explosives on his person to blow up himself and the Nazi leaders. Fritz von der Schulenburg found a volunteer for this assignment, a young officer from the Eastern Front, Captain Axel von dem Bussche-Streithorst, who met with Stauffenberg in Berlin in October and agreed to undertake the plan. The date for the demonstration was set but was postponed several times. Finally, at the end of November, Bussche was sent to East Prussia to await the arrival of the equipment. An air raid in Berlin destroyed parts of the new uniform and the explosive, and so once more the demonstration was postponed and Bussche returned to duty at the front. Shortly after Christmas he was again alerted, but once again there was a postponement. Captain Bussche returned to his regiment at the front and was severely wounded.

Another volunteer, Lieutenant Ewald von Kleist, agreed to take on the assignment and a date was set for February 11. Both Hitler and Himmler were to be present. At the last minute the demonstration was canceled and the plan had to be abandoned. Following the failure of the July 20 plot Lieutenant Kleist was arrested by the Gestapo. Captain Bussche, at that time still a patient in an army hospital, escaped arrest.[54]

After several failures the conspirators decided that a plan must be devised which did not depend on proximity to Hitler by virtue of a special occasion. Someone who had regular access to him must assassinate him. On July 1, 1944, Stauffenberg was appointed chief of staff of the Home Army and was, thereafter, occasionally required to attend conferences at Hitler's headquarters. From this time on Stauffenberg decided that he himself would carry out the assassination of Hitler. He made his attempt on July 20, 1944.

The date of the Putsch had depended on several factors. The

[54] Interview with Baron Bussche in Washington, D. C., April, 1957. See also FitzGibbon, *op. cit.*, pp. 70-74.

Beck-Goerdeler group had decided that they must wait until the Allies had achieved a decisive victory so that the German public would realize that eventual defeat was inevitable and that it had been the policy of Hitler and his government which had led Germany to defeat. On the other hand, they did not want to wait until the Allies had achieved so much success that they would no longer have anything to gain from a compromise peace settlement. By the end of March, 1944, Field Marshal Rommel and his staff in the West had been convinced that the time had arrived when Germany must make peace.[55] On June 17 Rommel had sent a message to Beck warning that the Normandy Front was in danger of imminent collapse, that if action was to be taken against Hitler it must be taken immediately.[56] By the first week in July Beck, Goerdeler, and Stauffenberg were preparing their final plan for the assassination.

The plan was carefully detailed.[57] Stauffenberg was to carry a bomb concealed in a briefcase into Hitler's staff meeting at headquarters in East Prussia. If possible, he was to choose a meeting at which Himmler and Goering, as well as Hitler, would be present. After depositing his briefcase under the table close to which Hitler would be standing, Stauffenberg would be called from the room to receive a telephone call from a coconspirator in Berlin. He would wait for the explosion, make sure of Hitler's death, and then inform the contact in Berlin. This would be the signal for *Operation Walküre,* the assumption of control by the resistance forces. General Fellgiebel, communications chief at the East Prussian headquarters and a member of the conspiracy, would cut off communications for at least two hours so that the Nazi survivors of the explosion could not contact their aides in Berlin or broadcast to the German people. In Berlin, Beck and his group would take over the High Command, reliable Wehrmacht troops would be deployed to the capital, ministries would be surrounded, and high-ranking party leaders would be arrested. The SS and Gestapo would be disarmed and the resistance

[55] Liddell Hart, *The Other Side of the Hill,* pp. 269 f.

[56] Wilmot, *The Struggle for Europe,* p. 369.

[57] See, especially, Fitz Gibbon, *op. cit.,* pp. 3-16, 65 ff., 154-213, and Schlabrendorff, *They Almost Killed Hitler,* pp. 109 ff.

leaders would proclaim a change of regime. On all fronts commanders friendly to Beck would arrest SS officers, Gestapo and security forces, and leading Nazis. The success of the plan and the lives of the conspirators depended on the smooth functioning of every phase of the operation, on the success of each detail.

After several delays the plan was implemented on July 20. At 12:42 on that date the bomb in Stauffenberg's briefcase exploded but failed to kill Hitler. July 20 was a warm day, and consequently all the windows had been open in the wooden barracks in which the conference was held. This may have weakened the force of the explosion. Nevertheless, the bomb exploded with sufficient force to demolish the barracks, to kill four officers, and to injure several others including Hitler and Jodl. Stauffenberg later said that the destruction was the equivalent to that of a direct hit by a 150-millimeter shell.[58] Stauffenberg assumed that Hitler must have been killed. He reported to Berlin that the Führer was dead and then returned by plane to Berlin. Fellgiebel cut communications.

In Berlin Beck and Witzleben and their military coconspirators took command of the War Ministry at the Bendlerstrasse. General Fromm, Commander of the Home Army, refused to co-operate and so he was disarmed and placed under arrest together with other pro-Hitler officers. The new army chiefs began to issue the orders for *Operation Walküre;* Wehrmacht troops under generals considered reliable to the conspiracy began to pour into Berlin. In Paris the conspirator General von Stülpnagel ordered his troops to arrest the security and Gestapo forces, high-ranking SS officers, and Nazi party officials. Only a single shot was fired by Stülpnagel's troops, no one was injured. By midnight of July 20 they had placed 1,200 top Nazis under arrest.[59]

In Berlin Wehrmacht troops surrounded government buildings and drew up their lines in front of SS barracks and Gestapo headquarters. Orders went out to every key city in Germany and to all German-occupied areas of Europe for similar army operations against the party's forces, but throughout Germany the re-

[58] FitzGibbon, *op. cit.*, p. 19.
[59] *Ibid.*, p. 205.

12 : 42 P.M. 7/20/44

sponses of troop commanders were dilatory and doubtful. Officers who were parties to the conspiracy urged and implored their commanders to act, but usually without success. In East Prussia General Fellgiebel was unable to prevent the re-establishment of communications between Hitler's headquarters and Berlin; Hitler got a message through to Goebbels informing him that he was alive and that he wanted to broadcast to the German people that night. Goebbels convinced the young major who had been sent to arrest him that Hitler was still alive and that the major was becoming involved in treason. Goebbels got Hitler on the telephone and let the young officer hear the Führer's voice. Instead of arresting Goebbels, the major turned his battalion against the rebellion. A few young officers loyal to Hitler recaptured the War Ministry on the Bendlerstrasse, released and rearmed Fromm and the other officers who had been interned, and then placed Beck and his coconspirators under arrest. General Beck was permitted to take his own life.[60] Count Stauffenberg and three other key conspirators were tried by Fromm in an *ad hoc* court-martial and were executed in the courtyard of the War Ministry by SS troops. The famous commando leader, Otto Skorzeny, arrived in Berlin, assumed command of the Berlin SS, and led the counterrevolution. The Gestapo began to round up the remaining resistance leaders, confiscate their papers and files, and a wave of arrests, of torture, and of executions followed.

The trial of the remaining major conspirators before the People's Court ended in August. Carl Goerdeler, Wilhelm Leuschner, Julius Leber, Count Peter Yorck von Wartenburg, Count Fritz-Dietlof von der Schulenburg, Adam von Trott zu Solz, and many other resistance leaders [61] were found guilty and were executed. Between July 20, 1944, and May, 1945, approximately five thousand men and women died for their complicity or alleged complicity in the unsuccessful plot. Many others were imprisoned. This final failure of *Operation Walküre* virtually ended organized anti-Nazi resistance in Germany.

!

[60] For further details see FitzGibbon, *op. cit.*, pp. 209 ff.

[61] This is by no means a complete list. For fuller details see Leber, *op. cit.*, or any other works on the Resistance.

THE EFFECTS OF UNCONDITIONAL SURRENDER ON THE RESISTANCE PLANS

The Attempts of the Resistance Nucleus to Negotiate with the Western Allies

Throughout the years of silent resistance the leaders of the German anti-Nazi opposition had made many attempts to negotiate with representatives of Allied governments to try to win support for their movement. Ever since the tense prewar years, agents of the resistance movement had maintained contact with English and American diplomats and laymen in neutral countries and especially in Rome through the unofficial good offices of the Vatican. In 1938 and 1939 Carl Goerdeler and Ulrich von Hassell engaged in frequent discussions with English and American officials and received unofficial encouragement but no official commitment. Goerdeler continued to correspond with friends in foreign countries and he made extensive visits to France, England, and the United States as long as that was possible. Hassell was in constant touch with Anglo-American diplomats in Rome, Berlin, and Switzerland.[62]

In 1939 Adam von Trott zu Solz, member of the Kreisau Circle and an official of the Foreign Office, visited friends and relatives in England and the United States under the cover of attendance at a meeting in Virginia of the Institute of Pacific Relations. During the course of this visit Trott arranged for two interviews with Messersmith, the American Assistant Secretary of State. He delivered to Messersmith a detailed memorandum which summarized the views of the German resistance leaders[63] on the question of the peace settlement that would follow the European war which had just begun and on America's role in influencing that settlement.

Briefly, Trott urged the United States to exploit its "tremendous authority" by sponsoring "a fair and durable peace settlement." He stated: "'America, not divided as we [in Europe] are by social and national boundaries, may well raise the standard of all peace

[62] Hassell, *op. cit.*, pp. 18, 20, 127 ff. See also Rothfels, *op. cit.*, pp. 132 ff.
[63] Presumably the Beck-Goerdeler group and the Kreisau Circle.

discussion above our complex prejudices of the past." He proposed that the United States, then neutral, use its influence to persuade the Allies, Great Britain and France, to issue a clear statement of their war aims. Such a statement at the beginning of the war would, he believed, serve two vital purposes: It would crystallize Allied policy at a time when the attitude of the public was rational and detached, when the passions inevitably aroused by war had not yet destroyed the possibility of announcing constructive and reasonable aims. It would also strengthen the hand and the enthusiasm of the anti-Nazi forces in Germany against the Nazi propaganda that the Allied aim was the destruction of the German state.[64]

The memorandum indicates that Trott was very likely of the view that the rise of Hitler and the outbreak of the Second World War had, to a large degree, been the result of the economic and political repercussions of the Versailles settlement. If his view was correct, if the Versailles Treaty and "the spirit of its application" had largely been responsible for National Socialism and for the war, then he suggested the peace settlement following the Second World War ought to "avoid all stimuli to a repetition of the aftermath of Versailles. Germany . . . should be granted a fair basis for national existence. Measures which might rekindle her persecution complex and supply new material for demagogues must be avoided." He warned that if this argument is accepted one must avoid plans for dividing Germany into separate states: "Never, in the long run, would the German people submit to forced partition." In this view a peace which would last must be based on radical departure from the "power politics" of the past and must rest on a thorough analysis of the underlying social and economic factors in the European situation which had been the genuine cause of both World Wars.[65]

The memorandum takes account of the fact that an opposing view of the situation is possible, that one can conclude from the resort of Germany to war that Germany "has now given final

[64] The entire document is published in "Adam Trott und das State Department," ed. by Hans Rothfels, *Vierteljahrshefte für Zeitgeschichte* (Stuttgart: Deutsche Verlags-Anstalt, July, 1959), pp. 322 ff.

[65] This is a free paraphrase from the memorandum.

proof of her inability to live on equal terms with other European states." Under this view the subsequent peace must "weaken Germany beyond hope of recovery," perhaps by dividing Germany into separate states. He recognized that the choice between the two opposing views of the war and of Germany lies in the hands of the Allies. He stated:

> The Allied Governments, and each Government which will participate directly or indirectly in any eventual settlement, must decide between the merits of those two points of view before they on their part approach the problem of peace terms.
>
> If the theory is accepted that Germany is bound to remain a nefarious element in the European family of nations, any proclamation of war aims on this basis can only do harm. Such an act can only contribute to the prolongation of the war. Even though the German people are increasingly opposed to the National-Socialist Government and embittered by its policies, it is clear that only a negligible minority of Germans will deny their support even to the present regime, if the preservation of the German nation is at stake.[66]

Should the Allies decide to depart from the philosophy of Versailles, Trott suggested: (1) a speedy end to the war; (2) the reduction of friction within Europe by a negotiated peace; and (3) the encouragement of intra-European co-operation. He continued:

> The extreme importance of a timely clarification of war aims derives not merely from the fact that it would reassure and consolidate opposition in Germany and thereby contribute to the discrediting and undoing of Nazi domination. It is of vital importance also for the future internal situation within the Allied states themselves.[67]

He warned that the Nazis were encouraging the popular German fear that the Allies intended to destroy Germany, that this fear "still holds the majority of Germans in the thrall of Nazi war measures so long as they appear to be the only means to national survival." He believed that if the Germans were assured that the overthrow of Hitler would enable them to secure "a tolerable position for Germany in a new Europe," this would provide the

[66] *Ibid.*, p. 323.
[67] *Ibid.*, p. 323.

German people "with a psychological prerequisite without which the instinct of national preservation must outrule even the most passionate urge to liberate themselves." However, if the German search for some alternative to Hitler is met with "continued vagueness and intransigence from the Western powers, their desperate hopes are bound to turn eastwards once more" and the dominance of Bolshevism in Europe might be the result.[68]

Trott was aware that the culmination of the promise of Wilson's Fourteen Points in the practice of the Versailles Treaty posed a problem, but he was certain that an explicit and unequivocal commitment to specific terms by the Allies endorsed by the moral prestige of the neutral United States would allay German skepticism.

Assistant Secretary of State Messersmith received Trott courteously and forwarded the memorandum to Secretary Hull and Undersecretary Welles. Although Messersmith records that he was personally favorably impressed with Trott and tended to regard him as "an honest man" he was of the opinion that "no person who is permitted to leave Germany and to return, as is true in the case of Mr. von Trott, can be entirely a free agent."[69] The files indicate that Supreme Court Justice Felix Frankfurter, who had known Trott at Oxford where Trott had been a Rhodes scholar, was extremely suspicious of him.[70] Rothfels, who has edited and interpreted these documents from the United States State Department files, writes that Frankfurter described Trott's friends in England as "certain 'clever' quarters in Oxford" and regarded them as appeasers.[71] Since it is true that Justice Frankfurter was a close and confidential adviser of President Roosevelt, it is very possible that his influence at least contributed to the suspicion which gradually dampened Roosevelt's initial interest in the plans and views of Trott and of the German resistance movement generally. Trott returned to Germany and continued his work with the resistance.

[68] *Ibid.*, p. 325.

[69] *Ibid.;* State Department memorandum dated Dec. 8, 1939.

[70] "Adam Trott and the State Department," p. 329, quoted from a memorandum from Messersmith to the Secretary and Undersecretary of State marked Strictly Confidential, dated Nov. 20, 1939.

[71] *Ibid.*, p. 320.

At the end of the same year, in December, 1939, the former Centrist Chancellor of Germany, Dr. Heinrich Brüning, visited the White House to appeal to President Roosevelt to give support to the anti-Nazi forces within Germany. Brüning reports that at first he found the President sympathetic and that he expressed interest in the anti-Nazi movement, but that he later changed his view and discouraged further contact with any anti-Nazi representatives, "apparently on the advice of men close to him." [72]

One of the reasons for this rebuff may have been the failure of early negotiations between the Allies and German oppositionists which took place under the auspices of the Vatican. At the beginning of 1940 negotiations had been initiated by German State Secretary von Weizsäcker without the knowledge of German Foreign Minister von Ribbentrop. Secret meetings between a German agent and the French Ambassador to the Holy See, Marshal Pétain, were arranged through the good offices of the Spanish Ambassador to the Vatican, Don José de Janguas. The details of these negotiations have not been released by the Vatican, but apparently the English as well as the French expressed interest in peace at this time.[73] These early negotiations collapsed after a meeting between Ribbentrop and Pope Pius XII in the Vatican in March, 1940. Ribbentrop informed the Pope that he would be interested only in an outright bid for peace from England and France and he confidently said that he expected to receive such an offer before the year was out.[74]

The official negotiations collapsed in the face of Ribbentrop's intransigence, but the unofficial efforts of the anti-Nazi opposition to win Allied encouragement continued. Two agents of the German Abwehr [75] who had been sent to Rome on official business pursued as well the unofficial business of the resistance; they were Dr. Josef Müller, a Munich lawyer, and Wilhelm Schmidhuber, former Portuguese Consul in Munich. Through Vatican channels they made contact with Sir Francis Osborne, English Minister to the Holy See, to inquire under what circumstances

[72] Rothfels, *op. cit.*, pp. 139 f.
[73] Konstantin Prinz von Bayern, *Der Papst*, pp. 112 f.
[74] *Ibid.*, pp. 117 f.
[75] The Abwehr was the intelligence branch of the Wehrmacht.

the British government would be willing to make peace with an anti-Nazi German government. The English reply was precise: the anti-Nazi German resistance movement must obligate itself to overthrow Hitler before the outbreak of the "hot war," they must prevent the implementation of the planned German offensive in the West. The German agents said that the resistance was strong enough to accomplish this if the Allied peace terms were favorable, and they committed their group to an immediate attempt against the Nazi government. When the coup did not occur immediately, the British warned that the time was running out. The launching of the German spring offensive against Norway and then France shattered English faith in the sincerity or, in any case, in the strength, of the German resistance and thereafter they were skeptical of further dealings with anti-Nazi agents. The Vatican circles, too, were angered and disappointed by the German failure to act.[76]

In July, 1943, Ernst von Weizsäcker, former German State Secretary, became German Ambassador to the Holy See. A former imperial naval officer, a diplomat of the old school and a conservative, Weizsäcker had always opposed the aggressive and stubborn policy of his chief, Ribbentrop. Although by July, 1943, Weizsäcker feared that it was already too late to achieve peace on the basis of reasonable terms from the enemy in return for the German overthrow of the Nazi government, he also believed that when Central Europe was destroyed it would then be too late for the Allies.[77] Through Vatican channels he made a specific proposal to the Allied commanders in Italy: he suggested that an anti-Nazi government in exile be established composed of German refugees living in England and the United States, that there should be no dictated peace, but rather a peace settlement negotiated with these unquestionably anti-Nazi Germans. Within a few days he had the Allied answer: "The highest political and military leaders of the Allied Occupation Army oppose this." The Allies rejected further negotiation.[78]

Independent of these efforts in Rome, other representatives of

[76] Konstantin von Bayern, *op. cit.,* pp. 120-23.
[77] *Ibid.,* pp. 149-52.
[78] *Ibid.,* p. 160.

the resistance had undertaken to contact the British government through the good offices of the Protestant Church. In May, 1942, two German pastors, Hans Schönfeld and Dietrich Bonhoeffer [79] met separately with the Bishop of Chichester in Sweden. Both pastors told the Bishop of the composition and the aims of the resistance and assured him that the opposition group had sufficient strength to overthrow the Nazis. They inquired regarding the attitude of the British government to an anti-Nazi Germany and asked whether the English would be prepared to negotiate with a succession government. They pointed out the extreme danger of the plot against a totalitarian regime and stressed the psychological importance of some assurance of Allied support. The pastors realized that Germany must atone for the evils of the Nazi period, that reparation must be made, but Bonhoeffer pleaded for a clear statement of Allied war aims and a commitment of Allied willingness to negotiate with an anti-Nazi German government.

Upon his return to London the Bishop of Chichester conferred with Eden, the Foreign Secretary, and gave him his account of the discussions with the German clergymen. Eden said that some of the information about the German opposition was already known to the Foreign Office, that peace feelers had already reached him from other neutral states. He reminded the Bishop that the British government was committed not to negotiate without the co-operation of the United States and the Soviet Union, but he promised to consider the question carefully. In July he wrote to the Bishop informing him that no action could be taken.[80]

As the war progressed, the possibility of a negotiated peace settlement grew less likely. The announcement of the Unconditional Surrender Formula in January, 1943, seemed to exclude all hope of an arrangement between the resistance movement and the Western Allies. Ambassador von Hassell had warned his coconspirators that the group must not wait until the inevitabil-

[79] Pastor Bonhoeffer was arrested after the July 20, 1944, failure and was murdered by the Gestapo in Flossenburg Concentration Camp in April, 1945. Leber, *op. cit.*, p. 190.

[80] Bishop of Chichester, *op. cit.*

ity of German defeat had become clear to the world or the chance for an acceptable peace would be lost.[81] As early as May, 1941, he had warned that, while at that time the English were still interested in a reasonable peace settlement, the time for such a settlement was running out.[82] Hassell reports that in December, 1942, he and his circle of friends still considered a negotiated peace a possibility, especially with England, but by January, 1943, he seemed to have lost hope. At that time he described as "very small indeed" the prospects for an agreement with the Allies for an acceptable peace. By August he seemed convinced that the Anglo-Americans had determined to destroy Berlin and to carry on the war to its ultimate end. He sent instructions to one of the resistance agents in Switzerland to stress to the Allies that the complete destruction of Germany would not serve either American or British interests in Europe, that "air bombardments such as that of Hamburg can only produce chaos." [83]

Apparently, however, Hassell and his friends received no encouragement from the Western Allies, and in the face of this adamant attitude even the conservative Hassell was tempted to think in terms of "an Eastern solution." He wrote:

> Actually a healthy European heart is in the interest of the East as well as the West. . . . I prefer the western orientation, but if necessary, I would also consider an agreement with Russia. . . . The fact that the Enemy does not seem to be treating Badoglio any better than Mussolini will not have an encouraging effect on our generals.[84]

Adam von Trott zu Solz, who after his return to Germany had resumed his work with the underground, visited Allen Dulles, the American intelligence chief in Switzerland and expressed similar discouragement with the Western attitude. He warned Dulles that the opposition was growing disheartened by the repeated failure to arrive at any agreement with England and the United States. He said that the German anti-Nazis were beginning to believe that the Anglo-Saxon governments were "filled with bourgeois prejudice and pharisaic theorizing" and that they, them-

[81] Hassell, *op. cit.*, p. 229.
[82] *Ibid.*, p. 204.
[83] *Ibid.*, pp. 283 ff., 287 f., 321.
[84] *Ibid.*, p. 321.

selves, were therefore seriously tempted to turn toward the East.[85] Basically, however, the German resistance forces were anti-totalitarian and had no illusions about the nature of Communism in the Soviet Union. Despite continued Anglo-Saxon indifference, the resistance agents continued their efforts to bring about an agreement with the British and Americans.

Throughout 1943 and until July, 1944, Dulles had frequent and repeated discussions with the representatives of the movement, and he regularly submitted detailed reports of these discussions to Washington. In April, 1944, Dulles reported to his superiors that the Beck-Goerdeler group represented the only possible opportunity of overthrowing Hitler because only they had both military force at their disposal and the facility of access to Hitler. He warned that the group was prepared to take action only if they could achieve some recognition from the Western Allies, that they did not want to deal directly with Moscow. He cited the recent Finnish surrender as a precedent: Finland had been at war with both the Soviet Union and Great Britain but had surrendered only to the U.S.S.R. The German group wished to surrender only to Great Britain and the United States in order to prevent Central Europe from coming under Russian control. Soviet domination, they feared, would destroy Christian culture and personal freedom in Europe; the Nazi dictatorship would have been overthrown in exchange for a new Communist dictatorship. In order to achieve this surrender on one front, the commanders in the West would be willing to facilitate Anglo-Saxon landings in France; Allied paratroops might also be landed in key points throughout Germany; resistance would be continued in the East.[86]

During the same month, April, 1944, Adam Trott warned Dulles that Communist propaganda was receiving a wide audience among the German laborers. The more hopeless the German workers became the greater would be the danger of the growth of Communism among their ranks. He suggested that the Allies address a series of appeals to the German workers promising at least local self-government and freedom of trade-unionism. He

[85] Dulles, *op. cit.*, pp. 131 f.
[86] *Ibid.*, pp. 130-36.

further suggested that leaflets be dropped to the German workers and that contact be inaugurated between the Allied governments and German Socialist leaders to counterbalance the contact between the U.S.S.R. and German Communists.[87] Trott made several other similar suggestions which proved equally fruitless.

The following month another courier of the resistance movement, Hans Bernd Gisevius, approached Dulles with a renewed request for surrender in the West and with assurances that the German military commanders on the Western Front and in Berlin would co-operate fully. Since Dulles could offer the group no commitment on behalf of his government, Gisevius was instructed by the resistance leaders to "take no further action." [88]

Despite the consistent Allied rejection of every bid for an agreement, Trott made one final attempt at the end of June, 1944, in Stockholm. For the last time he contacted Anglo-American representatives to inquire whether the Allies intended to pursue their demand for unconditional surrender, whether this demand might not be modified to permit an opposition government to establish control throughout Germany before the initiation of an Allied military occupation. He said that many members of the opposition felt that they would be unable to accept the responsibility of an internal armed rising in the face of the unremitting Allied demand for unconditional surrender. They felt further that the anti-Nazi movement as a whole must not allow itself to be maneuvered into the position of a quisling government, appointed by the victor powers, acting as their puppets and regarded as traitors by the bulk of the German public. This they felt might be the case if no agreement could be reached with the Allies before the coup d'état or if Allied armies were to occupy Germany and later appoint anti-Nazis to local control.[89]

The final inquiry, the final appeal, received the same inflexible reply given to all previous inquiries. The Allied powers could offer no encouragement or make no commitment to the German opposition forces. Although Prime Minister Churchill had per-

[87] *Ibid.*, pp. 137-38.
[88] *Ibid.*, p. 139.
[89] Reported in the English periodical *The Week*, Sept. 15, 1944, "Inside Germany."

suaded President Roosevelt not to issue the statement that "the United Nations would never negotiate an armistice with the Nazi Government, the German High Command, or any other group or individual in Germany," this in effect remained American policy and apparently the British were willing, or were compelled, to follow suit. The policy of Unconditional Surrender applied to anti-Nazi as well as Nazi Germany.

The Reaction of the Allies to the Negotiation Attempts of the German Anti-Nazi Resistance Movement

There was apparently a split in the Anglo-American alliance regarding the German opposition. Let us examine this briefly:

Churchill and the English

Throughout the war years and until July, 1944, the leaders of the German resistance tended to regard Churchill as their most likely ally in the search for an agreement with the West to end the war on terms other than Unconditional Surrender. It is possible that Prime Minister Churchill personally inclined toward such a commitment, that he would have been happy to see a stable and anti-Nazi government in Germany, that he would have preferred a negotiated peace which would have preserved some remnant of German strength to act as a counterweight against the rising tide of Communism in Europe. In any case, before the outbreak of the war, before Churchill had become prime minister, he had indicated that he would have welcomed a step by the "peace-loving and moderate forces in Germany, together with the chiefs of the German army" to re-establish "sane and civilized" conditions in that country.[90]

In January, 1942, Ulrich von Hassell's diary records a conversation with an agent of the resistance who had just returned from England. Although the agent had warned that hatred for Germany had become "almost pathological" among the English upper classes and said that any negotiation or compromise with Nazi Germany was unthinkable, he believed that in government circles in England, especially in those circles around Churchill

[90] Quoted in Rothfels, *op. cit.*, p. 130, from the (London) *Times*, Oct. 17, 1938, p. 16, col. 2.

and at the court, the idea was gaining ground that an arrangement with a decent Germany must be made. The agent said that the English of these circles kept inquiring about "the generals." In answer to their inquiry concerning the peace terms that at that time the anti-Nazi Germans would consider reasonable, the agent reported that the British seemed to regard a request for a return to the 1914 imperial boundaries (presumably in the East) as modest.[91]

In November, 1943, Hassell again records a report of Churchill's interest in the resistance movement. At that time Goerdeler had assured Hassell that Churchill had made an authentic statement to the effect that, although he could not make a prior commitment to the opposition, he believed that "a practicable way could be found" in the event of a successful overthrow of the Hitler government.[92] In December of 1943 Hassell again records Goerdeler's report that Churchill had instructed an agent to say that he would "look with benevolent interest" upon a new regime in Germany.[93]

In July, 1944, the opposition received faint encouragement from a statement by Clement Attlee in the House of Commons to the effect that a new Allied view of the German situation would depend on the action taken by the Germans to rid themselves of their criminal government. Churchill also publicly recommended that the Germans overthrow the Nazi government, thus encouraging the opposition to continue to hope that they might win his more definite support.[94]

However, after the failure of the July 20 assassination attempt Churchill joined with Roosevelt and the Anglo-American press, as well as with the Nazis, in disparaging the plot. He referred to the attempted revolution as a case of the highest persons in the German Reich "murdering each other." [95]

The U.S.S.R.

The policy of the Soviet Union differed markedly from that of the Western Allies. As early as 1943 the leaders of the German

[91] Hassell, *op. cit.*, p. 249.
[92] *Ibid.*, p. 325.
[93] *Ibid.*, p. 334.
[94] Dulles, *op. cit.*, p. 141.
[95] Rothfels, *op. cit.*, p. 152.

resistance were aware of the fundamental split between East and West regarding policy toward Germany. Stalin was careful not to associate himself with the repeated Western demands for unconditional surrender, and instead he publicized his Free Germany Committee.

Some of the Socialists and other less conservative members of the opposition began to insist, after 1943, that since no commitment seemed to be forthcoming from the Anglo-Americans, they should turn their attention to the East.[96] The Soviets actively encouraged this attitude: captured German officers broadcast regularly over the Russian radio appealing to German troops to surrender, the Soviets made earnest attempts to indoctrinate German prisoners of war in Communist ideology, and Moscow sought to encourage the German resistance by speedy recognition of the Badoglio government in Italy in advance of the Anglo-Americans. In June of 1944 the German Officers' Committee in Moscow appealed to the Germans to defend themselves against the Western invasion but to surrender in the East to prevent the Anglo-American domination of Europe.[97]

While the Western radio continued to broadcast demands for unconditional surrender and while the Anglo-American air forces continued around-the-clock saturation bombing of German cities, Moscow radio made the following appeal:

> The Soviet Union does not identify the German people with Hitler. . . . Our new Germany will be sovereign and independent and free of control from other nations. . . . Our New Germany will place Hitler and his supporters . . . before the judgment of the people, but it will not take revenge on the seduced and misguided, if, in the hour of decision, they side with the people. . . . Our aim is: a free Germany. . . . For people and for Fatherland. Against Hitler's war. For immediate peace. For the salvation of the German people.[98]

Adam Trott warned Dulles that, while constructive plans for rebuilding Germany after the war were continually emanating from the Soviet Union, the West demanded only destruction and

[96] Hassell, *op. cit.*, p. 321, and Gisevius, *To the Bitter End,* pp. 280 f.
[97] Hassell, *op. cit.*, pp. 347, 351.
[98] Dulles, *op. cit.*, p. 171.

that this was causing a gradual drift toward Communism among the German masses. He urged the Western powers to fill the vacuum created by the negative demand for unconditional surrender by a concrete statement of war aims.[99]

The Soviet promises of a constructive peace settlement were not policy but propaganda. Genuine Soviet policy toward a defeated Germany was reflected in the demands made by Stalin at Teheran and Yalta: annexations, partition, expulsion of millions of German-speaking inhabitants, mass trials, reparations, and forced labor. The reassuring propaganda was simply an instrument of war, an outright lie. But it was a well-timed lie, a lie which filled the gap of desperation produced by the negative propaganda from the West. The Soviets continued this line of propaganda until they arrived in Berlin. The rape and plunder of that city took place beneath placards proclaiming Stalin's statement: Hitlers come and go, but the German people and the German state remain.

At the time of the July 20 plot, Moscow radio broadcast a tribute to the resistance by the captured General Seydlitz:

> The die has been cast. Courageous men rose against Hitler. They have thus given the signal for the salvation of Germany. The power which Himmler holds can be taken from him only by the German people. . . . Generals, officers, soldiers! Cease fire at once and turn your arms against Hitler. Do not fail these courageous men.[100]

The Soviet Union missed no opportunity to attempt to exploit the anti-Nazi resistance as a weapon in their effort to destroy Nazi Germany and to bring Communism to Central Europe. It was only the fundamental opposition of the majority of oppositionists to any form of totalitarianism that prevented an agreement which might have proved disastrous to the Anglo-Americans.

The United States

The United States was probably the source of the Western attitude toward the anti-Nazi resistance. While Moscow was hail-

[99] *Ibid.*, p. 137.
[100] *Ibid.*, pp. 172 f.

ing the July 20 uprising, the official attitude in Washington and London was indifference and skepticism. Churchill commented cynically about the mutual murder of high-ranking Germans; Washington scarcely commented. Official American policy denied the existence of a genuinely anti-Nazi German resistance movement and, despite the flow of reports of American intelligence agents to the contrary, American propaganda described the German opposition forces, when they were referred to at all, as a small clique of reactionaries and militarists.[101] Roland Freisler, notorious judge of the People's Court before whom the key conspirators were tried after July 20, 1944, was able to taunt the defendants whom he was about to sentence to death with a quotation from a Western propaganda leaflet concerning the plot: "those who co-operated, those who engineered it, all of them are not worth anything. At best, they had a perverted love of Germany!"[102]

Perhaps this hostility dates back to the suspicions aroused by Trott's visit to Washington. In any case, official American policy ignored the German resistance and attempted to prevent the circulation of information concerning the size, the scope, and the aims of the movement. Throughout the war and in the immediate postwar period, the subject of the German anti-Nazi movement was taboo in American political thinking. President Roosevelt refused any official dealing with the movement and preferred not to hear of it.

Louis P. Lochner, former chief of the Berlin office of the Associated Press, had occasion to experience Roosevelt's attitude on this subject. In Berlin in November, 1941, Lochner had been invited to attend a meeting of the steering committee of the Beck-Goerdeler group. He had been introduced to some of the movement's leading figures. They had explained to him their aims and ideals and had requested him to approach President Roosevelt to inquire what sort of anti-Nazi government would be acceptable to the United States. After his return to the United

[101] Regarding American propaganda vis-à-vis Germany, it is perhaps significant that this propaganda emanated from the German section of the Office of War Information which was then headed by Gerhard Eisler, Communist party member who later defected to East Germany.

[102] Dulles, *op. cit.*, p. 173.

States in June, 1942, Lochner attempted to secure an appointment with the President. After five attempts he put his request in writing. He received a reply which indicated that the entire subject was "most embarrassing" and requesting him to drop the matter.[103]

Toward the end of 1944, when Lochner visited Paris as a war correspondent, he discovered that a group of anti-Nazi Germans living in Paris maintained contact with their group in Germany, that they often sent agents into Germany. He considered this an excellent news story and wanted to publish an account of it, but the report was censored. He took up the matter with the chief censor at SHAEF, questioning how such a story would violate American or Allied security. He was told that there was a special regulation, "a personal one from the President of the United States in his capacity of Commander in Chief, forbidding all mention of any German resistance." Lochner comments:

> Stories of a resistance movement did not fit into the concept of Unconditional Surrender. My belief that President Roosevelt was determined to establish the guilt of the entire German people, and not only the Nazi regime, for bringing on World War II had already received confirmation in the summer of 1942.[104]

The policy of silence was effective. The memoirs of American statesmen and military leaders of the period of the Second World War contain sparse reference to an anti-Nazi resistance movement. For example, Admiral Leahy, Roosevelt's personal chief of staff, seemed to have been uninformed on the subject. A note in his diary dated October 12, 1943, reports that he heard from Lisbon that "some high-ranking German Generals" were planning a revolution in Germany. He commented that "if there were any truth in this it would mean that some of the German military officials had become convinced that they would lose the war and were trying to save Germany from destruction." [105] Despite this limited view of the aims of the resistance, Admiral Leahy seems to have favored a compromise with this German group on the

[103] Rothfels, *op. cit.*, p. 139. Confirmed in an interview with Mr. Lochner in Fair Haven, N. J., April, 1958.

[104] Lochner, *Always the Unexpected*, pp. 294 f.

[105] Leahy, *I Was There*, p. 188.

grounds that peace with Germany would have freed American forces to deal with Japan, a task he regarded as more vital to United States' interests.[106] Leahy's view, of course, did not prevail.

On July 21, 1944, Leahy reported having read in the press about "a considerable revolt in Germany." He commented that apparently this heralded the disintegration of German military morale and that a surrender of the Nazis might be expected soon afterward.[107]

Admiral Leahy's comments indicate that he had not been informed of the American intelligence reports on the German anti-Nazi movement. The memoirs of many other American generals and diplomats seem to indicate even less knowledge of the movement, or less attention to it. Perhaps this was because the official policy was one of silence. After the war the policy of silence continued: the American occupation forces in Germany imposed censorship on anti-Nazi as well as on Nazi literature. In the summer of 1946 a former inmate of a concentration camp failed to secure permission to publish an article on the role of workers in the July 20 plot. Radio stations in the United States Zone of Occupation of Germany were forbidden to mention the existence of an opposition movement or any attempts to assassinate Hitler.[108] The policy remained one of silence. It is therefore not startling that American policy had rejected any commitment to the resistance agents, that Allen Dulles had received no encouragement from Washington in his negotiations in Zurich.

What was the effect of this policy of nonrecognition, of nonencouragement, on the strength and vitality of the anti-Nazi movement within Germany?

The Effect of the Policy of Unconditional Surrender on the German Anti-Nazi Resistance Movement

None of the leaders of the German opposition has left a clear-cut analysis of the effect of the Western refusal to negotiate, refusal to agree to any specific commitment on the strength and

[106] *Ibid.*
[107] *Ibid.*, p. 249.
[108] Rothfels, *op. cit.*, pp. 21 f.

efficacy of their movement, but many of them have mentioned Unconditional Surrender. The Casablanca Formula and the policy it represented may have influenced the resistance in several ways: it may have undermined the will and the morale of dedicated anti-Nazis; it may have weakened the resonance of the anti-Nazi movement with the masses of the German people; and it may have deterred certain non-Nazis, and especially military leaders, from joining the opposition. Baron Schlabrendorff has suggested that the effect of Unconditional Surrender must be weighed in these three separate categories: its effect on the Nazis, on the non-Nazi general public, and on the anti-Nazi resistance forces.[109] Let us accept these categories and examine each in turn.

Effect on the Nazis

To the Nazis the slogan was a godsend. In the first place, men like Hitler and Goebbels had no difficulty in understanding the psychology of such a categorical slogan. The identification of all Germans with a single party represented a philosophy which must have been familiar to them: Nazi attitude toward Jews and Slavs was similar, and similarly uncompromising.

In the second place, the phrase was ready-made for Goebbels. He soon twisted "Unconditional Surrender" into "Total Slavery." [110] Again and again he warned the German people that the price of military defeat would be the destruction of Germany and the enslavement of the German nation. In his diary he congratulated himself on the fact that the Allies had devised no compelling peace slogan such as Wilson's Fourteen Points.[111] He welcomed the Allied statements about drastic war aims:

> These press commentaries suit us exactly. Nothing better could happen to us than to have the English . . . openly proclaim their intention to destroy Germany completely, that is, not only the Nazi regime, but the entire German people.[112]

[109] Letter from Fabian Freiherr von Schlabrendorff to the author dated April 8, 1950. Confirmed in a letter dated July 26, 1960.

[110] Dulles, *op. cit.*, pp. 131 f.

[111] *The Goebbels Diaries: 1942-43* (ed., trans., and with an intro. by Louis P. Lochner) (New York: Doubleday, 1948), p. 47.

[112] *Ibid.*, p. 92.

He rejoiced in the speeches and writings of Vansittart:

This fellow Vansittart is really worth his weight in gold to our propaganda. After the war a monument ought to be erected to him somewhere in Germany with the inscription, "To the Englishman who rendered the greatest service to the German cause during the war." [113]

He considered every Allied threat to destroy Germany grist for his propaganda mill and "music for our ears."

The more radical the English are in prophesying a disgraceful peace for Germany, the more easily I succeed in toughening and hardening German resistance. We'd be in a dangerous fix now if British propaganda from the beginning of the war . . . had respected the German will to live and the German concept of honor. That's how Chamberlain began on the first day of the war. Thank God the English did not continue along that line. Even though we would always try to discredit them by citing 1918 as an example, they would, nevertheless, find foolish adherents here and there, especially since the domestic situation becomes more strained the longer the war lasts.[114]

The *Völkischer Beobachter* of April 12, 1943, stated the official Nazi view of Unconditional Surrender: "The Axis has conducted this war from the beginning not to achieve a compromise solution." It warned that such a compromise would only lead to a third and still more destructive world war by the enemy.

The Enemy at Casablanca proclaimed the Unconditional Surrender of the Axis and made it clear that their aim must be the total destruction of the German, Italian, and Japanese peoples. It goes without saying that great people acknowledge only one unequivocal answer to such an infamy: the total mobilization of all the vital forces they possess to achieve their victory.[115]

In June the newspaper repeated the theme:

Churchill and Roosevelt since Casablanca speak incessantly of the "unconditional surrender" of the Axis, but this new trumpet of Jericho will not blow down any walls. The fanfares are only the signal for an embittered struggle for the defeat of an enemy which proclaims

[113] *Ibid.*, p. 342.
[114] *Ibid.*, pp. 144-45.
[115] Munich ed., lead editorial, "Kompromisslos," by Dr. W. Koppen, p. 1.

the destruction and enslavement of great and free peoples and is prepared to throw Europe to Bolshevism.[116]

On August 8, 1943, the *Völkischer Beobachter* declared that the same forces which had been responsible for the destruction of the possibility of peace by the Treaty of Versailles in 1919 now spoke of Unconditional Surrender "so that their crimes can be repeated tenfold." It pledged, however, that the world would be spared a demonstration of this experiment, that after this war the peace-making would be reserved to "cleaner and stronger hands."[117]

Again on August 19, 1943, the editorial warned that the war aim of the enemy was not the overthrow of the regime or a change in the internal structure of Germany but rather the destruction of Europe,[118] and on August 28:

Dishonor, mass murder, suffering and total helplessness—this is the least that is inherent in the shameless demand of Churchill and Roosevelt for Unconditional Surrender.[119]

There is no question that Propaganda Chief Goebbels, who knew his Germans and was a master of the art of propaganda, believed that, had the Allies made it clear that their intention was to destroy National Socialism and punish only those directly responsible for its crimes but that they had no desire to punish or to enslave the German people as a whole, had they instead appealed to the honor and decency of the German people and exhorted them to overthrow their Nazi leadership, this would have caused great internal dissension and unrest.[120] Goebbels wrote that, had the Allies been able to arrive at a clever propaganda slogan along these lines and had they repeated it consistently, "we would face great difficulties every time we were

[116] *Ibid.*, lead editorial, "Hass gegen Hass," by Dr. W. Koppen, June 25, 1943, p. 1.

[117] *Ibid.*, lead editorial Dr. W. Koppen, "Unser Weg," Munich ed., p. 1.

[118] Helmut Sündermann, "Das Kriegziel unserer Feinde," *ibid.*, Munich ed., p. 1.

[119] "Das Kriegziel unserer Gegner: Weltdiktatur mit der Hungerpeitsche," *ibid.*, Munich ed., p. 1.

[120] *Ibid.*, derived from the editorial note by Louis P. Lochner, p. 145.

under a new, heavy strain." [121] He thanked God that the British and Americans did not pursue this course. He considered it his task to keep the German people convinced, "as indeed the facts warrant, that this war strikes at their very lives and their national possibilities of development, and they must fight it with their entire strength." [122]

Each time the Allied press issued some new demand against postwar Germany, such as reparations, forced labor, or the Morgenthau Plan, Goebbels rejoiced. He called the reparations demanded by the Moscow Conference

> so insane that one can vividly imagine the threat against us . . . if we were to weaken. I am having these . . . demands published prominently in the German press. The German people should realize clearly what fate is in store for us in case of defeat.[123]

He said that the plan to use German labor in the Soviet Union "will frighten our people":

> Demands like that are wonderful for our propaganda. They stir German public opinion deeply. The idea that our soldiers might not return home at all but might have to remain in the Soviet Union as forced labor is a terrible thought for every wife and every mother. The German people would prefer to fight to their last breath.[124]

Goebbels greeted the announcement that the Morgenthau Plan had been approved at the Second Quebec Conference with banner headlines in the *Völkischer Beobachter:* "Morgenthau surpasses Clemenceau: 'Forty Million Germans Too Many': Roosevelt and Churchill accept the Jewish Murder plan at Quebec." [125] He quoted American and English newspaper articles to the effect that the proposed plan for converting Germany into a purely agrarian and pastoral economy would require the reduction of the German population by about forty millions and that if the deindustrialization were forced and were implemented suddenly,

[121] *Ibid.*, p. 147.

[122] *Ibid.;* see also pp. 197, 227, 325 and 510.

[123] *Ibid.*, p. 510.

[124] *Ibid.*, p. 519.

[125] *Völkischer Beobachter*, Vienna ed., No. 268, Sept. 26, 1944; similar articles in the same publication, Sept. 26 and 29, 1944, and in the *Hamburger Fremdenblatt*, No. 22, Sept. 26, 1944.

the surplus population would simply starve. He said that an article had, in the London *Spectator,* described as only right that Germany should be crippled for all time, even if this would require that German women and children starve. Goebbels concluded that the German people had always been aware that a fanatical desire to destroy Germany was present among private circles in America and England and that this attitude had been exploited for propaganda purposes. Now, however, he stated, this attitude had been accepted as actual public policy.[126] The implied conclusion was that Germany clearly had no choice but to fight to the end. There was no preferable or acceptable alternative.

Hitler himself echoed this view. In the summer of 1944 he told his closest advisers that "in this war there can be no compromise, there can only be victory or destruction. And if the German people cannot wrest victory from the enemy, then they shall be destroyed." He added that "then they deserve to perish. . . . Germany's end will be horrible, and the German people will have deserved it." [127] Shortly before the launching of the last German counteroffensive in the Ardennes in December, 1944, Hitler told his army commanders that Germany stood in a fateful position between the East and the West:

> If Germany loses, it will have proved itself biologically inferior and will have forfeited its future existence. It is the West that forces us to fight to the last. However, it will transpire that the winner will not be the West, but the East.[128]

To the totalitarian Nazi mentality the war was one of existence for the entire German nation as well as for themselves and their ideology. The Western enemy reinforced this view by its announced war aims and by the repeated demand for unconditional surrender. A war for survival demands the exploitation of every available means of defense. A war of survival waged by a nation of 80,000,000 against a coalition in which the population of only the three major opponents exceeds 400,000,000, a nation whose

[126] *Ibid.*

[127] Reported by Walter Schellenberg, Nazi secret service chief, in his *Memoirs,* pp. 375-76.

[128] *Ibid.,* p. 376.

industrial potential is far outweighed by the combined productive capacity of its chief opponents, soon becomes a war of desperation. After the Goebbels proclamation of Total War at the Sportspalast in Berlin on February 18, 1943, the entire German economy, the entire German nation was mobilized for all-out war; from that time on no consideration was given to any argument except that of victory. Defeat meant total destruction. Victory required total effort, Total War with no holds barred. The Total End justified Total Means.[129]

The Nazis intensified their war effort. As the sense of desperation increased, the power and the fanaticism of the party-government increased. The numbers of arrests and executions mounted, the atmosphere of terror intensified. It was in the final years of the war that the campaign against the Jews became one of extermination, that resistance in occupied territories was met with unmitigated repression. The war of survival and of desperation became war *à outrance.*

Effect on the General Public

The reaction of the German public in general to the call for unconditional surrender is certainly difficult, if not impossible, to measure. Some facts are clear. Despite the increasing severity of economic and military circumstances, despite around-the-clock bombing and the consequent devastation of German cities, despite the constant news of battlefront and home casualties and of military defeats, despite the terror waged by the Gestapo, the German people continued to obey the law, to work at their assigned posts, to fulfill their duty. There was no open revolt, no measurable lowering of morale. During the period of greatest devastation, the final quarter of 1944, German war production reached its peak.[130]

Schlabrendorff writes that during the early years of the war many private German citizens had begun to distinguish between the cause of National Socialism, on the one hand, and the fate of Germany, on the other, but that the pronouncement of the Un-

[129] For details of the total mobilization orders see Max Seydewitz, *Civil Life in Wartime Germany*, pp. 232 ff.

[130] Fuller, *The Second World War: 1939-45*, p. 226.

conditional Surrender demand had compelled them to conclude that the Allies were not willing to make this distinction, but instead threw all Germans into one pot with the Nazi party. Therefore, they felt that they had no choice but to continue to fight in defense of their country.[131] He concludes that many private German citizens who might otherwise have thrown in their lot with the opposition circles were disillusioned by the negative demands of the Allies:

> I am . . . convinced that the theme "Unconditional Surrender" had an exclusively negative effect on the various groups of the German people. On the other hand, the prospect of an honorable peace would have dealt a death blow to National Socialism in Germany forever.[132]

Effect on Anti-Nazis

There is no question that the insistence by the Western powers on Unconditional Surrender even in the event of a successful overthrow of the Nazis was a serious deterrent to the growth and the morale of the opposition movement, even to the inner core of the conspiracy. Hassell said that the policy of the Anglo-Americans in identifying all Germans with Hitler destroyed every reasonable chance for peace.[133] The persistent attempts of the underground to make contact with Western agents and to secure some sort of prior agreement concerning peace terms before launching their attempt against the Nazi regime indicate how serious a factor they considered such an agreement. Again and again Goerdeler and his representatives requested at least a tentative commitment or some substantial indication of encouragement. Consistently such a commitment, such encouragement was refused. There is little question that this failure on the part of the underground leadership to secure a commitment weakened their negotiations with non-Nazis. General Guderian and Colonel General Jodl specifically cited this lack of an Allied promise of honorable peace terms as a major reason for refusing to join the plot. Whether or not this was in fact their major reason, the unmitigated insistence of the Allies on Unconditional Surrender pro-

[131] Letter from Baron Schlabrendorff previously cited.
[132] *Ibid.*
[133] Hassell, *op. cit.*, p. 219.

vided an eloquent excuse. Field Marshal Fritz Erich von Manstein states unequivocally that a coup d'état by the military leaders as a whole would have been thinkable only if previous assurance of acceptable peace conditions had been extended by the Allies. He believes that the chances of success of the assassination attempt of July 20 would have been entirely different if the demand for unconditional surrender had not been proclaimed, if there had been the prospect for undertaking immediate peace negotiations with a likelihood of achieving honorable conditions.[134]

During the actual unfolding of the tragedy of July 20 the phrase "Unconditional Surrender" again appeared as the Leitmotif of failure. One of the crucial points of *Operation Walküre* was the program to be carried out on the Western Front in France. One of the most crucial figures in the plan was the Commander in Chief on the Western Front, Field Marshal von Kluge. Kluge was sympathetic to the plot. He was an old associate of General Beck and of General von Tresckow, but Kluge was a man of caution and of vacillation. At the critical moment, during the evening of July 20, he hesitated. His aides argued and cajoled, attempting to persuade him to back the plot unequivocally and to undertake immediate negotiations with General Eisenhower for capitulation in the West. He hesitated.

Constantine Fitz Gibbon writes:

> Kluge was within an ace of declaring himself and his armies for Beck. It is at this point of time that one cannot help wondering what would have happened if the Western Allies had, in the past, given the conspirators the slightest encouragement. The balance, in Kluge's headquarters, was tipped now, though only slightly, in favour of revolt against Hitler and surrender to the West. Had there been any positive offer, or even any clear statement of Western aims, would not Kluge now have taken an irrevocable step? If there had been, for instance, some means arranged by which Kluge could get in touch with the Allied Command in Normandy, might he not now have used it, if only to inform Field Marshal Montgomery that he proposed stopping the discharge of V-1s? [135]

[134] Letter from Field Marshal von Manstein to the author, June 2, 1953.
[135] Fitz Gibbon, *op. cit.*, p. 198.

He goes on to speculate what the effect on the final outcome might have been if such a means of communication had existed. Without such means, Churchill remained uninformed of the historic developments; had he known he might have seized the initiative in the situation. No plans for such an eventuality had been made, no machinery had been established, no promises had been extended. Kluge vacillated and finally decided against the conspirators.[136]

Schlabrendorff writes that the slogan of Unconditional Surrender was "especially painful" to the German anti-Nazis. It seemed to indicate that the Western powers intended to destroy anti-Nazis as well as Nazis. Since this was so, he said, many anti-Nazis believed that it was foolish to attempt overt action against Hitler; they preferred to remain passive and simply wait until the Nazi system collapsed.[137]

Some of the oppositionists, including, for example, former Ambassador to Moscow Count Werner von der Schulenburg, concluded that Western inflexibility left them no alternative except an approach to the East. He said that it was foolish to rely on an "American solution" in the light of the apparent lack of understanding in official American circles about developments inside Germany or even of their own true interests. He warned that American policy, or rather lack of policy, provided no secure foundation for stability in Europe and he frankly advocated turning to the East.[138] Adam Trott, disillusioned by his many attempts to arrive at a settlement with Western representatives, reported that the Soviet Union was not dominated by the fixed idea of Unconditional Surrender and was apparently willing to negotiate.[139] However, the majority of conspirators would not allow even desperation to drive them into the arms of another form of totalitarianism.

In general the resistance leaders feared Bolshevism and opposed it as strenuously and unequivocally as they opposed National Socialism. It was precisely this fear of Communism which

[136] The full account is given *ibid.*, pp. 197 ff.
[137] In the letter previously cited.
[138] FitzGibbon, *op. cit.*, p. 141.
[139] *Ibid.*

complicated their plans for action against Hitler. During the early years of the war they wished to remove Hitler and dislodge the Nazi party, but they did not want to destroy German military power to resist in the East. Had they been able to arrive at an agreement with the Western powers to permit the cessation of the war in the West, they might have been able to continue to fight defensively in the East and protect Central Europe from Soviet domination. They still hoped for such a solution at the beginning of 1943.

The news of the disaster at Stalingrad seems to have been the psychological turning point of the war. One young officer of the conspiracy reports that the officers in his sector of the front were convinced after Stalingrad that the war had been lost. The army on the Eastern Front was in the mood for negotiations.[140] Albrecht von Kessel writes that the shattering losses at Stalingrad affected the entire German people; there was almost no German family without a loss, all because of the blindness and stubbornness of a single man. This, he says, was a moment of inner change, many eyes were opened.[141] Then, just at this crucial moment, came the announcement from Casablanca that the United States and England would accept nothing less than the unconditional surrender of Germany and Japan.

Kessel reports that the repercussions of this demand on the opposition were devastating. The work of three years was imperiled. Three days after the Casablanca announcement the active nucleus of the anti-Nazi resistance movement had dwindled to one small circle.[142] The oppositionists were confused by the Unconditional Surrender Formula. What precisely did it mean? A fortress can surrender unconditionally: this means that the defenders will be interned as prisoners of war until the end of the war, but what did Unconditional Surrender mean in the case of a state? Did it mean that the entire nation would be enslaved? [143]

Goebbels promptly announced that Unconditional Surrender

[140] Interview with Baron Axel von dem Bussche, German Embassy, Washington, D. C., March, 1957.

[141] Albrecht von Kessel, unpublished manuscript (diary), "Verborgene Saat: Das 'Andere' Deutschland," pp. 227-28.

[142] *Ibid.*, p. 230.

[143] *Ibid.*

meant precisely that, and apparently many of the German people believed him. Many anti-Nazis believed that they did not have the right to overthrow Hitler and weaken German military resistance, causing defeat, if the enslavement of their people would be a possible result. Others felt that they could not accept the responsibility of precipitating a civil war which might result from popular misunderstanding of the cause of their action: the people, fearing the threat of Unconditional Surrender, might regard the conspirators as traitors and might embrace a new "stab in the back" legend.

Still others felt that their religious convictions would permit rebellion and tyrannicide only if such actions promised a better solution for their people than would have been possible without the action. According to one theological interpretation,[144] tyrannicide can be justified only if success can be foreseen and if the action is intended to prevent a catastrophe, not to precipitate one. The unrelenting demand for unconditional surrender might well have given pause to the conscientious Christian who pondered the problem of whether or not to join in the plans of the resistance movement.

Surely even the core of the resistance leaders considered these questions. Even the most uncompromising anti-Nazis must have wondered whether in the face of an uncompromising enemy they had the right to divide their people and weaken their nation's power to resist the national destruction threatened by that enemy. Baron Schlabrendorff describes the Unconditional Surrender slogan as painful. Clearly the decision to proceed with the revolt in spite of the failure to win mitigation of this demand must have been arrived at painfully.

In the final analysis men like Beck, Witzleben, Goerdeler, Stauffenberg, Tresckow, Trott, and many others arrived at their own unconditional decision: despite their bitter disappointment with what they were forced to regard as the pharisaic attitude and political inepitude of the Western powers, despite the prob-

[144] The theological arguments regarding tyrannicide offered by both Catholic and Protestant theologians are reported in FitzGibbon, *op. cit.*, pp. 150 ff. See also *Die Vollmacht des Gewissens*, ed. Europaischen Publ. (Bonn: Rinn, 1956), esp. Chap. I.

able cost to their nation's future in economic, political, and cultural terms, despite the doubt concerning their own positions in the future history of Germany, they determined that they must act, if not to prevent a catastrophe then at least to remove one. Many of them were puzzled, shocked, or disheartened by the announcement of the Casablanca Formula and by the Allied persistence in it, but they were not deterred by it. When they finally acted in July, 1944, it was in spite of Unconditional Surrender. It was solely to take one action to salvage what still remained of German honor.

Again, it is impossible to measure the effect of the policy of Unconditional Surrender on their action. It did not deter the most convinced anti-Nazis, but one is tempted to wonder how many others, anti-Nazis and non-Nazis, military commanders, officials, perhaps some in crucial posts, had withheld their support because of this formula, because of fear of what revolt might mean to the future of their people, and one wonders what might have happened on July 20, 1944, or perhaps earlier if just a few more key commanders had been persuaded to participate in the plot.

It is impossible to measure accurately the effect of the policy of Unconditional Surrender, but it is interesting and perhaps instructive, if also painful, to speculate.

CHRONOLOGY
of
Postwar Events in Germany

1945	
5 June	Statement of assumption of authority in Germany by the victors; Allied Control Council must be unanimous
17 July-2 August	Potsdam Conference of Three Powers
November	Nürnberg Trials of major war criminals begin
1946	
15 February	Zone Advisory Council, a German committee to advise British occupation authorities on economic affairs established in Hamburg
25 April-19 May	Paris Foreign Ministers' Conference; Molotov rejects Western plans for a German peace treaty
25 May	General Clay orders cessation of shipments of reparations to the U.S.S.R. from U.S. Zone
15 June-15 July	Second Foreign Ministers' Conference; Molotov opposes merger of four zones
5 September	U.S. and Great Britain agree to economic merger of their two zones
6 September	Secretary Byrnes delivers his Stuttgart speech calling for the revival of the German economy

1947

1 January	German Economic Council takes over economic affairs of the Bizone
24 January	First trade agreement with Holland
1 March	Local political autonomy extended to Länder in U.S. Zone
26 March	Herbert Hoover calls for the revival of the German economy
10 March-24 April	Moscow Conference of Foreign Ministers; no agreement
5 June	Announcement of the Marshall Plan
6-8 June	Meeting of representatives of all German Länder in Munich; Soviet Zone delegates withdraw
17 July	General Clay issues new directives assigning greater economic and political autonomy to U.S. Zone
28 August	Revised Level of Industry Plan for the Bizone
25 November-15 December	London Conference of Foreign Ministers; no agreement reached

1948

6 March	London Conference decides to establish a federal government in West Germany
19 March	Soviets withdraw from Allied Control Council
1 April	Soviet Blockade of Berlin begins
30 June	Allies initiate Airlift to Berlin
22 September	Marshall Plan agreement announced

1949

4 April	Atlantic Pact signed by twelve nations (Germany not included)

8 May	Acceptance of the Basic Law (Constitution) of the German Federal Republic
23 May	Basic Law goes into force
14 August	First Bundestag elections
22 August	Announcement of full West German participation in the Marshall Plan
12 September and 15 September	Election of Theodor Heuss as President and Konrad Adenauer as Chancellor of the Federal Republic
20 September	Adenauer announces his first Cabinet
21 September	Promulgation of the Occupation Statute
6 October	Mutual Defense Assistance Pact signed (Germany not immediately a party)
1950	
26 January	First West German Consuls General appointed to Paris, London, and Washington
25 June	Korean War begins
7 August	West Germany invited to join the Council of Europe
24 October	Dedication of Freedom Bell in West Berlin
19 December	West Germany invited to join NATO
1951	
1 January	India becomes first state to terminate a state of war with Germany
2 May	West Germany assumes full membership in the Council of Europe
21 June	Federal Republic invited to join UNESCO
9 July	Great Britain ends state of war with Germany
19 October	U.S. ends state of war with Germany

1952

26 May — Bonn Convention replaces Occupation Statute

1953

17 June — Popular uprising in East Berlin and East Germany

27 July — Korean Armistice signed

1955

5 May — German sovereignty recognized in the German Federal Republic; Western High Commissioners resign former status, assume status of Ambassadors

CHAPTER 5

Conclusions

War, according to Clausewitz, is nothing but a continuation of political intercourse with a mixture of other means; it is an instrument of policy, it is "policy itself, which takes up the sword instead of the pen, but does not on that account cease to think according to its own laws." [1] War is a resort to violence to compel the enemy to accept a political objective that could not be obtained by peaceful means. Victory in war implies the successful attainment of the political goal by means of appropriate military operations; all strategy is directed to this end. In the view of Clausewitz there is only one result by which the success of a war can be evaluated—the final result. From the first day of hostilities strategy must be directed to one objective: the peace conditions that will emerge from the war. The final goal is not simply the military defeat of the enemy's forces but rather the defeat of the enemy to some political purpose. According to the logic of Clausewitz, then, a successful war would be one in which the original political objective is achieved by appropriate means and at proportionate cost.[2] From the viewpoint of these standards let us review the results of the Second World War and of its policy: Unconditional Surrender.

[1] Clausewitz, *On War*, Vol. III, p. 121.
[2] *Ibid.*, pp. 79, 87, 123-25, 127.

THE POSTWAR SITUATION IN GERMANY

Germany in 1945

On May 8, 1945, the United States achieved its strategic objective of the European phase of the Second World War; the representatives of the German Wehrmacht signed the official document of Unconditional Surrender. Allied strategy had achieved the objective that President Roosevelt had so often pronounced, the total defeat of Axis forces in Europe. German military power had been shattered. The victorious troops of Great Britain, the U.S.S.R. and the United States marched in triumph through the streets of Berlin. The territory of the German Reich was carved into four zones of occupation. The members of the Doenitz Cabinet and the commanders of the Wehrmacht were placed under arrest. Supreme power in Germany passed into the hands of the Allied occupying powers. This was the immediate meaning of Unconditional Surrender.

The immediate result was chaos. Production in Germany was at a standstill, roads were blocked by physical wreckage and flooded with streams of refugees, transportation was halted, gas, electricity, and other public utilities were shut down. Many officials had left their posts and gone into hiding, leaving virtual anarchy in their wake. The German currency was inflated, banks were closed, factories and businesses were left without money to pay their employees. There was no way to move food from the farms into cities and population centers were threatened with starvation.

The years of around-the-clock saturation bombing had reduced German cities to rubble piles. More than 20 per cent of all housing throughout Germany had been totally destroyed and another 20 per cent had been so badly damaged as to be uninhabitable.[3] In large cities such as Cologne, Hamburg, and Essen the percentage of destruction ranged from 50 to 75 per cent. Factories and production centers had been similarly gutted. In one raid alone 5,000 acres at the center of Cologne had been leveled and in Hamburg 12½ miles of the city had been burned to the

[3] *Germany Reports,* p. 177.

ground in a single night. Twenty-four per cent of all the bombs which had been dropped by the Western Allied air forces during the war had been aimed at civilian targets. Sixty-one German cities had been attacked, leaving 7,500,000 people homeless.[4]

Into this maze of rubble poured the refugees from the East. The German-speaking populations of the Sudetenland, of the Volga region of Russia, and of Western Poland, as well as German nationals from East Prussia and from the territory east of the Oder-Neisse line were expelled or had fled from their homes. About 8,000,000 of these expellees survived their flight and arrived in Occupied Germany during the first postwar weeks.[5] Anti-Communists began to pour across the boundaries of the Soviet Zone of Occupation into West Germany so that by the end of 1945 more than 10,000,000 expellees and refugees were in the three Western zones.[6]

Obviously there was a severe housing and food crisis. During the immediate postwar years the average daily calorie consumption per capita in West Germany was less than 1,000, and often was as low as 700. In the cities there was virtual starvation. Tuberculosis and infant mortality rates soared. The birth rate dropped. Between 1945 and 1947 the United States and Great Britain were forced to spend more than a billion dollars a year simply to sustain life in their zones of occupation in Germany.[7]

The British and American armies of occupation established order in this chaos by swiftly re-establishing essential public services, restoring public utilities, and distributing relief supplies. There was no mass starvation, although there was general malnutrition, and there were no riots or uprisings.

The Economic Situation

Although order was quickly established and the worst economic disaster averted, the economy languished. Workers suffered from malnutrition, lived in overcrowded and often partially destroyed buildings. They lacked shoes, clothing, soap, heat, and

[4] Fuller, *The Second World War: 1939-45,* pp. 226-29.
[5] Stolper, *German Realities,* p. 26.
[6] *Germany Reports,* p. 177. By 1946 the number had grown to 12 million.
[7] Stolper, *op. cit.,* pp. 67-68.

medical supplies. Naturally this sapped the productive energy of the population. Plants suffered from physical destruction caused by bombing and by fires and by artillery shelling; they suffered, too, from shortages of supplies: there was no capital, there were no light bulbs, nails, wire, or spare parts, and certainly no new machinery. There was frequently no raw material. Consequently, by May, 1946, one year after Unconditional Surrender, industrial production in the British Zone had reached only 33 per cent of the 1936 level and in the United States Zone 46 per cent.[8] In the light of the postwar chaos, this represents great progress but for the German consumer the low level of production meant shortages and continued malnutrition.

The acute shortage of all consumers' goods produced its inevitable result—a black market. By 1946 about 20 per cent of all food sold was sold on the black market. Cigarettes, coffee, soap, and textiles were bartered for potatoes, coal, fat, or shoes. By 1947 the price of a carton of American cigarettes had reached 1,000 marks. The Düsseldorf Chamber of Commerce reported that about half the business transactions which took place in that city in 1946 and 1947 were outside normal commercial channels.[9] The official value of the currency, the Reichsmark, gradually declined. Two years after the surrender the German economy was in a state that seemed hopeless. A distinguished American economist who toured the Western zones at the request of the American government shook his head sadly and predicted privately that recovery to a prewar standard of production and prosperity was virtually impossible.[10]

To this war-born destruction and dislocation was added the purposeful destruction of the policy of dismantling. JCS/1067, the directive under which the United States Zone was administered, had borrowed at least an element of the philosophy of the Morgenthau Plan: the level of industry would not be permitted to rise beyond the level necessary for subsistence, German con-

[8] *Ibid.*, p. 69.

[9] *Ibid.*, pp. 98-100.

[10] This judgment was expressed to the author in Munich in 1948. The comments on the black market and shortages derive from personal observation of German conditions in 1947 and 1948.

sumption would not be permitted to exceed the European average. The occupation forces were to take no steps to raise the German standard of prosperity or to revive the German economy. In addition, the West had promised approximately 25 per cent of West German factory equipment, machines, and machine tools to the Soviet Union as reparations.

The "level-of-industry plan" announced in March, 1946, set a ceiling for German industrial production at the level of 1932, a depression year in which about half Germany's labor force had been unemployed. This would amount to about 50 to 55 per cent of the 1938 level of production.[11] In 1932, however, Germany still had reserves of foreign investments, capital, and capital goods which did not exist in 1946. Under the level-of-industry plan, although theoretically there was to be sufficient production to prevent starvation, the food crisis mounted. Theoretically agriculture may seem not to be dependent on the level of industry, but in practice the farmers required tools, tractors, and equipment as well as shoes and clothing and household goods. Farms needed fertilizers, which had to be imported, but there were no industrial goods to be exported to pay for the vitally needed imports. The plan and the German economy foundered.

Secretary of State Byrnes, who journeyed to Germany after the failure of the Second Paris Foreign Ministers' Conference, was shocked by the situation he found in Germany. At Stuttgart on September 6, 1946, he made a speech calling for the revival of the German economy. In Washington the men who had originally opposed Morgenthau's view now supported Byrnes and urged President Truman to abandon the attempt to maintain German production at the subsistence level. Stimson warned that such punitive measures would endanger stability and Forrestal stanchly opposed any further weakening of the German economy.[12]

Former President Hoover's report on the German economic situation was published in Washington in March, 1947, recommending the removal of all restrictions on production. This had

[11] *Germany Reports*, p. 344.

[12] Stimson, *On Active Service in Peace and War*, pp. 582-83, and Forrestal, *Diaries*, p. 378.

a serious effect on Congressional opinion. Meanwhile the smaller nations of Europe which had previously depended on imports of German heavy industrial products began to join the protest. In January, 1947, the government of the Netherlands had issued a detailed memorandum which concluded with the proposal that all restrictions be removed from German production of iron and steel.[13]

Demands mounted for a revision of the level-of-industry plan. In August a revised plan was announced under which production would be established at the 1936 level. Steel production was to be virtually doubled. Under the new plan the economy did not revive overnight. The black market, shortages, malnutrition, and dismantling continued, but the revision had marked the beginning of a change.

In June, 1948, the Western zones undertook a currency reform. The unstable Reichsmark was replaced by a new Deutsche Mark. Former government restrictions on enterprise were liberalized and a virtually free market was restored. In August the West Germans were admitted to full participation in the European Recovery Program. In Washington Secretary Forrestal and others criticized continued dismantling, maintaining that it was absurd for American policy to attempt to rebuild Germany through the ERP with one hand while continuing the "ripping up" of industrial plants for dismantling with the other.[14] Pressure to suspend dismantling mounted and the practice gradually subsided. In April, 1951, the last West German plant was dismantled at Watenstedt-Salzgitter.[15]

The currency reform, the influx of Marshall Plan aid, and the suspension of dismantling had their effect. German production grew and then soared. The black market disappeared, stores were

[13] Stolper, *op. cit.*, pp. 164-65.

[14] Forrestal, *op. cit.*, p. 379.

[15] *Germany Reports*, p. 203. This report gives the following statistics for the total percentages of 1945 plant facilities which were dismantled between 1945 and 1951:

in the Soviet Zone	45
in East Berlin	33
in West Berlin	67
in the 3 western Zones	8

full of consumers' goods, exports poured out to markets throughout the world. The "German miracle" of economic recovery had begun. The first danger created by the chaos of war had been outrun.[16]

The Political Situation within the Western Zones

Immediately following the surrender in May, 1945, the political situation in Western Germany also was chaotic. Major government officials had been interned, many had gone into hiding, and so there was virtual anarchy. Under JCS/1067 both high-ranking and insignificant Nazis and also economic and financial leaders, landowners, and professional men were interned. The directive ordered that in the absence of evidence to the contrary it might be assumed that anyone who had held a position of influence, even in private life, during the era of the Third Reich had been a Nazi or Nazi sympathizer. Consequently, so many thousands were arrested that prompt trials, even hearings and indictments, were impossible. Two years after the surrender thousands were held in internment camps; many of these prisoners had not yet been questioned after twenty months' confinement.[17]

In March, 1946, the Länder of the American Zone passed a law titled "Law for Liberation from National Socialism and Militarism." Under this measure all German citizens over eighteen living in the U.S. Zone were required to file a questionnaire which contained 131 questions regarding political activities from 1933 to 1945. However, not only were citizens required to report membership in the Nazi party and in party-affiliated organizations such as the SS, SA, and Hitler Youth, but they were also required to state their incomes, property holding, university and fraternity affiliations, promotions and honors in business and in the professions and publications during the Nazi period. Once again it was assumed that anyone who had prospered or won distinction during the Nazi period, whether in the field of public life or of paleontology, must have done so by collaboration with

[16] *Ibid.*, p. 204.

[17] See, for example, Stolper, *op. cit.*, pp. 19-20, 61-63.

the party. It was further assumed that aristocrats, industrialists, and financiers had been morally and politically responsible for the rise of Hitler and were therefore as dangerous to democratic society as Nazi activists.[18]

According to their answers to this questionnaire and to the subsequent verification of the answers by investigation, citizens were divided into five categories: major offenders, offenders, lesser offenders, followers, or not affected. Depending on the seriousness of their category, offenders were punished by imprisonment, confiscation of property, loss of pensions, loss of position, and/or by disqualification from holding political office or from serving in a position of economic, social, or cultural influence.

In the United States Zone alone 450 special courts were established to hear denazification cases. One year after the trials had begun 200,000 cases had been tried but 1,300,000 still remained on the docket. Those awaiting trial were usually interned, consuming food however frugal, unable to contribute to production. Meanwhile society was deprived of the skills of technicians, engineers, scientists, and teachers who might later be judged innocent or merely followers. The trials added to the financial burden of occupation: Germany, which had formerly produced 85 per cent of the food consumed within her borders, by 1947 was producing only 25 per cent. The deficit, to the extent of preventing starvation, had to be made up by imports from the United States.[19] In addition, the inevitable delays in denazification trials produced the unfortunate political result of engendering sympathy for the internees among the masses of the German people. John J. McCloy, High Commissioner for the American Zone, rendered his judgment in retrospect on the denazification program. In his report for the last quarter of 1950 he wrote that it would have been wiser "to have applied the penal aspects . . . more promptly and effectively to the real activists . . . treating the great mass of lesser Nazis more leniently."[20] The official

[18] Eugene Davidson, *The Death and Life of Germany* (New York: Knopf, 1958), pp. 127-29.

[19] *Ibid.*, pp. 158-59.

[20] *Ibid.*, p. 277.

HICOG history of military government arrives at the negative conclusion that as a whole the denazification program failed to fulfill the objectives of American policy: minor offenders were punished quickly and often severely, while many major offenders were tried later in a period when postwar bitterness had subsided and so received relatively mild sentences.[21] Not only was this in itself unjust but it inevitably produced an attitude of cynicism regarding denazification.

With such an overwhelming number of courts and trials there was always an insufficient number of trained personnel. Duty on denazification courts was unpopular; those who could do so avoided the duty, leaving it for less qualified and often less reputable people. In many cases genuine Nazis achieved acquittal by bribing witnesses to testify to their innocence; butchers and bakers, for example, compelled customers to exonerate them in order to receive food.[22] In other cases widows of party members who themselves had never been involved in any political activity were deprived of pensions.

Denazification, logical and necessary in theory, was implemented with more enthusiasm than practicality. In practice it weakened rather than enforced anti-Nazi sentiments among the masses of the people, undermined rather than bolstered the prestige of the German anti-Nazis. By 1948, 85 per cent of those who had been removed from office in Bavaria under the denazification program had been reinstated.[23]

The Nürnberg Trials

Throughout the war Roosevelt, Churchill, and Stalin had warned that Germans guilty of atrocities would not escape punishment. After Germany's unconditional surrender all members of the German Cabinet, ranking civil servants, the General Staff, the OKW, high-ranking Wehrmacht officers, SS officers and men, Gestapo officials, and major industrialists, as well as any others who were accused of war crimes, were interned and screened. Of the total number interned the 23 most prominent or repre-

[21] *Ibid.*, pp. 277-78.
[22] Stolper, *op. cit.*, pp. 20, 61.
[23] Davidson, *op. cit.*, p. 278.

sentative were brought to Nürnberg to the Palace of Justice for trial before the International Military Tribunal, a court composed of justices representing each of the four occupying powers. The defendants, including Cabinet members, party officials, and Wehrmacht officers, were indicted on charges of having committed war crimes in occupied areas, of crimes against humanity within Germany, and of having participated in a conspiracy to wage aggressive warfare. The trial lasted 216 days, one of the longest trials in history. Ten million words were entered into the court record. The verdicts, pronounced in October, 1946, condemned eleven defendants to death, seven were sentenced to prison terms ranging from ten years to life, and three were acquitted.

The trials launched a controversy which still rages. The controversy is part of the heritage of the policy associated with Unconditional Surrender. Although supporters of the Nürnberg proceedings contend that they established a precedent "unique in the history of the jurisprudence of the world"[24] and mean by that that they represent a step forward in the direction of justice and civilization, critics contend precisely the opposite. Lord Hankey, for example, calls the precedent established "deplorable" in that it established "one law for the victors and another for the vanquished. Vae victis!"[25] Field Marshal Montgomery's comment was blunt: the Nürnberg decisions made the waging of an unsuccessful war a crime in which the defeated generals would be hanged.[26]

Military men, international lawyers, historians, and political leaders have contributed to the argument. Admiral Leahy expressed sympathy for the condemned soldiers, writing that to a professional soldier "his country's appeal to the force of arms is final. A soldier carries out the orders of his government. He defends his country to the best of his ability."[27] Secretaries Stimson and Byrnes both indicate that the question of the punishment of

[24] Quotation from a statement by the British prosecutor at Nürnberg, Sir Hartley Shawcross in Davidson, *op. cit.*, p. 102.

[25] Hankey, *Politics: Trials and Errors*, p. 56.

[26] *Ibid.*, p. 60.

[27] Leahy, *I Was There*, p. 315.

war criminals had been directly linked with the Morgenthau Plan. The Morgenthau memorandum of September 6, 1944, had proposed that the leading Nazi criminals be shot upon identification, without a trial. Stimson found this, like the Morgenthau Plan itself, "deeply disturbing" and used his influence to support the principles of traditional Anglo-Saxon jurisprudence.[28] A few days later the President asked James Byrnes to consider taking on the assignment as United States High Commissioner for Germany after the war and Byrnes, in considering the decision, asked to see the State Department's plan for occupation. Mr. Byrnes found the plan punitive: "One provision struck me particularly. Its phraseology was tantamount to saying that the principal war criminals should be tried and hanged. I asked if any consideration had been given to the possibility that some of those charged might be acquitted." He reports that he was informed that much of the plan, including that section, had been prepared by representatives of the Treasury Department. Byrnes declined the invitation to become High Commissioner.[29]

Even today there is by no means unanimity of judgment on the Nürnberg trials. Were they a landmark in the march toward international justice and morality or were they the barbaric and hypocritical vengeance of the victor upon the vanquished? Whichever contention is nearer to the truth, like so many other events of the postwar era the Nürnberg trials added fuel to the growing controversy between the East and the West. As Lord Hankey commented, the trials had established a precedent; the Soviet government used the language of Nürnberg in denouncing the Atlantic Pact, the United Nations actions in the Korean War, and the arming of West Germany.

The Beginning of the East-West Discord

The Soviet Zone

Order No. 1 of the Soviet Military Administration on June 10, 1945, established a new order in the Soviet Zone of Germany. In the field of politics, four non-Nazi parties were organized and

[28] Stimson, *op. cit.*, pp. 584-89.
[29] Byrnes, *Speaking Frankly*, pp. 182-83.

the first elections were scheduled for September, 1946. Meanwhile the population of the Soviet Zone was encouraged to join the "anti-fascist democratic mass organizations" such as the Free German Youth, the Democratic Women's Association, and the Free German Trade-Unions. The aim was to create a Socialist society for which the mass organizations were to act as an advance guard. Just before the first election the German Social Democratic party (SPD) was forcibly merged with the German Communist party (KPD) to form the Socialist Unity party (SED). Despite this measure and despite the advantages given the SED in campaigning, the Soviet-sponsored party polled only 52.4 per cent of the vote.[30]

On October 5, 1949, a provisional government was established with Otto Grotewohl as Prime Minister, Walter Ulbricht, Secretary-General of the SED, as Deputy, and Wilhelm Pieck as President. On October 13 the U.S.S.R. recognized the status of the new German Democratic Republic by changing the name of the SMA to the Soviet Control Commission and by sending an ambassador to Berlin.

The position of the non-Communist parties was gradually undermined. The concentration camps at Buchenwald and Sachsenhausen, which at first had been used for the internment of major Nazis, gradually began to number among their inmates non-Communists, especially Socialists. The numbers of political refugees to the West mounted. In 1950 a total of 142,000 were admitted to the Federal Republic; in 1951 the number was 161,386.[31]

In January, 1950, the National Council of the National Front abolished the pretense of political opposition within the Soviet Zone. In subsequent elections there would be a single list of candidates. In the ensuing election, 99 per cent of the voters endorsed the proposed list.[32] The Soviet Zone had begun to conform to the standards of Soviet satellites.

The economic aim of the Soviets in their zone was sovietiza-

[30] For example, the SED received a larger ration of newsprint, more radio time, etc., *Germany Reports*, pp. 70-71.
[31] *Germany Reports*, p. 77.
[32] *Ibid.*, pp. 72-73.

tion. They organized a form of corporation in which the stock was owned outright by the U.S.S.R. In this manner a branch of the Soviet state economy has been established within East Germany. These Soviet corporations were organized into twelve holding companies which dominated key industries and by 1947 these corporations accounted for approximately 20 per cent of East German production. In addition, most other large-scale plants have been socialized; by 1947 approximately 40 per cent of all workers were employed in state-owned companies.[33]

The collection of reparations by dismantling was carried out by the Soviets in a thorough but haphazard manner in their zone and resulted in tremendous dislocation of the economy. For example, it was the custom in Germany for investors to leave their stocks in a central depot. Russian officials raided these depots, confiscating some stocks and bonds, leaving no record of what had been taken. The result was financial chaos in all Germany.[34]

The Soviets tore up the second tracks of all but three of the main railroads in their zone. In the Berlin area fifteen railroad lines were put out of service entirely because even the single line had been uprooted. The East German railroads were essential for the distribution of food and supplies and to connect Baltic and North Sea ports. The dislocation of rail transport proved a great handicap to the European economy and provided little gain to the Russians.[35]

In addition, the East Zone was stripped of livestock and rolling stock, of works of art and capital goods. Factories were dismantled and machinery and machine tools were shipped to the East. Able-bodied young men and boys were rounded up and prisoners of war were detained for labor in the Soviet Union, and hundreds of thousands of Germans were employed as forced labor within the Soviet Zone, especially in uranium mines. Although no accurate account of the confiscated goods has been kept, the West German government estimates the worth of the dismantled and expropriated items as approximately $12 billion.

[33] Stolper, *op. cit.*, pp. 113-14.
[34] *Ibid.*, pp. 109-10.
[35] *Ibid.*, p. 112.

In addition, the Soviets profited from German patents and from the knowledge and labor of German scientists and technicians.[36]

The Question of Berlin

The location of Berlin, capital of the German Reich and site of the Allied Control Authority, within the Soviet Zone of Occupation has provided a major instance of controversy between East and West. The decision regarding the allotment of the zones was arrived at at the Quebec and Yalta Conferences, but these decisions made no reference to the question of Western access to Berlin.

In January, 1944, the United States Department of State had proposed that the zone boundaries be drawn so that all zones would intersect in Berlin, but the War Department opposed the plan. In February, 1944, the British government proposed that a corridor be established for Western access to Berlin, but once again the American War Department objected.[37] Apparently at this juncture Harry Hopkins suggested that the Russians simply be requested to issue a guarantee of free access to the city. Cables were exchanged between Roosevelt and Stalin and agreement was reached in principle that the United States and Great Britain were to have the right of entry of persons and goods to Berlin, that a written commitment to this effect would be drafted by the military commanders in the area at the end of the war, but this was never done.[38]

On March 28, 1945, when Allied troops stood on the Rhine, 300 miles from Berlin, General Eisenhower proposed that American forces push forward as far as the Elbe to meet the Red Army and simultaneously American and French troops would move on Bavaria and Austria to prevent a last-ditch German stand in the Alps. The British meanwhile would move northward to cut off Wehrmacht forces in Denmark and to seize North German ports. Churchill objected strongly to the plan. He proposed that the Allies push toward Berlin to try to capture the city before the Red Army arrived there. Eisenhower contended that the de-

[36] *Germany Reports*, p. 75.
[37] Baldwin, *Great Mistakes of the War*, pp. 48-50.
[38] Forrestal, *op. cit.*, pp. 251-52.

cision was purely military, that there was danger in the German concentration of forces in the Alps. Washington supported Eisenhower and Churchill was overruled.[39]

After the Americans had crossed the Rhine they pushed on swiftly, reaching the Elbe and by April 12 establishing a bridgehead on the eastern side, one hundred miles from Berlin. The Russians were still on the Oder. The Americans waited on the Elbe for three weeks, until April 25, for the arrival of the Red Army. The Soviets did not win the battle for Berlin until early May.[40]

As the war moved to its end, General Patton, commander of the American troops which had penetrated into Czechoslovakia, was ordered not to pass beyond Pilsen. He writes: "I was very much chagrined, because I felt, and still feel, that we should have gone to the Moldau River and, if the Russians didn't like it, let them go to hell." [41] However, American policy was committed to the fulfillment of Big Three decisions; the Red Army was allowed to take Prague and United States forces voluntarily relinquished Vienna. Forrestal reports that when Churchill learned that the Americans planned to withdraw from territory they had conquered he wept.[42]

Admiral Leahy's comments reflect a typical American attitude of the time: "I do not believe any of us . . . thought that three years later a state of virtual armed truce would exist in Berlin." [43] Joseph Davies interpreted Churchill's concern over growing Soviet power as narrow British nationalism rather than genuine concern for peace, and Leahy writes that this, too, was often the judgment on Churchill of the American Joint Chiefs.[44]

On May 2, 1945, the battle of Berlin subsided, leaving the smoking remnants of the city in the hands of the Red Army. For the first weeks of the occupation the Soviets alone controlled Berlin. It was the Soviet city commander who established the first municipal government in the Reich capital. In July the first

[39] Baldwin, *op. cit.*, pp. 52-54.
[40] *Ibid.*, p. 55.
[41] Patton, *War As I Knew It*, p. 327.
[42] Forrestal, *op. cit.*, p. 496.
[43] Leahy, *op. cit.*, p. 382.
[44] *Ibid.*, p. 380.

Western troops arrived in Berlin and a four-power joint command was established. Under the new system unanimity was required for all decisions, and so the Soviet commander retained a strong measure of control through the threat of a veto.

The provision requiring unanimity meant that no controversial issues could be resolved, and eventually repeated obstructionism by the Soviet commander and obstructionism by Communist members of the Berlin city government led to a split in the administration of the city. In the fall of 1948 the Berlin Parliament moved its headquarters to Schöneberg in the Western sector of the city. Ernst Reuter, a Socialist and staunch anti-Communist, was elected mayor of West Berlin. A separate Communist-dominated government was established in East Berlin.

On April 1, 1948, tension between the U.S.S.R. and the Western powers flared into crisis in the Soviet blockade of Berlin. The city, virtually an island within the Soviet Zone, was cut off from the West by a blockade of the canals and highways which connect Berlin with the British and American zones. On June 30 the Allies launched the Airlift to fly vitally needed supplies of food and raw materials into blockaded Berlin. The air-supply service reached an unheard-of height of precision: at its peak the planes were landing every 63 seconds at West Berlin's Tempelhof airfield; in a single day 12,849 tons of goods were delivered.[45] The Airlift marked a new high in Allied-German understanding and inaugurated a new era of co-operation.

The Cold War

Despite the many toasts drunk to Allied unity during the war and despite the satisfaction expressed by President Roosevelt and his aides at the degree of compromise arrived at during the wartime Big Three Conferences, relations between the Eastern and Western partners of the coalition remained strained throughout the war. There was constant fear in London and Washington that Stalin would arrange a separate peace with Hitler, and this fear may not have been entirely groundless. Peter Kleist, former

[45] *Germany Reports*, p. 59. For a detailed account see W. Phillips Davison, *The Berlin Blockade: a Study in Cold War Politics* (Princeton Univ. Press, 1958).

high-ranking German civil servant, has recently reported a firm offer early in 1943 by Stalin to Hitler of peace assuring Germany the 1914 Imperial German boundary in the East, but Hitler and Ribbentrop rejected the offer.[46] Whether or not the Soviet Union had intended to negotiate with the Germans in good faith, the rumors of such offers and negotiations which circulated through the chancelleries created an atmosphere of tension. The Soviets, in turn, were suspicious of any contact between Western officials and representatives of the German anti-Nazi movement or of the German government. The exchange of telegrams between Stalin and Roosevelt at the time of the negotiations with SS General Wolff for the surrender of German forces in Italy was acrimonious.[47]

This suspicion penetrated the festive atmosphere of the celebration of victory in Europe. The second, official signing of the Unconditional Surrender instruments by the German representatives at Berlin on May 8, after the original signing on May 7 at Reims, was necessitated by Soviet suspicion. General Deane, who was charged with the preparations for the ceremony of the official ratification of the surrender, reports that relations between the Anglo-Americans and the Soviets were extremely delicate, that there was great concern in Washington that Stalin might be offended because the original signing had been in the West.[48]

No sooner had the surrender been implemented and four-power control begun than the tension mounted. For example, one source of controversy was the fact that at the end of the war thousands of Soviet citizens who had served in the German Wehrmacht had fallen into Western captivity. At first the Soviet Union had denied that there were any such Soviet citizens in the Wehrmacht, and so the Allies treated them as German prisoners of war. Later the U.S.S.R. objected to this and demanded that these prisoners receive preferential treatment. Finally they demanded their repatriation. Almost all the Soviet prisoners of war refused repa-

[46] Dr. Peter Kleist, "Nach Stalingrad bot Josef Stalin Hitler den Frieden an," *Deutsche Soldaten Zeitung*, December, 1959, 1st ed., pp. 1, 4.

[47] See, for example, the account of Deane, *The Strange Alliance*, pp. 162-65.

[48] *Ibid.*, pp. 169-73.

triation to the Soviet Union and claimed German citizenship. *Pravda* sharply criticized the Anglo-Americans for violating the Yalta agreement, which had called for mutual repatriation of Western and Soviet citizens. The bitterness over this issue led to a series of misunderstandings and to a stream of accusations against the Western powers by Stalin, Molotov, and Soviet generals.[49]

From July 17 to August 2 the representatives of Great Britain, the U.S.S.R., and the United States met at Potsdam to implement the Yalta decisions regarding the administration of Germany and to establish a program for four-power occupation. Stalin and Molotov represented the Soviet Union, President Truman and Secretary Byrnes represented the United States, and Churchill and Eden began the conference as British representatives. Midway through the conference the change of government in England resulted in the withdrawal of Churchill and Eden and the arrival of Attlee and Bevin.

The major decision at Potsdam was that, although every attempt should be made to pursue a uniform policy in all four zones, in practice each of the zones would be autonomous. In addition, the West agreed that Poland should administer the German territory east of the Oder-Neisse line until the conclusion of a final peace treaty. The ethnic Germans to be expelled from Poland, Czechoslovakia, East Prussia, and from the territory east of the Oder-Neisse were to be transported in an "orderly and humane manner." [50] The West further agreed that 25 per cent of the factories and equipment dismantled in their zones would be sent to the U.S.S.R. as reparations. The conference concluded with an agreement that the final treaty with Germany would be drafted by a Council of Foreign Ministers of the Big Five, including China, to be convened in London not later than September, 1945.

The Western Allies were by no means satisfied with the agreements reached on the surface at Potsdam. Churchill objected even to the tentative acceptance of the Oder-Neisse boundary,

[49] *Ibid.*, pp. 187-90, 200-2, 213-20.

[50] U.S. Department of State, *Making the Peace Treaties: 1941-1947* (Washington, 1947), pp. 12-14.

insisting that this loss of one-fourth her arable land would severely cut the German food supply and that the influx of more than a million additional refugees into the West would put a serious burden on the already overcrowded and impoverished Western zones.[51] Secretary Byrnes also was unhappy with the Oder-Neisse line, but he said that the West had encountered a fait accompli. It was one thing to protest in principle that the Yalta agreement had been only tentative, it would be quite another matter to evict the Poles, who were supported by the Red Army.[52]

From April 25 to May 19, 1946, the Foreign Ministers of the four occupying powers met in Paris. Secretary Byrnes, representing the United States, warned his colleagues that, unless action were taken promptly, disaster faced all four zones during the next winter. He proposed that machinery be set up immediately for the administration of all Germany as a single economic unit as envisioned by the Potsdam agreement. The fundamental disunity of East and West objectives clearly made this impossible, and so the discussions bogged down in dissension. Senator Vandenberg, who had been a member of the American delegation at Paris, summarized the results of the conference as "no runs, no hits, and a lot of errors." [53] However, the conference marked a new turning point in Anglo-American policy. The British and American delegates had stopped compromising on points they considered matters of principle.

A second Foreign Ministers' Conference convened in June, 1946, and, although some agreements were arrived at concerning Trieste and the Italian borders, there was "appalling disagreement" on Germany. East-West suspicion mounted. No prospect for unification seemed in evidence.

When the conference closed Secretary Byrnes and Senator Vandenberg traveled to Germany. The senator reports that he was astonished by the conditions he observed in the defeated country. He was profoundly shocked by the degree of devastation in Berlin and in the industrial areas, and he described the

[51] Byrnes, *op. cit.*, p. 81.
[52] *Ibid.*, pp. 79-80; full discussion of the Potsdam decisions, pp. 81-87.
[53] Vandenberg, *Private Papers*, pp. 281-84.

destruction as "past comprehension." [54] It was during this visit that Secretary Byrnes made his famous Stuttgart speech calling for an end to the philosophy of Morgenthauism and for the revival of the German economy.

The American attitude toward the aims and policies of the Soviet Union had begun to change. The American policy toward Germany, not unconnected with the question of the U.S.S.R., began to shift. The American Secretary of State called for the reconstruction of the German economy; the British and American Zones were merged into a bizonal economic unit; political autonomy was restored to the American Zone; West Germany was admitted to full participation under the Marshall Plan; eventually the Federal Republic was established and became a full partner in the European economy and in NATO. Co-operation with West Germany emerged as a pivotal point of American foreign policy in direct relation to the tension with the Soviet Union.

President Eisenhower, who in 1945 had been fearful lest the English and Americans be deceived by Goebbels's propaganda that the Soviet designs in Europe were sinister, which he considered merely a tactic to divide the wartime coalition,[55] had by 1952 arrived at a vastly different view of history. He stated:

> We must call to mind some of the historical facts that have weight and meaning to the men shaping Soviet policy today.
>
> The last two hundred years tell a simple, sensational story about Russia's relationship to Europe. Through all this time one of the commonest ways of measuring Russia's pressure upon the Continent has been in terms of the distance of the Russian frontier from Europe's center at Berlin. In 1750 that frontier was 1,200 miles from Berlin. In 1800 the distance was but 750 miles; in 1815, only 200 miles. Since then the Russian frontier has moved farther westward until it now includes Berlin within its limits. Thus, under Communist impulse, the old Russian vision of an empire spanning two continents—"from Aachen to Vladivostok"—has come close to being realized.[56]

American policy has swung full circle. Not only had the United States come to an appreciation of the danger to American na-

[54] *Ibid.*, pp. 297-99.
[55] Butcher, *My Three Years with Eisenhower*, p. 827.
[56] *Germany Reports*, p. 128.

tional interest and to Western Europe of further Soviet expansion, either physical or political, but also the basic American view of foreign policy seems to have shifted. The very Americans who had once criticized Churchill and the British chiefs for narrow nationalism, imperialism, and for thoughts of power politics had begun themselves to think in terms of the balance of power and began hastily to reconstruct German economic, political, and finally military power as a bastion of the West. The realities of the Cold War destroyed the last official vestiges of the policy and mentality of Unconditional Surrender.

RECAPITULATION

The Casablanca Formula of Unconditional Surrender is symptomatic of an attitude toward war which tends to divide strategy from political goals. In the Second World War American long-range political objectives played a secondary role. In the major conferences of the war, at least until the last year, strategy took precedence over diplomacy. Decisions of the greatest political importance were made primarily, even solely, on the basis of military considerations, as, for example, the routes the invading Allied armies would follow or which ally would take Berlin. It is true that the American planners were dedicated to a final goal in the war, but they perceived that goal as simply total victory, the total destruction of the military power of the Axis enemy.

There appear to have been at least three roots of this "win the war first" mentality: military, political, and ideological. In retrospect it may be difficult to take the military basis seriously, to grant that sheer military necessity dictated the attention first to strategic planning. In retrospect it is difficult to recapture the tensions and fears of 1943 but certainly, to some degree at least, the focusing of Allied planning on immediate military problems, on the marshaling of troops, the sinking of submarines, and the achievement of air superiority rather than on diplomatic objectives was due to the psychology engendered by the dazzling German victories in the war's early years, to the blitzkrieg in the West, and the rapid advance of the Wehrmacht to the gates of

Moscow and Leningrad and Stalingrad. The argument that military victory which does not secure the political conditions essential for peace or for the preservation of national safety and interest is not strategic victory is not answered by a reference to the psychology of 1943, but such an explanation can, at least, make the error intelligible.

The political roots of the doctrine of winning the war first were complex and serious. The Western fear that the U.S.S.R. might withdraw from the alliance by arranging a separate peace with Germany was apparently not entirely groundless. Whether or not the Soviets intended to negotiate with the Nazi government they did not hesitate to use the threat that they might do so as a weapon in winning concessions from the West. It was certainly in the Western interest to keep the U.S.S.R. in the war. Critics of the concessions made will probably quarrel with the degree and the method of bargaining rather than with the aim.

Even within the Anglo-American alliance there was some degree of suspicion and division. The Americans, on the one hand, seemed to fear that British interest in the Mediterranean and the Balkans represented narrow British nationalism, imperial interests, and power politics, and therefore they often opposed British proposals to side with the Soviet Union. The English, on the other hand, were often forced to regard their American partners as naïve and shortsighted, guided more by enthusiasm than by experience and sagacity. However, within the American camp itself there was division: General Wedemeyer, for example, opposed the doctrine of Unconditional Surrender and General Clark favored the British plan for a Balkan invasion route; Secretaries Hull and Stimson differed sharply with Morgenthau on plans for Germany. Within the American Senate isolationism was by no means dead, Roosevelt's postwar plans were never sure of unquestioning acceptance.

The ideological root of a doctrine of total defeat of the enemy, that is, in the doctrine of moral war, seems to lie in the nature of modern democracy. Modern war requires mass participation in the armed service, in industry, and in war work. In a democracy, and probably also in a dictatorship, this requires the moral support of the general public for the war. One of the ways in which such popular support can be secured is by making the war a clear-cut moral issue, by asserting that it is being fought to right a wrong, by branding the enemy as totally guilty, as criminals, aggressors, and militarists. Throughout the war stories of the enemy's atrocities are used to increase public willingness to make sacrifices. Popular emotions of fear and hatred are evoked, and these emotions once evoked become in themselves a political force which may make rational political decisions unpopular or even impossible. In the instance of the Second World War the propaganda offensive seems to have been so successful that even the makers of policy themselves seem to have accepted the tenets of propaganda as the bases for policy. The dogma that Prussia-Germany was the perpetual aggressor in European warfare, the official view of the exaggerated political importance of the German General Staff, the theory of the dangers to democracy, lawful government, and peace inherent in Prussia and especially in its ruling class, the doctrine of the conspiracy of the industrialists, Junkers, and militarists to push Hitler into power, a dogma that was at least open to question and critical historical analysis, seems never to have been criticized in official circles during the war, at least not in the recorded public discussions of memoranda or memoirs. The dissension from Morgenthauism was made on grounds of impracticality; it was criticized as an ineffective means not as an end.

The basic assumptions of Roosevelt's aims in Germany—the assumptions that Germany alone had been primarily responsible for all recent international war and tension, that peace could be established by destroying the roots of aggression in Germany—seem never to have been questioned. There were arguments over the degree of control, the extent of dismantling, the exact nature of the Nürnberg trials but never, publicly, over the view of history and of warfare on which these plans were based. There was no open questioning of the total guilt of the enemy, no questioning of the moral right of the United States to bring what would amount to a social, legal, and economic revolution to the center of Europe. This was the unchallenged right of the victor, of the innocent nation. Within the framework of this attitude, which can be described as Calvinistic or naïve, there was no alternative to the war aim of total defeat of the enemy.

Since the war is viewed as a massive struggle of the forces of good against the forces of evil, no compromise is thinkable. Compromise is possible only between human beings who recognize each other as human, as mutually fallible, not between abstract forces, and most certainly not between abstract Good and Evil.

Such a categorical view renders flexibility of policy almost impossible. Not only is compromise with the Nazi government in Germany unthinkable, but also compromise with any group or faction within Germany, certainly a group centered around Junkers and militarists. The very existence of an anti-Nazi group within Germany became a cause of embarrassment for the Roosevelt administration. Compromise concerning the ends of war policy rather than merely the details of the means became impossible.

Throughout the war there were suggestions by American generals, American Cabinet officials, the Soviet and British governments that the Casablanca Formula be abandoned or modified or at least explained. These were not demands for the alteration of the basic aim of the war; that would remain the total defeat of the enemy. These demands were for the modification of the phrase "Unconditional Surrender" as a propaganda slogan. Consistently the President rejected all demands for the abandonment or modification of Unconditional Surrender, repeating again and again the anecdote about Lee and Grant at Appomattox. Although the presidential version of the historical origin of Unconditional Surrender was inaccurate, it revealed a symbolic truth: the President thought of the Second World War as at least analogous to the American Civil War. Traditionally diplomacy has distinguished sharply between civil wars—which are essentially rebellions in which the rebels have acted in violation of established order, have committed a criminal act by the resort to violence, and in which there can be no compromise—and a war between two or more sovereign states. The President seems not to have made this traditional distinction. For him the Second World War was a species of civil war, a war of the forces of law against the forces of totalitarianism and aggression. That the struggle was being waged in coalition with a power that had been a full partner in the aggression of 1939 and that was at least as totalitarian as Nazi Germany seems not to have disturbed the logic of Unconditional Surrender. The policy and the demand remained.

The demand was fulfilled in May, 1945. The total power of Germany had been destroyed. The victorious armies of the four powers marched through the streets of Berlin. The four powers assumed supreme authority in Germany. Total victory had been achieved.

What had been its costs? Was the achievement worth the cost? Had there been a practicable alternative which might have produced more favorable results? It is impossible to answer these questions with any degree of accuracy. Even the specific military question of whether the demand for unconditional surrender lengthened and intensified the war cannot be answered absolutely. If the phrase "Unconditional Surrender" is interpreted as the policy of refusal to compromise, of rejecting a negotiated solution, then it seems quite clear that it did lengthen the war, or at least that the leaders of the German Wehrmacht, had they been in a position to make their decisions effective, would have been willing to negotiate on the basis of compromise much earlier than May, 1945. Three German field marshals have recorded their opinions that Germany had lost all chance of achieving strategic victory in the war after the Stalingrad disaster, that they would have considered a compromise solution at that time intelligent. After the defeat of the German and Italian forces in North Africa, in spring, 1943, Rommel concluded unequivocally that the German cause was hopeless. By July, 1944, when the Allies broke through the German encirclement of their Normandy beachhead and secured the open plain leading to Paris and Germany, dozens of German generals on both the Eastern and the Western Front concluded that total eventual defeat of the Wehrmacht had become inevitable. In the East the Red Army was driving toward the German border, the Crimea had been lost, the Soviets had penetrated into Rumania. Keitel confessed: "Even I know that there is no more to be done." On July 15 Rommel prepared a memorandum for Hitler urging him to accept the political consequences of the military situation. Hitler refused.

No one succeeded in estimating the political consequences of the military situation. Germany had lost the war, but the fighting continued for nine months longer. The impressive list of German generals who insist that Germany could not have secured victory after Stalingrad, January, 1943, and conclude that Germany had decisively lost the war by July, 1944, state that they, as commanders, would have been willing to participate in and agree to negotiations for a compromise settlement, but rather than submit to Unconditional Surrender they and their troops continued the hopeless struggle until May, 1945. It seems clear that had the German generals been able to act to end the war and had the Allies been willing to negotiate, the war might have ended earlier, nine months to two years earlier depending on the degree of compromise.

The exact nature of the peace that might have ensued at an earlier date than that of Germany's unconditional surrender cannot be accurately constructed in retrospect. Since it would have been a solution arrived at by the process of bargaining, based on mutual compromise, it is difficult to know what details of final settlement might ultimately have been accepted. However, the generals interviewed were in substantial agreement that in July, 1944, they would have been willing to accept in principle the payment of reparations for war damages, the surrender of all territory gained by conquest, disarmament, and the trial of alleged war criminals under accepted principles of existent international law. A compromise solution could very likely not have included the unconditional surrender aims of four-power military occupation of the German Reich, and of Allied assumption of full power to pursue the policy of denazification, demilitarization, and punishment of war criminals. The compromise solution would very likely have been a treaty with the West alone.

It is also impossible to prove the exact degree of effect the Allied Unconditional Surrender policy had on the German anti-Nazi resistance movement, but it is clear that the leaders of this movement were in agreement that the effect was negative. The anti-Nazis could hope to succeed in overthrowing Hitler and the

SS and Gestapo only if they could secure the active co-operation of sufficient troop commanders to throw the balance of military strength for and not against a possible coup d'état. Although they did succeed in winning the support of many military leaders, many crucial commanders withheld active support. Kesselring, although not approached in regard to the plan, writes that he would not have participated as long as the alternative to Hitler remained unconditional surrender. Manstein agreed, and both Guderian and Jodl gave as explicit reasons for their refusal to co-operate with the plot the alternative of unconditional surrender. Even Field Marshal von Witzleben, an original member of the conspiracy, was shaken by the final refusal of the Allies to compromise or to negotiate. He felt that no honorable man could overthrow the government in the face of the demand for unconditional surrender and was ready to withdraw support from the plot, but he was convinced by Schlabrendorff's argument that by then the stakes were no longer German existence, but German honor.

The choice was not a simple one. Many key commanders refused to join the conspiracy. Despite this, *Operation Walküre* was launched and ran its tragic course. It cannot be proved with historical accuracy that the participation of a few more military commanders would have ensured the victory of the plot nor that the commanders who refused co-operation on ground of unconditional surrender would actually have brought themselves to act had an alternative policy been extant; however, there is room to speculate that some truth might lie in the twin deductions. In any event, the uncompromising demand for unconditional surrender was at least a factor in the failure of the plot and certainly did not strengthen the hand of the resistance leaders.

Had the plot succeeded, had the anti-Nazi leaders succeeded in their plan to assume control in Germany, arrest the Gestapo and SS leadership, and intern the heads of the Nazi government, they certainly intended to sue for peace. Their plans included the re-establishment of constitutional government in Germany, the denazification of the government and public life, and the trial under established law of alleged war criminals. The new provisional government would have sought a peace which would guarantee German sovereignty and unity on the basis of the prewar boundaries. Whether such a solution would have been more in the interests of the United States and of the West is a question that can be more dispassionately answered now, perhaps, than would have been possible in 1945. The failure to achieve such a solution, the failure of the 1944 plot, was costly to Germany if not to the West. The loss of leadership involved in the execution of men like Beck, Goerdeler, Stauffenberg, Witzleben, Trott, Moltke, Leuschner, and hundreds more has been felt in postwar Germany. The failure to end the war in 1944 brought about the death and torture of thousands of Germans and non-Germans in Gestapo prisons and concentration camps month by month until the final end in May, 1945.

The cost of the failure of the plot and the costs of the continuation of the war cannot be attributed solely to the Casablanca Formula, but surely the facts seem to warrant the conclusion that had the Allies been in a frame of mind to seek a solution there were Germans who would have been eager to meet them at least halfway.

ALTERNATIVES

The proposition that a policy other than the demand for the total defeat of Germany might have resulted in the saving of lives, the sparing of cities from complete devastation, the preservation of valuable human and cultural and economic resources important to all Europe and to the West, as well as to Germany, depends for its validity on the assumption that an alternative policy would have served better the interests of the United States and of the West and on the further assumption that such an alternative would have been practicable.

The acceptance by the United States of an alternate policy to Unconditional Surrender would have necessitated a basically different view from that of war as the punishment of the guilty by the innocent. Had the American planners accepted the traditional view of Clausewitz—that military operations in war are the servants of policy, that the goal of all war is to achieve a political objective by one means or another, and that the defeat of the enemy on the field of battle is only one such means—there might have been less tendency to rivet attention on the means rather than on the ends. If the dominant question of the policy makers had been "What ends would best serve American interests?" the answer might have been not the punishment of aggression, the destruction of the enemy, but rather the prevention or at least the discouragement of future war and the establishment in Europe of conditions which would tend to foster peace.

What were the basic American and Western interests in Europe? Perhaps, in general terms, these: (1) the creation of conditions less likely than those of the 1930's to precipitate war and international crisis; (2) the abolition of totalitarianism in Germany; (3) the establishment of a system in Europe which would add to the security and independence of smaller states; (4) a relatively prosperous and stable European economy as a prerequisite to political stability and freedom; (5) the furtherance of the principles of international law and of civilized intercourse among states.

Surely aims not greatly different from these seem to have underlain the American wartime plans for the occupation of Germany, for denazification, and for the Nürnberg trials. Such aims are realistic and moral. How successful were the means? Did the policy of Unconditional Surrender and the implementation that it implied lead to stability and peace or to chaos and to the Cold War?

The conclusions of those most closely associated with denazification, for example, indicate that the zealous American attempts to revamp German society in the postwar era proved costly and far from overwhelmingly successful. The Nürnberg trials have provoked serious criticism by jurists of many nations and now form the precedent for Soviet charges that the West is currently engaging in a conspiracy to wage aggressive warfare against the Communist nations. The four-power occupation that had been designed to bring democracy to Germany and peace to Europe has brought Communism to East Germany and a hostile division between East and West to the world. The small nations of Eastern Europe have been rescued from the theories of Rosenberg only to be delivered over to the theories of Lenin and the practice of Stalin. The war, begun to secure the independence of Poland and Czechoslovakia, ended with Soviet domination of Eastern and Central Europe.

Could there have been an alternative policy which would more nearly have fulfilled the original aims of American planners? Many writers assert that there could have been. As early as 1943 the English military analyst Basil Liddell Hart urged his government to consider the future balance of Europe, warning that the preponderance of Russian power in postwar Europe would pose a menace to British interests. He contended that the predominance of any one nation in Europe has always tended to precipitate wars: "Acton's famous dictum that 'absolute power corrupts absolutely' applies to nations as well as to individual rulers." He pointed out the growing emphasis on military power in the Soviet system as demonstrated, for example, in the increased attention given to military training under the revised Soviet educational system, and he concluded that postwar Soviet imperialistic expansion might be the ultimate result. By 1943 it was clear that Russia intended to absorb the Baltic States and a large part of Poland, and he warned that the "process of extending frontiers for greater security easily develops a habit of further extensions for greater power—as history reminds us." [57] Victory in Europe would be in a large measure due to the efforts of the Red Army, or at least the U.S.S.R. would believe so, and would result in Soviet occupation of the whole of Central Europe and a large part of Germany. Liddell Hart was afraid that a political crisis in Western and Southern Europe might result because the parties of the left in those areas would gravitate to the Soviet sphere of influence and might appeal to the Soviet government for aid in struggles with their own governments. He concluded that unfortunately the only state which could provide a stable element in Europe and could effectively serve as a buffer against Soviet expansion was "the one we are now aiming to smash." He concluded that German aggressive power had been broken:

[57] Basil H. Liddell Hart, "The Future Balance of Europe—a Reflection," unpublished memorandum, dated Oct. 1, 1943, pp. 1 and 2.

> . . . It was curbed before the winter of 1941, and crippled before the winter of 1942. Indeed, it was a plant that had shallow roots even when it looked most impressive, and could only flourish when nourished by easy success—as was pointed out in successive estimates of the situation that I wrote both before the war and in the autumn of 1939. Its shallowness was clearly shown by the lack of enthusiasm among the mass of the German people at the time their army had its most striking run of success; many neutral observers in Germany have borne witness in 1940-41 to the prevalence of this underlying depression.
>
> While Germany's offensive power has long since waned and could only be revived by blunders on our part, her resources still suffice to provide a large measure of defence power. It is sustained by fear of the consequences of unconditional surrender. . . . The underlying paradox of the situation today is that this defensive power which we are trying to break, and which still presents a formidable obstacle athwart our "path to victory," is at the same time the only Continental element that has sufficient strength to form a stable buttress in Western Europe.

He concluded that the "natural effect of destroying the German Army will be to establish the overwhelming military predominance of the Red Army." [58]

The British generally seem to have taken the view that the aim of the war was to prevent any single power from achieving a position of predominance on the Continent. To prevent Soviet hegemony in Central Europe, Churchill urged Western penetration of the Balkans and Anglo-American capture of Berlin, but such arguments were regarded with suspicion in Washington, at least by President Roosevelt. Roosevelt constantly warned that all anti-Soviet propaganda emanated from the pen of Goebbels and at least some of his official associates shared this view. Eisenhower reportedly feared that the Anglo-Americans might be seduced by the German warnings of Soviet intentions,[59] and in May, 1945, Ambassador Joseph E. Davies confided to Admiral Leahy his concern over Churchill's "vehement and violent criticisms" of the Soviet Union:

[58] *Ibid.*, p. 3.
[59] Butcher, *op. cit.*, p. 827.

. . . I said that frankly, as I had listened to him inveigh so violently against the threat of Soviet domination and the spread of Communism in Europe, and disclose such a lack of confidence in the professions of good faith of Soviet leadership, I had wondered whether he, the Prime Minister, was now willing to declare to the world that he and Great Britain had made a mistake in not supporting Hitler, for as I understood him, he was now expressing the doctrine which Hitler and Goebbels had been proclaiming and reiterating for the past four years in an effort to break up allied unity and "divide and conquer" . . . I simply could not bring myself to believe that his considered judgment or expressions would ultimately confirm such an interpretation.[60]

Ultimately the official view of the American government came to accept and to share the British Prime Minister's fears, but during the Second World War the view of Roosevelt and of his close advisers was that the war must be fought in close co-operation with both major allies, Great Britain and the Soviet Union, and that it was somehow lacking in good faith to express skepticism regarding the political intentions of an ally. There were surely experts in both the Department of State and the army who prepared memoranda based on a realistic appraisal of Soviet intentions, but these did not affect policy. Sumner Welles, wartime Undersecretary of State, later complained that State Department plans to prevent the worst dangers of the Russian domination of Europe were never implemented[61] and that frequently American policy makers had been outmaneuvered by the Soviets simply because they did not know sufficient history.[62]

Secretary Forrestal also decried his government's lack of realism in planning policy: "The great mistakes were made during the war because of American failure to realize that military and political action had to go hand in hand. Both the British and the Russians realize this fact." He concluded that the Churchill plan to invade Europe by way of the Balkans might have proved militarily costly, "but it would have prevented the Russian domination of the Balkans."[63] Forrestal's over-all conclusion on American wartime policy was that diplomatic planning had been "far

[60] Quoted by Leahy from an official report by Davies, *op. cit.*, pp. 378-79.
[61] Forrestal, *op. cit.*, p. 53.
[62] Welles, *Seven Decisions That Shaped History*, pp. 205-9.
[63] Forrestal, *op. cit.*, p. 496.

below the quality of planning that went into the conduct of the war" and that "comparatively little thought" had been given to the political conditions that would emerge from the destruction of Germany and Japan. He wrote that "the ominous developments in Europe could have left no thoughtful person too happy with the results of 'unconditional surrender.'"[64]

Undoubtedly thought had been given to political objectives and to the realities of history, but the thinking had been done by experts whose views were simply not consulted. There seem to have been two major reasons why no alternative to Unconditional Surrender was even openly discussed during the Second World War: first, that the major decisions regarding aims of policy were made by the President and by his personal advisers as more or less an afterthought to strategic decisions and, second, because the emotions and enthusiasms engendered by the war seem to have blurred the realism of the planners' analysis of German and of Russian history. The statements of President Eisenhower in 1952 sound nothing like the statements of General Eisenhower in 1944 and 1945. The reactions of Truman and Byrnes to the fait accompli they encountered at Potsdam were realistic and relatively quick. The revolution in the official American view of both Germany and Russia which began slowly in 1945 and 1946 has gathered momentum. The shock of the Cold War has engendered a realism which could not thrive in the heat of the Second World War. This American *renversement diplomatique* has, in a sense, been a repudiation of both the theory and the content of Unconditional Surrender. It has been an acknowledgment de facto of the realities of the balance of power, and an implicit acknowledgment that perhaps the moral basis of the doctrine of total victory was neither historically nor philosophically sound.

The acceptance of an alternative to the policy of Unconditional Surrender during the Second World War would have demanded a more flexible and a more realistic attitude toward both Germany and Russia, a view of war as the instrument of policy rather than of policy as the handmaiden of strategy, an attitude toward both

[64] *Ibid.*, entry for April 25, 1947, p. 53.

war and policy less sentimental, less categorical, and less emotional, a policy designed to achieve ends and not one which became entangled with means. The words "Unconditional Surrender" and the specific aims those words convey, the rejection of compromise, the total defeat of the enemy, total occupation, punishment and re-education of the enemy nation, and total reorganization of enemy society, the pursuit of war to its ultimate conclusion—all this indicates a kind of thinking, an attitude toward war, inimical to a policy of alternatives. The words and the policy Unconditional Surrender reveal the wartime atmosphere of idealism, of enthusiasm, and of hatred, an atmosphere open to criticism on two serious grounds.

It was the realist Bismarck who warned that in politics emotions make a good servant but a bad master. During the Second World War it was a different realist, Pope Pius XII, who in June, 1944, warned President Roosevelt through his envoy, Myron Taylor, that the temple of peace would stand and endure only if established on the foundation of Christian charity, not alloyed with vindictive passion or any elements of hatred.[65] The Pope explained to Taylor that he considered the demand for unconditional surrender incompatible with Christian doctrine.[66]

[65] *Wartime Correspondence between President Roosevelt and Pope Pius XII* (New York: Macmillan, 1947), p. 97.

[66] Konstantin von Bayern, *Der Papst*, p. 211.

APPENDIX A

Additional Notes on the German Anti-Nazi Resistance

A thorough and detailed study of the facets and plans of the German anti-Nazi resistance movement is not germane to an analysis of the effects of the wartime policy of Unconditional Surrender. A selected list of books on the subject is given in the Bibliography. Perhaps, however, a few words should be added here for the interested reader to add to the material presented in the body of the study on the specific subjects of the Inner Emigration, the Church Opposition, and the army.

The Inner Emigration

Since this movement was a state of mind rather than an organization, it is difficult to document its existence. It produced no records, it held no meetings, it published no identifying works, and it took no overt political action. The Inner Emigration was an intellectual reaction, a spiritual withdrawal from the beliefs and values of the Nazi era and the Nazi leadership. It was a movement primarily of intellectuals and artists.

Artists and intellectuals who fled from Germany during the Nazi regime are often hostile toward their colleagues who remained behind and skeptical of the genuineness of their claimed opposition. Those who remained have several justifications. In the first place, it was not physically or financially possible for every intellectual to leave Germany. Many were forced to stay for family reasons or because they simply did not have the money to leave. Others were fully absorbed in their art or their science, they regarded politics as something foreign, something removed from their own world. Many German intellectuals lived in an ivory tower, and these became only gradually aware of the full human and moral import of the doctrines and practices of National Socialism. By the time they realized it, it was too late. The dictatorship was in a position to silence opposition and to prevent flight. Only then did many traditionally nonpolitical scientists and artists realize that the Nazi state enveloped art and science and that whether they willed it or not, as scientists and artists, they were involved in politics.

It was only gradually that they became aware that they would be forced to make a choice on the basis of intellectual and artistic integrity and on the basis of moral and human standards. In the final analysis, those who had courage as well as conviction were able to make that choice. It is of these that we speak.

Perhaps because a unified German state was a very recent development in German culture, politics and the running of the state were regarded by most German intellectuals as a subject unworthy of their consideration. Politics were not dignified. Serious artists and professors dedicated themselves to their work and to their private concerns and left politics to the government and to party leaders. By the time the tragedy of this viewpoint had become apparent to many German intellectuals, in the mid-1930's, the National Socialist government had grown into a behemoth, an apocryphal monster which had swallowed the German state and had at its disposal the total power to coerce and control inherent in the apparatus of a modern totalitarian government. Every radio broadcast, every play, every film, even every concert and art exhibit stood under the aegis of the Ministry of Propaganda and Enlightenment. No meeting could convene, no lecture could be presented at a university or professional society without infiltration by the secret police. No scientific findings and no creative works could be published without the approval of the censor. The party had invaded and brought under its supervision and control the entire cultural and scientific life of the nation. Writers who did not conform were silenced by being denied publication. Professors who ignored polite warnings were retired prematurely. The most persistent and stubborn critics were arrested or were forced to flee. Those who remained and wished to continue actively in their professions had to conform outwardly, at least, to the ideology and to the pressure of the party.

Under this system of total control, hidden and indirect resistance was all that was possible. To the embarrassment of the Nazis and in particular of Propaganda Chief Goebbels, audiences flocked to pre-Nazi and classical plays. Often they applauded loudly any criticism of tyranny or praise of liberty. During the presentation of Schiller's *Don Carlos* in Berlin during the war years audience reaction to a speech by the hero was violent. In one scene the prince, Don Carlos, challenges his father, King Philip of Spain, to give greater freedom to the subject people of the Netherlands: "Give them freedom of thought!" The Berlin audiences shouted and clapped.

Writers of the time frequently resorted to using fables and analogies. They criticized the tyranny of Napoleon, praised the civic virtue of Demosthenes in defending Athenian democracy, attacked the censorship of the medieval church. For example, in 1935, Adam von Trott zu Solz edited the works of Heinrich von Kleist. He underscored Kleist's attacks on Napoleon's power and ambitions in such a way that the parallel to Hitler was unmistakable.[1] Ernst Jünger produced an even more outspoken parable in his novel, *On the Marble Cliffs.* Jünger, once a German nationalist whose earlier works had found favor with the Nazis, had come to realize that romantic nationalism had prepared the way for the excesses and brutalities of the National Socialists. Together with many intellectuals he turned away from the spirit of German nationalism and toward a broader spirit of humanism and Europeanism.

Many former nationalists saw in National Socialism the destructive fruits of their romantic hopes for Germany and for German culture. Many former skeptics and relativists saw in the Nazi

[1] Rothfels, *The German Opposition to Hitler,* pp. 38-39.

philosophy the moral bankruptcy of skepticism turned to cynicism, relativism to nihilism. Atheists, deists, and agnostics began to seek for an answer, an alternative, in the realm of theology: the church, Catholic and Protestant, offered an answer which was supranational and absolute. For many intellectuals Christianity became the symbol of ideological sanctuary from the dehumanization of the period. Intellectuals, who had regarded religion as superstition, and Socialists, who had called the church the tool of the capitalist class, began to attend church services and to meet with leaders of the Christian resistance. Many of the inner emigrants came to believe that the loss of spiritual values had made possible the rise of National Socialism, and that the re-establishment of order and decency in Europe would be possible only by strengthening religious faith among the people and by establishing a new regime dedicated to basic religious principles. The concepts of *Una Sancta* and of Christian Socialism flourished underground during the worst period of Nazi terror.

The Church

The basic Nazi philosophy and program is clearly contrary to Christian teaching. Both the Catholic and the Protestant clergy, church organizations, and conscientious laymen realized this; however, in Germany the tradition of rendering to Caesar the things that are Caesar's is strong. Devout German Christians, although they might reject Nazi teaching, would very likely not have been led into direct opposition to the legal government if the government had not directed its program specifically against the church and against the Christian religion.

Top Nazi party leaders were violently anti-Christian. Goebbels regarded the Catholic Church as the next enemy to be attacked after the Jews had been extirpated.[2] Martin Bormann, Reichsleiter of the party, was a bitter and determined enemy of all churches. When the war began in 1939 he argued military necessity as an added reason for restricting the church and urged stern anti-church measures under the "Law of Patriotic Discipline" which had been drafted to meet war needs. More property was sec-

[2] Paul Joseph Goebbels, *Diaries*, pp. 121-22; W. Adolph, *Im Schatten des Galgens*, pp. 13 f, 374.

ularized, more restrictions made in publications, more clergymen were interned.

In June, 1941, Bormann issued a secret Nazi party decree to all the gauleiters in Germany concerning Christian churches. The decree states that, since the basic ideals of Christianity and those of National Socialism are totally incompatible, the power of the churches in Germany must be rooted out. Bormann stated that the NSDAP must win the German people away from obscurantism and from superstitious faith in an unscientific creed, win them for progressive, scientific National Socialism.[3]

In October, 1943, Heinrich Himmler, Commander of the SS, addressed a gathering of SS gruppenführer in Posen, Poland. In a violent speech exhorting the SS to pursue victory even at the cost of traditional morality, he warned that all convinced Christians were the natural enemies of the regime. He predicted that following the war the Christian Church in Germany would be entirely destroyed.[4]

In 1941, as part of the German occupation of Poland, an anti-religious plan was introduced in the province of Warthegau. If the plan proved successful in this district, Nazi party leaders hoped to adopt similar regulations for all German-held territory after the war. In the first place, all bishops [5] were placed under house arrest or were imprisoned. Many priests were arrested and some were shot; in the city of Posen only four priests remained to minister to approximately 200,000 Catholics. Monks were shot, arrested, or deported. Nuns were conscripted for forced labor. All church schools were secularized; major theological seminaries were closed and their property was confiscated; children were not permitted religious instruction except with the express consent of police authorities; church publications and lay organizations were banned; marriage was entirely secularized; all remaining church activities were strictly supervised by the Gestapo.[6]

In September, 1941, Reinhard Heydrich called a secret meeting

[3] Adolph, *op. cit.*, pp. 14-18.

[4] *Ibid.*, pp. 19-20.

[5] Since this was a predominantly Catholic district, these regulations were directed primarily against the Catholic Church.

[6] Adolph, *op. cit.*, pp. 29-30.

of the Gestapo chiefs in Berlin at which he outlined his plans against German churches. He too said that the final destruction of the church would have to be postponed until after the war, but he insisted that troublesome clergymen, "hetzende Pfarrer," must be restrained immediately. He outlined a new program of increased severity in the supervision of the church: more pastors were to be silenced, more were to be interned.[7]

Roland Freisler, President of the People's Court, the special Nazi court which had been established to deal with political crimes, typified the party's attitude toward the Christian churches.[8] Within a six-month period, from summer, 1943, until winter, 1944, Freisler sentenced to death twenty-five priests and a number of Protestant clergymen, and laymen of both confessions.[9] In presiding over the trial of Dr. Max Joseph Metzger, the founder of the *Una Sancta* or one-faith movement, Freisler summarized the Nazi view of Christianity: he shouted at the defendant in a loud and sharp voice, "Una Sancta! Una Sancta! Una! Una! Una! That is us! There is nothing more!"[10] In the trial of the resistance leader Count Helmuth James von Moltke, Freisler revealed the basis for his hatred of the church: "In only one respect is Christianity like us [the party], we both demand the whole man."[11]

This was the issue. No man could sincerely serve both the Christian Church and the Nazi party, both God and Hitler. The party realized this from the first days of the regime. Higher party leaders were not permitted to be church members, and pressure was put on lesser members to sever their church affiliation. Resignations from the churches reached a peak in 1937, when church membership dropped to a low of 94 per cent.[12] However, anti-church measures and anti-Christian propaganda were not popu-

[7] *Ibid.*, pp. 32-33.

[8] *Ibid.*, p. 37.

[9] *Ibid.*, p. 37.

[10] *Ibid.*, p. 41, literally, "Das sind wir! Und sonst gibt es nichts!" See also Heinz Kuhn, *Blutzeugen des Bistums Berlins* (Berlin: Morus Verlag, 1950), pp. 141-42.

[11] Helmuth J. Graf von Moltke, *Letzte Briefe*, p. 51.

[12] *Germany Reports*, p. 288. It should be kept in mind that church membership in Germany is automatic unless an individual specifically declares otherwise. Hence many of the 94 per cent were merely nominal members.

lar with the people, so an all-out offensive against the churches was postponed until after the war.[13] The Catholic Church had signed a concordat with the Nazi government during the early days of Nazi control, but this established at best an armed truce. Inevitably the claims of the Total Government conflicted with the prerogatives which the Roman Church demanded: sole authority over the faith and morals of its members. The Nazis infringed on the church's property, discouraged young people from joining Catholic Youth groups or even from attending services, interfered in Catholic hospitals and schools and orphanages, spied on the clergy and attempted to censor sermons, and sponsored practices, such as euthanasia, which the church regarded as immoral.

The tradition of the Catholic Church made conflict inevitable. The Roman clergy, led by cardinals such as Preysing of Berlin and Faulhaber of Bavaria, openly protested. The Pope and his nuncio added their voices to the protest and sometimes succeeded in delaying the confiscation of a monastery, the arrest of a priest, and to a great extent slowed down the anti-Christian offensive.[14] Many private citizens and parish priests were forced by their convictions to join with other facets of the opposition in underground activities designed to help victims of the regime or to plot the overthrow of the Nazi government. Many sincere Catholics co-operated with Protestants in the *Una Sancta* movement in the belief that only unified Christian action could combat the moral onslaught of National Socialism. The Gestapo hunted Catholics and Protestants alike on the grounds that they were Christians and taught men and women of different confessions to co-operate and to respect each other. In 1937 Cardinal von Preysing, Archbishop of Berlin, said that "never before . . . have we been so deeply linked in love and sympathy with our brothers who differ from us in creed." [15]

The Protestant tradition in Germany provided no historical precedent for church resistance against the government. There

[13] There are repeated references in the *Goebbels Diaries* to the need for caution in anticlerical activities during the war but the intention to "take care of the sky pilots" once the war had been ended.

[14] *Ibid.*, pp. 120, 196, 374.

[15] Quoted by Rothfels, *op. cit.*, p. 45.

were several reasons for this. In the first place, the Protestants had always represented a majority within the German Empire, their church had been the state church established by the princes and linked with the authority of the state. In addition, Lutheran doctrine taught that the kingdom of the Christian is not of this world, the citizen should "render unto Caesar the things that are Caesar's" without expecting perfection from a government of imperfect human beings. The Protestant, and especially the Pietist, tradition in Germany emphasized the personal spiritual relation of the individual to God. Regarding the state, it encouraged respect for law and obedience and loyalty to the established authority. For these reasons, and also because the Protestant churches do not possess the unity and hierarchy of the Roman Catholic Church, Protestant resistance to Hitler grew slowly and tended to be individual rather than institutional.

Gradually individual Protestants began to realize that under the Nazis the government itself defied law and state, that it repeatedly violated the Constitution under which it had come to power. They saw, too, that Nazi teaching was the antithesis of Christian dogma. The most conservative Protestants, the group called the Confessional Church,[16] although traditionally the most withdrawn from party politics, became the pivotal group of Protestant resistance. The faith of the Confessional Church rested on the Bible and on the teachings of Christ. A government which demanded belief contrary to Scripture or actions contrary to the spirit of Christ could not be obeyed.[17]

As early as 1935 the Confessional Church made its position clear by issuing a manifesto which was read from pulpits throughout Germany. The manifesto stated unequivocally that Christianity and the ideology of National Socialism were incompatible. Following this announcement seven hundred pastors were arrested.[18]

[16] "Bekennende Kirche" in German.

[17] Although the Confessional Church represented only a minority of German Protestants, it was a substantial minority. For example, in 1937 in Berlin, center of the Confessional Church, 160 pastors belonged to the Confessional Church; 40 were of the Nazi-controlled German Christians; about 200 belonged to other Protestant groups. Rothfels, *op. cit.*, p. 42.

[18] *Ibid.*, p. 41.

On Whitsunday, 1936, the leaders of the Confessional Church sent to Hitler a memorandum which stated the objections of their group to the teachings of National Socialism: Christians cannot accept blood, race, and nationality as eternal values; all men, even Aryans, are sinful and in need of salvation; a Christian must love his neighbor and therefore cannot hate Jews. A new wave of arrests followed the delivery of the memorandum. Many pastors were executed or died in prison or in concentration camps as a result.[19]

Following this incident, the remaining leaders of the Confessional Church were forced to conceal their opposition. Many of them began to co-operate with the Catholic clergy and with other resistance groups. Since the regime interfered with the training of pastors for this oppositionist church, Pastor Dietrich Bonhoeffer organized an underground seminary. This secret seminary was discovered and dissolved twice by the Gestapo, and in 1940 Pastor Bonhoeffer was prohibited from delivering public sermons; however, he was well acquainted with underground methods. He was able to reorganize the illegal seminary and to maintain contact with other elements of the political opposition. Pastor Bonhoeffer was arrested in 1943 and was murdered in April, 1945, in the Flossenburg Concentration Camp.[20]

The number of Christians, clerics and laymen, Protestants and Catholics, who were arrested, died, or were executed because of their opposition to the Nazi regime is not known. No one pastor or layman can be called typical of the Christian opposition, but perhaps one lay leader was better known than any other. Count Helmuth James von Moltke, the leader of the circle of anti-Nazis who took their name from Kreisau, Moltke's country estate in Silesia, was executed in the Plötzensee prison in Berlin in January, 1945.[21] Moltke, an aristocrat, a landowner, a lawyer, had gradually gathered around him a circle of leaders of many backgrounds, of varying viewpoints: Jesuit fathers, Protestant pastors,

[19] *Ibid.*

[20] Bishop of Chichester, "The Background of the Hitler Plot," *Contemporary Review*, Sept., 1945, pp. 204-205; A. Leber, *Das Gewissen Steht Auf*, pp. 190-92.

[21] Moltke, *op. cit.*, p. 66. Leber, *op. cit.*, p. 202.

Trade-Unionists and Socialists, aristocrats and Christian laymen of both confessions. From 1940 on this group met regularly, not to plan the overthrow of the Nazi regime but rather to plan spiritually for the Germany that would survive the Nazi period. Moltke was arrested and tried for high treason, not because his group plotted revolution but because they offered spiritual resistance to the National Socialist movement. In his own words, he stood before Special Justice Freisler "not as a Protestant, not as a landowner, not as a Prussian, not as an aristocrat, not as a German . . . but simply as a Christian, and as nothing else." [22]

From 1933 until the end of the regime in 1945 many thousands of Germans stood before Freisler and before similar but less notorious judges to be sentenced simply as Christians. The Christian churches formed an important link in the chain of resistance.

The Position of the Army

The consideration of the role of the German Army in the political developments of the Third Reich must be based on an accurate impression of the importance of the army in Nazi Germany. The political significance and power of the army and especially of the General Staff is often exaggerated.

The General Staff, always a research and advisory organization, had less than its usual authority during the Nazi period. The chief of the General Staff ranked as one among five department chiefs subordinate to the Supreme Commander of the army, who in turn shared the command of the armed forces with the supreme commanders of the navy and of the air force; these in turn were under the direction of the Minister of War and of the Chief of State as Commander in Chief. The influence of the General Staff was limited within the army, the influence of the army was limited within the government (see chart [23]).

In addition to this weakness of its constitutional position, the army was hampered in any political action by the tradition that the Prussian-German officer is aloof from politics. In 1933 when the chief of the General Staff, Colonel General Kurt von Hammerstein-Equord, advocated army intervention to prevent the

[22] Moltke, *op. cit.*, p. 56.

[23] Wolfgang Foerster, *Ein General Kämpft gegen den Krieg*, pp. 19-20. (Chart derived from facts given in this work.)

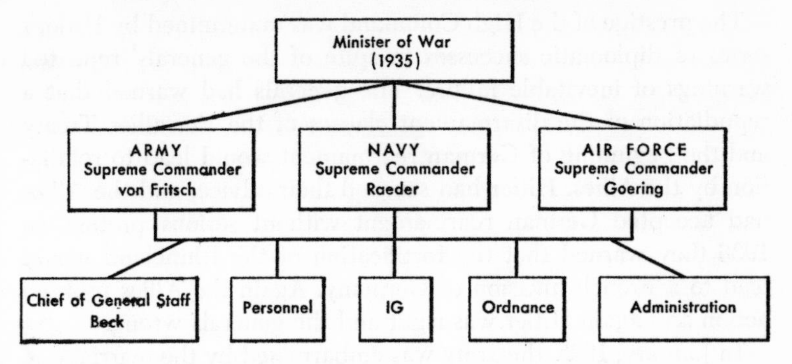

appointment of Hitler as chancellor he was rebuked by the President, Field Marshal Paul von Hindenburg, and reminded that the army's business was military and not political.[24]

The realization that opposition to National Socialism was basically a moral and not a political question came slowly and gradually to the Officer Corps. By the time the true character of National Socialism had become apparent to a substantial proportion of the professional officers the party by a series of blows had already undermined the army's power to resist.

In 1934 Hitler forced the troublesome Hammerstein to retire. During the purge of June, 1934, a leading and ambitious general, Kurt von Schleicher, was assassinated together with his wife; the army stood by, shocked but silent. Following the death of President von Hindenburg the officers of the army were maneuvered into taking an oath of personal allegiance to Hitler instead of to the Constitution or to the German state. To many officers this oath constituted a barrier of conscience to any participation in an anti-Hitler plot. In 1935 universal military training was introduced, and the need for an expanded Officer Corps to meet the demands of the new and growing army made it possible for many party members to infiltrate the formerly closed ranks of the Reichswehr. Hitler was determined to create a "People's Army" and, although he did not entirely succeed, he was able to weaken the former sense of unity. In addition, he tried to win the support of officers by quick promotions, gifts, and estates.[25]

[24] Dulles, *op. cit.*, p. 26; Rothfels, *op. cit.*, p. 64.

[25] Rothfels, *op. cit.*, p. 68. For a discussion of this subject, see *ibid.*, pp. 55 ff., and Neumann, *Making the Peace*, pp. 382 ff.

The prestige of the High Command was undermined by Hitler's series of diplomatic successes in spite of the generals' repeated warnings of inevitable failure. The generals had warned that a repudiation of the disarmament clauses of the Versailles Treaty and the beginning of German rearmament would lead to retaliation by the Allies. Hitler had scorned their advice, and the Allies had accepted German rearmament without serious protest. In 1936 they warned that the fortification of the Rhineland would lead to a French invasion of Germany. Again the Allies took no action and again Hitler was right and the generals wrong.

In January, 1938, the army was embarrassed by the marriage of the War Minister, von Blomberg, to a woman of questionable reputation. Blomberg was forced to resign. This was followed by a charge of immorality against the Supreme Commander of the army, General von Fritsch, and by his trial before a court-martial. Fritsch was fully exonerated but nevertheless resigned his post and some stigma of the charge remained attached to the army as a whole. In February, 1938, Hitler reorganized the chain of command, assuming personal command of the armed forces. He appointed General Wilhelm Keitel, generally considered subservient to Hitler, as chief of the new High Command, or OKW. Many old-line generals were retired. One hundred regimental commanders and more than ten corps and division commanders were replaced.[26]

In 1938, despite its weakened position, the High Command opposed the annexation of Austria and Hitler's demand for the Sudetenland. General Beck, Chief of the General Staff, resigned in protest over Hitler's aggressive policy but Hitler remained adamant. In both cases Hitler was successful despite army warnings. In March, 1939, when Hitler decided to occupy the remaining territory of Czechoslovakia in violation of the Munich Pact of the previous September he did not even consult the OKW.[27]

During the campaign against Poland in the fall of 1939 the generals again warned Hitler that his plans were rash and overoptimistic, but even in the question of tactics Hitler emerged victorious over the professional advice of his army. From then

[26] Rothfels, *op. cit.*, p. 69.
[27] Chester Wilmot, *The Struggle for Europe*, p. 86.

on he was convinced that his generals were a collection of "hide bound pessimists who opposed his plans out of stubborn stupidity,"[28] and their advice had even less influence on his decisions. From then on the influence and prestige of the generals further decreased. This weakening of the power and confidence of the military leadership is a factor that must be taken into account in an analysis of the role of the military in the opposition movement, in evaluating the delays and hesitations of the generals.

[28] *Ibid.*

APPENDIX B

Excerpts from a Note About the July 20, 1944, Plot by Colonel General Alfred Jodl, Nürnberg, 1946

Opinions about the plot will always be divided, perhaps less on moral and ethical grounds than on the question of whether, had the plot led to Hitler's death, this would have been advantageous or disadvantageous for Germany. Aside from a few dark and ambitious but insignificant elements, I had no doubt either then or now that men like Beck and Witzleben, for example, thought only of Germany's welfare. For someone like Beck dishonor was impossible. What did these men expect? I have tried to discover their motives. I sent for the interrogation records of the arrested officers in order to study them and they disappointed me bitterly. They said that they had hoped by overthrowing Hitler to clear the way for a compromise peace with the enemy, but they realized that they had been disappointed or had deceived themselves, that they understood nothing of diplomacy and their act had been madness and they regretted it. At the time it did not occur to me that the interrogation records might have been falsified. Today I am not so sure. However, the view expressed by the occupation powers and by a segment of the German press, that these officers took the only action possible since Hitler was a criminal, is certainly false. In my interpretation of the circumstances this is not so. Hitler's criminal activities were carried out with unparalleled secrecy by a few members of the SS; the conspirators knew as little about them as the other officers of the Wehrmacht. Had they known about these activities they would have had a powerful argument to win the support of the mass of the German Officer Corps. However, their chief argument in every cautious contact with commanders was that the war was lost and that it could only be ended without Hitler. I had long since thought this, but along with the majority of responsible commanders I saw no way out. Our enemies did not seek the overthrow of the Nazi regime; they had proclaimed the destruction of Germany. Could we prevent this fate for Germany by overthrowing Hitler? This was the decisive question. Hope for a positive answer was the fateful error of the Beck group. Even if Hitler had been overthrown, the rest of the government would have remained. The navy and the air force would have continued to obey their commanders as would the SS and the Police . . . this would have led to civil war, the front would have collapsed at a time when as yet not a single foreign foot stood on German soil and when the people, correctly or incorrectly, still believed in the possibility of salvation. . . . It is my firm conviction that the people and especially the workers would have remained peaceful, but in the chaos of self-destruction the enemy could have invaded without the order of a capitulation. Exactly the same misery would have descended on Germany as has now arrived, perhaps in a still worse form, but the public might have believed that it was not the result of military defeat but of a "stab-in-the-back." . . . It could have happened that way. Even when I consider the losses which followed until May, 1945, I still believe that the way to the bitter end was better for Germany. It cannot give rise to false legends.

These notes were supplied to the author in typescript in German by General Jodl's widow, Luise Jodl.

Selected Bibliography

INTERVIEWS

Blumentritt, Günther. Marburg, Germany, September, 1958.
Bussche-Streithorst, Baron Axel von dem. Washington, April, 1957.
Hammerstein-Equord, Ludwig Baron von. Bonn, March, 1961.
Jodl, Luise. Munich, Germany, July, 1958.
Kessel, Albrecht von. Washington, April, 1957.
Kesselring, Albert. Bad Wiessee, Germany, July and August, 1958.
Leber, Annedore. Berlin, March, 1961.
Manteuffel, Hasso von. Garmisch-Partenkirchen, Germany, August, 1958.
Manstein, Fritz Erich von. Allmendingen über Ulm, Germany, September, 1953.
Müller, Josef. Munich, Germany, August, 1958.
Schlabrendorff, Fabian von. Rutherford, N. J., April, 1957.
Steelman, John R. Washington, April, 1956.
Warlimont, Walter. Rottach-Egern, Germany, August, 1958.
Weskamm, Bishop Wilhelm. Berlin, Germany, August, 1953.
Westphal, Siegfried. Bonn, May, 1961.
Witzleben, Hermann von. Munich, Germany, July, 1958.

UNPUBLISHED LETTERS AND DIARIES

Blumentritt, Günther. Letters dated Marburg, Germany, March 1 and April 18, 1950.
Guderian, Heinz. Letter dated Dietramzell, Germany, March 28, 1950.
Halder, Franz. Letter dated Königstein, Germany, March 22, 1950.
Jodl, Alfred. Personal notes dated Nürnberg, Germany, 1946.
Kessel, Albrecht von. "Verborgene Saat: das Andere Deutschland," unpublished diary of the war years.
Lünick, Baron Hermann von. Letter to Pater Max Pribilla dated Jan. 19, 1950.

Manstein, Fritz Erich von. Letter dated Allmendingen über Ulm, Germany, June 2, 1953.

Manteuffel, Hasso von. Letter dated Neuss, Germany, March 12, 1950.

Schlabrendorff, Fabian von. Letter dated Wiesbaden, Germany, April 8, 1950.

Speidel, Hans. Letter dated Freudenstadt, Germany, March 13, 1950.

THE BACKGROUND OF ALLIED POLICY IN THE SECOND WORLD WAR: CHAPTERS 1 AND 2

Baldwin, Hanson W. *Great Mistakes of the War.* New York: Harper, 1950.

Barth, Karl. *The Only Way: How Can the Germans be Cured?* New York: Philosophical Library, 1947.

Bernadotte, Count Folke. *The Fall of the Curtain.* London: Cassell, 1945.

Bismarck, Otto Fürst von. *Gedanken und Erinnerungen.* Stuttgart: Verlag der J. G. Cotta'schen Buchhandlung, 1898.

——. *Bismarcks Briefe an Seine Gattin aus dem Kriege 1870-71.* Stuttgart and Berlin: Cotta'sche, 1903.

Boetticher, Friedrich von. *Schlieffen: Viel Leisten, Wenig Hervortretsen, Mehr sein als scheinen.* Göttingen: Musterschmidt Verlag, 1957.

Brogan, Denis W. *The Era of Franklin D. Roosevelt.* A Chronicle of the New Deal and Global War. New Haven: Yale Univ. Press, 1950.

Bryans, J. Lonsdale. *Blind Victory.* London: Skeffington, 1951.

Bryant, Arthur. *The Turn of the Tide: A History of the War Years Based on the Diaries of Field-Marshal Lord Alanbrooke, Chief of the Imperial General Staff.* New York: Doubleday, 1957.

Bullitt, William C. "How We Won the War and Lost the Peace," *Life,* Aug. 30, 1948.

Butcher, Harry C. *My Three Years with Eisenhower.* New York: Simon and Schuster, 1946.

Byrnes, James F. *Speaking Frankly.* New York: Harper, 1947.

Chamberlin, William Henry. *America's Second Crusade.* Chicago: Regnery, 1950.

Churchill, Winston S. *The Hinge of Fate.* Boston: Houghton Mifflin, 1950.

——. *Closing the Ring.* Boston: Houghton Mifflin, 1951.

Clark, Mark. *Calculated Risk.* New York: Harper, 1950.

Clausewitz, Karl von. *On War.* Translated by Colonel J. J. Graham. London: Kegan, Paul, Trench, Trubner, 1911.

Clauss, Max Walter. *Der Weg nach Jalta: President Roosevelts Verantwortung.* Heidelberg: Vowinckel, 1952.

Corbett, Percy E. *War Aims and Postwar Plans.* London: Chatham House, Royal Institute of International Affairs, 1941.

Council on Foreign Relations. *The United States in World Affairs: 1945-47.* Series 1931–. New York: Harper, 1947.

Craig, Gordon Alexander. *The Politics of the Prussian Army: 1640-1945.* Oxford: Clarendon Press, 1955.

Craig, Gordon Alexander, and Gilbert, Felix (eds). *The Diplomats: 1919-1939.* Princeton: Princeton Univ. Press, 1953.

Dahms, Hellmuth Günther. *Roosevelt und der Krieg: die Vorgeschichte von Pearl Harbor.* Munich: Janus Bücher, Verlag Oldenbourg, 1958.

Day, Donald. *Franklin D. Roosevelt's Own Story.* Boston: Little, Brown, 1951.

Deane, John R. *The Strange Alliance: The Story of Our Efforts at Wartime Cooperation With Russia.* New York: Viking, 1947.

Decade of American Foreign Policy: Basic Documents, A. Washington: U.S. Government Printing Office, 1950.

Dennett, Raymond, and Johnson, Joseph E. (eds.). *Negotiating with the Russians.* Boston: World Peace Foundation, 1951.

Eisenhower, Dwight David. *Crusade in Europe.* New York: Doubleday, 1948.

Feis, Herbert. *Churchill, Roosevelt, Stalin: The War They Waged and the Peace They Sought.* Princeton: Princeton Univ. Press, 1957.

Fischer, John. *Master Plan, U.S.A.* New York: Harper, 1951.

Foreign Relations of the United States: The Conferences at Malta and Yalta. Washington: U.S. Government Printing Office, 1955.

Forrestal, James. *The Forrestal Diaries* (ed. Walter Millis). New York: Viking, 1951.

Fuller, John F. C. *The Second World War: 1939-45.* New York: Duell, Sloan, Pearce, 1948.

Gooch, G. P. *Studies in Diplomacy and Statecraft.* London: Longmans, Green, 1942.

Goodrich, Leland M., and Carroll, Marie J. (eds.). *Documents on American Foreign Relations.* Boston: World Peace Foundation, Vol. VI, July, 1943-June, 1944, 1945. Vol. VII, June, 1944-June, 1945. Princeton: Princeton Univ. Press, 1947.

Grenfell, Russell. *Unconditional Hatred: German War Guilt and the Future of Europe.* New York: Devin Adair, 1953.

Gunther, John. *Roosevelt in Retrospect.* New York: Harper, 1950.

Hammond, Paul Y. "The Origins of JCS 1067." Typescript. 1958.

Holborn, Louise W. (ed.). *War and Peace Aims of the United Nations.* Boston: World Peace Foundation, 1943, 1948.

Hoover, Herbert C. *Addresses upon the American Road: 1948-1950.* Stanford: Stanford Univ. Press, 1951.

Hull, Cordell. *The Memoirs of Cordell Hull.* New York: Macmillan, 1948.

Kennan, George F. *American Diplomacy: 1900-1950.* Chicago: Chicago Univ. Press, 1951.

Kingdon, Frank. *As FDR Said.* New York: Duell, Sloan, Pearce, 1950.

Leahy, William D. *I Was There.* New York: McGraw-Hill, 1950.

Lerner, Daniel. *Sykewar: Psychological Warfare against Germany, D-Day to V-E Day.* New York: Stewart, 1949.

Löwenstein, Prince Hubertus. *The Germans in History.* New York: Columbia Univ. Press, 1945.

MacLeish, Archibald. *American Opinion and the War.* New York: Macmillan, 1942.

Meissner, Boris. *Russland, die Westmächte und Deutschland: die Sowjetische Deutschlandpolitik, 1943-1953.* Hamburg: Nölke, 1953.

Morgenthau, Henry, Jr. "Our Policy Toward Germany," New York *Post,* Nov. 24, 1947.

Morley, Felix. *The Foreign Policy of the United States.* New York: Knopf, 1951.

Moseley, Philip E. "Dismemberment of Germany. The Allied Negotiations from Yalta to Potsdam," *Foreign Affairs,* Vol. XXVIII, No. 3 (April, 1950), pp. 487-98.

Muralt, Leonard von. *From Versailles to Potsdam.* Chicago: Regnery, 1948.

Mussolini, Benito. *The Fall of Mussolini.* Max Ascoli (ed.). New York: Farrar, Straus, 1948.

Neumann, Franz. *Behemoth: The Structure and Practice of National Socialism.* London and New York: Oxford Univ. Press, 1942.

Neumann, William L. *Making the Peace: 1941-1945.* Washington, D. C.: Foundation for Foreign Affairs, 1950.

Niebuhr, Reinhold. *The Irony of American History.* New York: Scribner, 1952.

Nizer, Louis. *What to Do With Germany.* Chicago and New York: Ziff-Davis, 1944.

Opie, Redvers. *The Search for Peace Settlements.* Washington: Brookings Institution, 1951.

Peffer, Nathaniel. "The United States and China. The Politics of Sentimentality." Columbia University *Forum*, Vol. II, No. 2 (Winter, 1959), pp. 28-34.

Pich, F. W. *Peacemaking in Perspective.* Oxford: Pen-in-Hand, 1950.

Roosevelt, Elliott. *As He Saw It.* New York: Duell, Sloan, Pearce, 1946.

Roosevelt, Franklin D. *Wartime Correspondence between President Roosevelt and Pope Pius XII.* Intr. and explanatory notes by Myron C. Taylor. New York: Macmillan, 1947.

——. *War Messages of Franklin D. Roosevelt: December 8, 1941, to April 13, 1945.* Washington: U.S. Government Printing Office, [1945].

——. *The Public Papers and Addresses of Franklin D. Roosevelt.* New York: Random House, 1938-1950.

Rosenman, Samuel S. *Working with Roosevelt.* New York: Harper, 1952.

Sherwood, Robert E. *Roosevelt and Hopkins.* New York: Harper, rev. ed., 1950.

Slessor, Sir John. "Grand Strategy and the Second World War," *The Listener,* Vol. LVI, No. 1443, Nov. 22, 1956.

——. *The Central Blue: The Autobiography of Sir John Slessor, Marshal of the RAF.* New York: Praeger, 1957.

Snell, John L. *Wartime Origins of the East-West Dilemma over Germany.* New Orleans: Hauser, c. 1959.

Statistischen Amt der Stadt Berlin. *Berlin in Zahlen, Taschenbuch.* Berlin: Neue Berlin Verlagsgesellschaft, 1947.

Stettinius, Edward R. *Roosevelt and the Russians, The Yalta Conference* (ed. Walter Johnson). Garden City, N. Y.: Doubleday, 1949.

Stimson, Henry L., and Bundy, McGeorge. *On Active Service in Peace and War.* New York: Harper, 1948.

Stolper, Gustav. *German Realities.* New York: Reynal and Hitchcock, 1948.

Thomas, Norman. *Appeal to the Nations.* New York: Henry Holt, 1947.

Truman, Harry S. *Memoirs.* Garden City, N. Y.: Doubleday, 1955.

United States Department of State. *Toward the Peace, Documents.* Department of State Publication 2298. Washington: U.S. Government Printing Office, 1945.

——. *Making the Peace Treaties, 1941-1947.* Washington: U.S. Government Printing Office, 1947.

United States Senate. *Interlocking Subversion in Government Departments* (The Harry Dexter White Papers). Committee on Judiciary. Washington: U.S. Government Printing Office, 1956.

Valentin, Veit. *The German People: Their History and Civilization from the Holy Roman Empire to the Third Reich*. New York: Knopf, 1946.

Vandenberg, Arthur H. *The Private Papers of Senator Vandenberg* (ed. Arthur H. Vandenberg, Jr., and Joe Alex Morris). Boston: Houghton Mifflin, 1952.

Wedemeyer, Albert C. *Wedemeyer Reports!* New York: Henry Holt, 1958.

Welles, Sumner. *Seven Decisions That Shaped History*. New York: Harper, 1951.

Wilmot, Chester. *The Struggle for Europe*. New York: Harper, 1952.

Wittmer, Felix. *The Yalta Betrayal*. Caldwell, Idaho: Caxton, 1954.

Wolfe, Thomas. *You Can't Go Home Again*. New York: Sun Dial, 1942.

The Military Development of the Second World War

Aron, Raymond. *The Century of Total War*. Garden City, N. Y.: Doubleday, 1954.

Assmann, Kurt, *et al*. *Deutsche Schicksalsjahre: Historische Bilder aus dem Zweiten Weltkrieg und Seiner Vorgeschichte*. Wiesbaden: Brockhaus, 1950.

Baldwin, Hanson. "Our Worst Blunders of the War." *Atlantic Monthly*, January, 1950, pp. 34 ff.

Bilanz des Zweiten Welt Krieges. Oldenburg: Hamburg, 1953.

Blumentritt, Günther. *Gerd von Rundstedt, the Soldier and the Man*. London: Odhams, 1952.

Boldt, Gerhard. *Die Letzten Tage der Reichskanzlei*. Hamburg: Rowolt, 1947.

Bradley, Omar N. *A Soldier's Story*. New York: Henry Holt, 1951.

Butow, Robert J. C. *Japan's Decision to Surrender*. Stanford, Calif.: Stanford Univ. Press, 1954.

Buttlar, Freiherr von, *et al*. *Weltkrieg, 1939-1945: Ehrenbuch der Deutschen Wehrmacht*. Stuttgart: Riegler, 1954.

Command Decisions. Kent Roberts Greenfield (ed.). Prepared by the Chief of Military History, U.S. Department of the Army. Introduction by Hanson W. Baldwin. New York: Harcourt, Brace, 1959.

Dickens, Sir Gerald Charles. *Bombing and Strategy, the Fallacy of Total War*. London: S. Low, Marston, 1947.

Dirksen, Herbert von. *Moscow, Tokyo, London: 20 Years of German Foreign Policy*. Norman, Okla.: Univ. of Oklahoma Press, 1952.

Doerr, Hans. *Der Feldzug nach Stalingrad*. Darmstadt: E. S. Miller and Son, 1955.

Dupuy, R. Ernest. *Men of West Point.* New York: Sloane, 1951.

Dupuy, R. Ernest, and Dupuy, Trevor N. *Military Heritage of America.* New York: McGraw-Hill, 1956.

Gilbert, Felix (ed.). *Hitler Directs His War.* New York: Oxford Univ. Press, 1950.

Goebbels, Paul Joseph. *The Goebbels Diaries, 1942-1943* (ed. Louis P. Lochner). Garden City, N. Y.: Doubleday, 1948.

Görlitz, Walter. *Der Deutsche Generalstab, 1657-1945.* Frankfurt am Main: Frankfurter Hefte, 1950.

——. *Der Zweite Weltkrieg, 1939-1945.* Stuttgart: Steingrüben, 1951, 1952.

Greiner, Helmuth. *Die Oberste Wehrmachtführung, 1939-1943.* Wiesbaden: Limes, 1951.

Guckenholz, Hermann. "Zur Zusammenbruch der Heeresgruppe Mitte im Sommer 1944," *Vierteljahrshefte fur Zeitgeschichte,* Vol. 3, No. 3 (1955), pp. 317-33.

Guderian, Heinz. *Erinnerungen eines Soldaten.* Heidelberg: Vowinckel, 1951. American edition: *Panzer Leader.* New York: E. P. Dutton, 1952.

Halder, Franz. *Hitler as Warlord.* London: Putnam, 1950.

——. *Gespräche mit Halder* (ed. Peter Bor). Wiesbaden: Limes, 1950.

Hayne, Friedrich. *Die Invasion, von Cotentin bis Falaise.* Heidelberg: Scharnhorst, Vowinckel, 1954.

Heusinger, Adolf. *Befehl im Widerstreit: Schicksalsstunden der Deutsche Armee, 1923-1945.* Tübingen: Wunderlich, 1950.

Hinsley, F. H. *Hitler's Strategy.* Cambridge, England: Cambridge Univ. Press, 1951.

Hossbach, Friedrich. *Zwischen Wehrmacht und Hitler, 1934-1938.* Wolfenbüttel: Wolfenbüttlerverlaganstalt, 1949.

Huntington, Samuel P. *The Soldier and the State: the Theory and Politics of Civil-Military Relations.* Cambridge, Mass.: Belknap Press of Harvard Univ. Press, 1957.

Kecskemeti, Paul. *Strategic Surrender, the Politics of Victory and Defeat.* Stanford, Calif.: Stanford Univ. Press, 1958.

Kern, Erich. *Dance of Death.* New York: Scribner's, 1951.

Kesselring, Albert. *Soldat bis zum Letzten Tag.* Bonn: Athenäum, 1953.

——. *Gedanken zum Zweiten Weltkrieg.* Bonn: Athenäum, 1955.

Kleist, Peter. *Zwischen Stalin und Hitler, 1939-1945.* Bonn: Athenäum, 1950.

——. "Nach Stalingrad bot Josef Stalin Hitler den Frieden an," *Deutsche Soldaten Zeitung,* December, 1959, 1 ed., pp. 1 and 4.

Koch, Lutz. *Erwin Rommel, die Wandlung eines Grossen Soldaten.* Stuttgart: W. Gebauer, 1950.

Konstantin Prinz von Bayern. *Der Papst, ein Lebensbild.* Frankfurt: Ullstein, 1952.

Kreipe, Werner, *et al. The Fatal Decisions.* New York: Berkeley, 1956.

Kuby, Erich (ed.). *Das Ende des Schreckens. Dokumente des Unterganges.* Munich: Süddeutsche Zeitung, 1955.

Liddell Hart, Basil Henry. *The British Way in Warfare.* London: Faber, 1932.

——. "A Reflection on Strategy and Policy—and Humanity—in Relation to the Past and Present." Typescript, July 3, 1943.

——. "The Background to 'Unconditional Surrender.'" Typescript, July 31, 1943.

——. "The Future Balance of Europe—a Reflection." Typescript, Oct. 1, 1943.

——. "The High Cost of 'Unconditional Surrender.'" Typescript, Nov. 21, 1947.

——. *The Other Side of the Hill.* London: Cassell, 1948. American edition: *The German Generals Talk.* New York: Morrow, 1948.

——. *Defense of the West.* New York: Morrow, 1950.

——. *Strategy: The Indirect Approach.* New York: Praeger, 1954.

Lüdde-Neurath, Walter. *Regierung Dönitz: die Letzten Tage des Dritten Reiches.* Göttingen: Musterschmidt, 1950.

Manstein, (Fritz) Erich von. *Verlorene Siege.* Bonn: Athenäum, 1955.

Marshall, George C. *General Marshall's Report, the Winning of the War in Europe and the Pacific: Biennial Report of the Chief of Staff of the U. S. Army, July 1, 1943-June 30, 1945.* New York: Simon and Schuster for the War Department, 1945.

The Memoirs of Field-Marshal the Viscount Montgomery of Alamein, K.G. Cleveland: World Publ., 1958.

Müller, Johannes. *Sturz in den Abgrund: die Letzte 10 Monate, vom 20 Juli 1944 bis zum 8 Mai 1945.* Offenbach am Main: Bollwerk Verlag, 1947.

Nebel, Gerhard. *Unter Partisanen und Kreuzfahrern.* Stuttgart: Klett, 1950.

Norman, Albert. *Operation Overlord.* Harrisburg, Pa.: Military Service Pub. Co., 1952.

OKW (German High Command). *OKW Bericht: Deutschland im Kampf* (eds. A. J. Berndt of Reichs Propaganda Ministry and Col. von Wedel of OKW). Berlin: Otto Stollberg, 1943 and 1944.

O'Neill, H. C. *A Short History of the Second World War.* New York: Praeger, 1950.

Paget, R. T. *Manstein: His Campaigns and His Trial.* London: Collins, 1951.

Papen, Franz von. *Memoirs.* New York: Dutton, 1952.

Patton, George S., Jr. *War as I Knew It.* Boston: Houghton Mifflin, 1947.

Picker, Henry. *Hitlers Tischgespräche im Führerhauptquartier, 1941-1942.* Bonn: Athenäum, 1951.

Pogue, Forrest C. *The Supreme Command.* Washington: Department of Army, Office of Chief of Military History, 1954.

Pratt, Fletcher. *War for the World.* New Haven: Yale Univ. Press, 1950.

Quint, Herbert A. *Die Wendepunkte des Krieges.* Stuttgart: Steingrüben, 1950.

Raeder, Erich. *Mein Leben.* Tübingen: Schlichtenmayer, 1957. American edition: *My Life.* Annapolis: United States Naval Institute, 1960.

Rintelen, Enno von. *Mussolini als Bundesgenosse.* Tübingen: Wunderlich, 1951.

Rommel, Erwin. *The Rommel Papers* (ed. Basil H. Liddell Hart). New York: Harcourt, Brace, 1953.

Root, Waverly. *Casablanca to Katyn: the Secret History of the War,* Vol. III. New York: Scribner's, 1946.

Schacht, Hjalmar. American edition: *Confessions of the Old Wizard,* Autobiography. Boston: Houghton Mifflin, 1956.

Schellenberg, Walter. *The Labyrinth: Memoirs of Walter Schellenberg.* New York: Harper, 1956.

Schultz, Joachim. *Die Letzten 30 Tage.* Stuttgart: Steingrüben, 1951.

Schwerin von Krosigk, Lutz Graf. *Es Geschah in Deutschland.* Tübingen: Wunderlich, 1951.

———. "Die 21 Tage der Regierung Dönitz," *Die Zeit,* Nov. 8, 1951, p. 9.

Seydewitz, Max. *Civil Life in Wartime Germany. The Story of the Home Front.* New York: Viking, 1945.

Sommerfeld, Martin. *Der OKW Gibt Bekannt.* Frankfurt am Main: Westdeutscher Verlag, 1952.

Speidel, Hans. *Invasion 1944. Ein Beitrag zu Rommels und des Reiches Schicksal.* Tübingen: Wunderlich, 1949.

Stieff, Helmut. "Ausgewählte Briefe von Generalmajor Helmut Stieff," *Vierteljahrshefte für Zeitgeschichte,* pp. 291-305.

Taylor, Telford. *Sword and Swastika.* New York: Simon and Schuster, 1952.

Thorwald, Jürgen. *Das Ende an der Elbe.* Stuttgart: Steingrüben, 1950.

Tippelskirch, Kurt von. *Geschichte des Zweiten Weltkriegs.* Bonn: Athenäum, 1956.

United States Department of the Army. *Army Battle Casualties and Nonbattle Deaths in World War II. Final Report, 7 December, 1941-31 December, 1946.* Washington. n.d.

Weizsäcker, Ernst Heinrich Freiherr von. *Memoirs* (trans. John Andrews). Chicago: Regnery, 1951.

Westphal, Siegfried. *The German Army in the West.* London: Cassell, 1951.

Wheeler-Bennett, J. W. *The Nemesis of Power.* London: Macmillan, 1953.

Wiener Library Bulletin. "Unconditional Surrender: Was it a Sensible Demand." London, Vol. X, Nos. 3-4, 1956, pp. 20-21.

Young, Desmond. *Rommel, the Desert Fox.* New York: Harper, 1951.

The German Anti-Nazi Resistance Movement

Adolph, Walter. *Im Schatten des Galgens, zum Gedächtnis der Blutzeugen in der nationalsozialistischen Kirchenverfolgung.* Berlin: Morus, 1953.

Andreas-Friedrich, Ruth. *Berlin Underground, 1938-1945.* New York: Henry Holt, 1947.

Anger, Walter. *Das Dritte Reich in Dokumenten.* Frankfurt: Europa, 1957.

"Aus den Akten des 20 Juli"—Der Bericht des Major Remer. *Das Parlament: Aus Politik und Zeitgeschichte.* B XXXXVI, 1954. Nov. 17, 1954.

Bonhoeffer, Dietrich. *Widerstand und Ergebung.* Briefe und Auszeichnungen aus der Haft (ed. Eberhard Bethge). Munich: Kaiser, 1951.

Bryan, J. Lonsdale. "Zur Brittischen Amtliche Haltung gegenüber der deutsche Widerstandsbewegung," *Vierteljahrshefte für Zeitgeschichte,* Vol. I (1953), pp. 347-51.

Chichester, Bishop of. "The Background of the Hitler Plot," *Contemporary Review,* September, 1945, pp. 203-8.

Delp, Alfred. *Im Angesicht des Todes* (ed. Paul Bolkovac). Frankfurt: Knecht, 1956.

Dokumente aus dem Kampf der Katholischen Kirche im Bistum Berlin gegen den Nationalsozialismus. Berlin: Morus, 1957.

Dulles, Allen W. *Germany's Underground.* New York: Macmillan, 1947.

Ehlers, Dieter. "Die Methoden der Beck-Goerdeler Verschwörung," *Das Parlament: Aus Politik und Zeitgeschichte.* B IV, 1955. Jan. 26, 1955.

Fitz Gibbon, Constantine. *20 July*. New York: W. W. Norton, 1956.

Foerster, Wolfgang. *Ein General Kämpft gegen den Krieg.* Aus dem nachgelassenen Papieren des Generalstabschefs Ludwig Beck. Munich: Dom Verlag, 1949.

——. *Generaloberst Ludwig Beck, Sein Kampf gegen den Krieg.* Munich: Isar Verlag, 1953.

Ford, Franklin L. "The Twentieth of July in the History of the German Resistance," *American Historical Review,* July, 1946.

Gisevius, Hans Bernd. *To the Bitter End* (trans., Richard and Clara Winstone). London: Jonathan Cape, 1948.

Gollwitzer, Helmut, *et al.* (eds.). *Du Hast mich heimgesucht bei Nacht. Abschiedsbriefe und Aufzeichnungen des Widerstandes, 1933-1945.* Munich: Kaiser, 1954.

Graml, Hermann. "Die Deutsche Militäropposition vom Sommer 1940 bis zum Frühjahr 1943," *Das Parlament: Aus Politik und Zeitgeschichte.* B XXVIII, 1959. July 16, 1959.

Hamburger Fremdenblatt. No. 22, Sept. 26, 1944.

Hassell, Ulrich von. *Vom Andern Deutschland.* Aus den nachgelassenen Tagebüchern, 1938-1944, von Ulrich von Hassell. Zurich: Atlantis, 1946. American edition: *The von Hassell Diaries, 1938-1944* (intro. by Allen W. Dulles). Garden City, N. Y.: Doubleday, 1947.

Hermelink, Heinrich (ed.). *Kirche im Kampf.* (Documents of the Resistance of the Evangelical Church, 1933-1945). Tübingen: Wunderlich, 1950.

Klonne, Arno. *Gegen den Strom.* (Report of youthful resistance in the Third Reich.) Hannover: Norddeutsche Verlag, 1958.

Knauss, Robert. "Soldaten und der 20en Juli," *Die Zeit,* Oct. 4, 1951.

Krausnick, Helmut. "Erwin Rommel und der deutsche Widerstand gegen Hitler," *Vierteljahrshefte für Zeitgeschichte,* I, 1953.

——. "Vorgeschichte und Beginn des Militärischen Widerstandes gegen Hitler," *Das Parlament: Aus Politik und Zeitgeschichte,* B XXXXVI, Nov. 16, 1955.

Leber, Annedore (ed.). *Das Gewissen Steht Auf.* Berlin: Mosaik, 1954.

Leber, Julius. *Ein Mann geht seinen Weg* (ed. by his friends). Writings, Speeches, Letters. Berlin: Mosaik, 1952.

Lochner, Louis P. *Always the Unexpected.* New York: Macmillan, 1956.

Moltke, Helmuth James Graf von. *Letzte Briefe aus dem Gefängnis Tegel.* Berlin: Henssel, 1950.

Neuhäusler, Johannes. *Kreuz und Hakenkreuz.* (The Struggle of National Socialism against the Catholic Church and the Church Resistance.) Munich: Catholic Church of Bavaria, 1946.

Niemöller, Wilhelm. *Die Bekennende Kirche sagt Hitler die Wahrheit.* Bielefeld: Bechauf, 1954.

——. *Die Evangelische Kirche im Dritten Reich.* Bielefeld: Bechauf, 1956.

Osas, Veit. *Walküre.* Hamburg: Deutschland Verlag, 1953.

Pechel, Rudolf. *Deutscher Widerstand.* Zurich: E. Rentsch, 1947.

Das Reich, Berlin, Feb. 1, 1943-April 1, 1945.

Ritter, Gerhard. *Goerdeler und die Deutsche Widerstandsbewegung.* Stuttgart: Deutsche, 1954.

Rothfels, Hans. *The German Opposition to Hitler.* Chicago: Regnery, 1948.

—— (ed.). "Adam von Trott und das State Department," *Vierteljahrshefte für Zeitgeschichte,* 7 Jahrgang, 1959, 5 Heft, July, pp. 318-32.

Schacht, Hjalmar. *Account Settled.* London: G. Weidenfeld and Nicolson, 1945.

Schlabrendorff, Fabian von. *They Almost Killed Hitler* (ed. Gero v.S. Gaevernitz). New York: Macmillan, 1947.

Schramm, Wilhelm Ritter von. *Der 20en Juli in Paris.* Bad Wörishofen: Kindler und Schiermeyer, 1953.

"SS Bericht über den 20en Juli": Aus den Papieren des S.S. Obersturmbennführers Georg Kiessel. *Nordwestdeutsche Hefte* 2, 1947.

Völkischer Beobachter. Munich edition, Jan. 24, 1943-April 1, 1945. Vienna edition, Sept. 26, 28, and 29, 1944.

Die Vollmacht des Gewissens (ed. by Europäischen Publikation). Bonn: Hermann Rinn, 1956.

Weisenborn, Günther (ed.). *Der Lautlose Aufstand, 1933-1945.* Hamburg: Rowolt, 1953.

Zeller, Eberhard. *Geist der Freiheit, der Zwanzigste Juli.* Munich: Rinn, 1954.

Zimmermann, Erich, and Hans-Adolf Jacobsen (eds.), *20, Juli 1944.* Bonn: Bundeszentrale für Heimatdienst, 1960.

Postwar Germany

THE NÜRNBERG TRIALS

Bardeche, Maurice. *Die Politik der Zerstörung. Nürnberg oder Europa.* Göttingen: Plesse, 1950.

Belgion, Montgomery. *Victor's Justice.* Chicago: Regnery, 1949.

Benton, Wilbourn E., and Grimm, George (eds.). *Nuremberg. German Views of the War Trial.* Dallas: Southern Methodist Univ. Press, 1955.

Ehard, Hans. "The Nuremberg Trial Against the Major War Criminals and International Law," *American Journal of International Law,* Vol. XLIII (April, 1949).

Hankey, Lord. *Politics. Trials and Errors.* Chicago: Regnery, 1950.

Stimson, Henry L., "The Nuremberg Trial, Landmark in Law," *Foreign Affairs,* Vol. XXV, January, 1947.

Trial of the Major War Criminals Before the International Military Tribunal, Nuremberg, 14 November, 1945-10 October, 1946. (Official text in the English language.) Nürnberg, 1947-1949.

General Postwar Conditions

Alexander, Edgar. *Adenauer and the New Germany.* The Chancellor of the Vanquished. New York: Farrar, Straus and Cudahy, 1957.

Am Abend der Demontage. Sechs Jahre Reparationspolitik. Bremen: Trüjen, 1951.

Arbeitsgemeinschaft Deutscher Wirtschaftswissenschaftlicher Forschungsinstitut. *The Condition of the West German and the World Economies at mid-Year of 1951.* Bonn, 1951.

Bidwell, Percy. *Germany's Contribution to European Economic Life.* Paris: M. Rivière, 1949.

Bindschedler, Rudolf L. "Die Völkerrechtliche Stellung Deutschlands." *Schweizerisches Jahrbuch für Internationales Recht.* Vol. 6 (1949), pp. 37-64.

Brandt, Karl. *Germany, Key to Peace in Europe.* Claremont, Calif.: Claremont College Press, 1949.

Bryan, J. Lonsdale. *Blind Victory.* London: Skeffington, 1951.

Clay, Lucius D. *Decision in Germany.* Garden City, N. Y.: Doubleday, 1950.

Davidson, Eugene. *The Death and Life of Germany.* New York: Knopf, 1959.

Fahy, Charles. "Legal Problems of German Occupation," *Michigan Law Review,* Vol. 47 (November, 1948), pp. 11-22.

Gembardt, Ulrich. "Zehn Jahre Danach." *Deutsche Universitätszeitung.* Vol. 8 (1953), No. 4, pp. 3-4.

Germany, Auswärtiges Amt. *Documents on German Foreign Policy, 1918-1945.* Washington: U.S. Government Printing Office, 1949.

Germany, 1947-1949. The Story in Documents. Washington: U.S. Government Printing Office, 1950.

German Federal Government. *Germany Reports.* Bonn: Press and Information Office, 1953.

Gollancz, Victor. *In Darkest Germany* (intr. by Robert M. Hutchins). Hinsdale, Ill.: Regnery, 1947.

Grewe, Wilhelm. *Ein Besatzungsstatut für Deutschland.* Stuttgart: Koehler, n.d.

Holles, Everett. *Unconditional Surrender.* New York: Howell Soskin, 1945.

Hoover, Calvin Bryce. "Germany and Europe's Recovery," *Yale Review,* Spring, 1948.

Howley, Frank L. *Berlin Command.* New York: Putnam, 1950.

Kaufmann, Erich. *Um Recht und Gerechtigkeit.* Stuttgart: Kohlhammer, 1950.

Knappen, Marshall. *And Call it Peace.* Chicago: Univ. of Chicago Press, 1947.

Liepelt, Klaus. "Die Oder-Neisse Line: Ein Ergebnis der Allierten Kriegziel." *Deutsche Universitätszeitung.* Vol. 8, 1953, Heft 5, pp. 9-13.

Litchfield, Edward H. *Governing Postwar Germany.* Ithaca: Cornell Univ. Press, 1953.

Meinecke, Friedrich, *The German Catastrophe* (trans. Sidney B. Fay). Cambridge: Harvard Univ. Press, 1950.

Merkatz, Hans Joachim von (ed.). *Germany Today.* Frankfurt am Main: A. Metzner, 1954.

"Military Government," *The Annals.* American Academy of Political and Social Science, Vol. 267, January, 1950.

Miksche, F. O. *Unconditional Surrender: The Roots of a World War III.* London: Faber, 1952.

Morgenthau, Hans (ed.). *Germany and the Future of Europe.* Chicago: Chicago Univ. Press, 1951.

Neumann, Franz. "German Democracy, 1950," *International Conciliation.* New York: Carnegie Endowment, No. 461, May, 1950.

Norman, Albert. *Our German Policy: Propaganda and Culture.* New York: Vantage, 1951.

Pollack, James K. *Germany in Power and Eclipse.* New York: Van Nostrand, 1952.

Pollack, James K.: Meisel, J. H.; Bretton, H. L. *Germany under Occupation.* Ann Arbor: George Wahr, 1949.

Pribilla, Max. *Deutsche Schicksalsfragen. Rückblick und Ausblick.* Frankfurt am Main: Knecht, 1950.

Royal Institute of International Affairs. *Documents on European Recovery and Defence, March, 1947-April, 1949*. London: Chatham House, 1949.

——. *Defence in the Cold War*. London: Chatham House, 1950.

——. *Documents on Germany under Occupation: 1945-1954* (ed. Beate Ruhm von Oppen). London: Oxford Univ. Press, 1955.

Salomon, Ernst von. *Fragebogen* (trans. Constantine FitzGibbon). Garden City, N. Y.: Doubleday, 1954.

Shub, Boris. *The Choice*. New York: Duell, Sloan, Pearce, 1950.

Starr, Joseph R. *United States Military Government in Germany*. Washington: U.S. Army, Historical Division, 1950.

Stödter, Rolf. *Deutschlands Rechtlage*. Hamburg: Rechts und Staatswissen-schaftlicher Verlag, 1948.

United States Department of State. *Occupation of Germany, Policy and Progress, 1945-1946*. Washington: U.S. Government Printing Office, 1947.

United States Office of High Commissioner for Germany. *Germany's Parliament in Action*. Washington: U.S. Government Printing Office, 1950.

Utley, Freda. *The High Cost of Vengeance*. Chicago: Regnery, 1949.

Vagts, Alfred. "Bedingungslose Kapitulation als geschichtliches Phänomen." *Vierteljahrshefte für Zeitgeschichte*. 7 Jahrgang, 1959, 3 Heft, July, pp. 280-309.

Die Vertreibung der deutsche Bevölkerung aus den Gebieten östlich der Oder Neisse. Bonn: Government Publications, I, 1953; II, 1955.

Wallich, Henry C. *Mainsprings of the German Revival*. New Haven: Yale Univ. Press, 1955.

Ward, Barbara. *The West at Bay*. New York: W. W. Norton, 1948.

——. *Policy for the West*. New York: W. W. Norton, 1951.

Weinstein, Adelbert. *Armee Ohne Pathos*. Bonn: Kollen, 1951.

Zbinden, Hans. *Um Deutschlands Zukunft, Gedanken eines Schweizers*. Zurich: Artemis Verlag, 1947.

Zink, Harold. *The United States in Germany, 1944-1945*. Princeton: Van Nostrand, 1957.

Glossary of Terms and Abbreviations

Abwehr. Wehrmacht Intelligence Service

Barbarossa. German invasion of U.S.S.R., June, 1941

BEF. British Expeditionary Forces

Bundestag. The Diet or lower house of the German Federal Republic

Gestapo. Geheime Staatspolizei—the Nazi Secret State Police, charged especially with investigating political crimes

HICOG. Office of U.S. High Commissioner for Germany; replaced Office of Military Government

JCS/1067. Basic directive of the U.S. Joint Chiefs of Staff governing the American occupation of its zone of Germany, 1945

KPD. Kommunistische Partei Deutschlands—German Communist party, now merged with SPD in the SED in Soviet Zone of Germany and East Berlin

Länder. The lands or states of the German Federal Republic (West Germany)

Luftwaffe. The German Air Force

Maginot Line. French defensive installations along German border

NATO. North Atlantic Treaty Organization

NKVD (later MVD). The Soviet secret (political) police

NSDAP. Nationalsozialistische Deutsche Arbeiterpartei—National Socialist German Workers' party—the Nazi party

OKW. Oberkommando der Wehrmacht: Supreme Command of the German Armed Forces

Organization Todt. German Engineers' Corps

OSS. Office of Strategic Services; American military Intelligence organization in World War II

Overlord. Allied Invasion of Normandy, June, 1944

SA. Sturm Abteilung—Storm Troopers, the original Nazi paramilitary street fighters, purged in 1934

SED. Sozialistische Einheits Partei—Socialist Unity party; the forced amalgamation of the SPD with the Communist party in the Soviet Zone of Germany and East Berlin

SHAEF. Supreme Headquarters Allied Expeditionary Forces

SMA. Soviet Military Administration in Soviet Zone of Germany

SPD. Sozialdemokratische Partei Deutschlands—Social Democratic party of Germany; comparable to British Labour party

SS. Schutzstaffeln—Protective Squads, originally Hitler's elite body guard. Later expanded to full military units

United Nations. During World War II this term referred to the nations allied with the United States, Great Britain and the Soviet Union against the Axis states

Waffen SS. The armed SS, regular military units composed solely of elite personnel: candidates must be perfect physical specimens, Nazi party members, and of pure "Aryan" ancestry. Later during the war, draftees were accepted into the Waffen SS

Wehrmacht. The German Armed Forces: combined army, navy, air force

Westwall—Siegfried Line. German defensive installations along French border, opposite Maginot Line

Index